St Patrick's Day 2023

To Alex
With all my affectionate compliments

WITH HOPE IN MY HEART

Musings of a Spirited Psychiatrist

François

FRANÇOIS MAI

One Printers Way
Altona, MB R0G 0B0
Canada

www.friesenpress.com

Copyright © 2022 by Francois Mai
First Edition — 2022

Phil Jenkins, Editor

The photo of Charles Huggins on page 190 held by David Teplica and Archives Canada and is reproduced with permission.

All rights reserved.

No part of this publication may be reproduced in any form, or by any means, electronic or mechanical, including photocopying, recording, or any information browsing, storage, or retrieval system, without permission in writing from FriesenPress.

ISBN
978-1-03-914928-1 (Hardcover)
978-1-03-914927-4 (Paperback)
978-1-03-914929-8 (eBook)

1. BIOGRAPHY & AUTOBIOGRAPHY, MEDICAL

Distributed to the trade by The Ingram Book Company

"The author's powerful message of hope is vital in these extraordinary, war-tainted days. It is an erudite yet highly readable account of why hope should play such a central role in all our lives. The book resonates because it speaks with the authentic truth of personal experience."

Paul Grof
MD PhD FRCP, Professor of psychiatry University of Toronto;
Director Mood Disorders Centre, Ottawa.

"Professor Mai's memoir about his unusual and interesting family and personal history relates the events, achievements, tragedies and relationships in his long life …. enabled him to register both as a physician and a psychiatrist. He recognises that trials and tribulations from trivial to catastrophic, can contribute to one's psychological growth …. underpinned by his conviction that faith, hope and optimism are crucial for an individual's mental health. *Sursum corda* (lift up your heart) a message sent to him by his father while he was still a youth has uplifted and supported him for many years. This book is an excellent read."

Jocelyne Kane-Berman MB, ChB. DCH. RCP(London) RCS.MA (Pub Admin); Formerly Chief Executive Officer, Groote Schuur Hospital, Cape Town, South Africa.

"Dr. Francois Mai …. has a great collection of anecdotal tales to tell. Apart from enjoyable, I found it very interesting and instructive. Highly recommended reading."

Beverley Barron – Family Physician, Victoria, BC.

"An impressive and inspiring autobiography by an author, physician, musician and athlete who left apartheid South Africa and pursued his medical studies in England and Scotland, eventually settling in Canada where he built a successful medical career as a psychiatrist and teacher."

Honourable R.E. Salhany, Q.C; Roger Salhany a former Judge of the Superior Court of Ontario.

"This is a grand tale, spanning the 20th century and beyond, touching on many of its major events and their effects on real people …. Dr Mai's diligent pursuit of better understanding and treatment of psychiatric disorders and his contributions to academic medicine produced new knowledge. His continued drive and creativity, post-retirement, in spite of major health challenges, produced a definitive book on the illnesses of Beethoven, an historical novel set in post-revolutionary France and now this intriguing autobiography which readers will find richly rewarding."

Thomas E. Feasby CM BSc (Med) MD DSc (Hon) FRCPC
Professor of Neurology and Past Dean, Cumming School of Medicine, University of Calgary.

"In spite of adversities, Francois became an outstanding professional and contributor to the well-being of those suffering from mental and physical disorders. Interacting with Francois for many memorable years has been my good fortune."

Yvon Lapierre, Former Head, Department of Psychiatry, University of Ottawa.

Hope springs eternal in the human breast;
Man never Is, but always To be blest.
The soul, uneasy, and confin'd from home,
Rests and expatiates in a life to come."
Alexander Pope,
1688-1744
An Essay on Man

DEDICATED

to my mentors

George Engel and William Sargant

Table of Contents

Foreword	xiii
Chapter One: With Hope in My Heart	1
Chapter Two: A Moment in Time	3
Chapter Three: My Tangled, Travelled Roots	7
Chapter Four: Bombs, Beethoven, and Backstroke	25
Chapter Five: Moving into Medicine	48
Chapter Six: Tempestuous Times	61
Chapter Seven: Love at Second Sight	75
Chapter Eight: My Brother's Keeper	88
Chapter Nine: Highs and Lows	99
Chapter Ten: A Slippery Slope	123
Chapter Eleven: Becoming Canadian	135
Chapter Twelve: A Capital Adventure	155
Chapter Thirteen: Physician, Heal Thyself	183
Chapter Fourteen: A Rocky Road	201
Chapter Fifteen: The Perils of Prophecy	207
Chapter Sixteen: Afterthoughts	213
Suggested Reading	219
Personal Bibliography	226
Website Links	229
Glossary	230
Acknowledgements	233
Index	234

Foreword

While the subtitle of François Mai's autobiography reveals his professional identity as a psychiatrist, early on we read that psychiatry is in fact a supplementary theme. I have known François since the 1980s—as a senior colleague and mentor—so this statement comes as no surprise. My early impression was of a man whose talents and range of interests extended beyond those of anyone I had previously encountered in my working life. The passage of time since has merely served to reinforce this opinion. Regardless of their personal or professional backgrounds, readers will be inspired by François' portrayal of a remarkably full and varied life and his insightful commentary on a range of universal concerns. The book challenges and informs, as much as it entertains.

At the outset, François describes his personal identity as confused, a consequence of what he refers to as his "tangled roots." The son of French immigrants to South Africa, with both English and French spoken in the home, he had childhood experiences that were diverse and sometimes painful, and included loss, homesickness, and early exposure to illness and death. From these roots, an introspective, sensitive "citizen of the world" emerged. François was close to his mother, a professional musician who nurtured his early and enduring love of classical music; he had a more distant relationship with his father. Teachers and other adult figures cultivated his life-long interest and later achievements in history and literature. Along with feeding childhood adventures in the warm sun and natural beauty of rural South Africa, these proved to be a wellspring for François' sustained physical energy and creativity well into his later years. In describing the early period of his life, he interweaves an enlightening historical perspective on the momentous global events of the time, on the origins of apartheid and South Africa's turbulent path toward modern democracy.

Hope is the manifest theme of the book. However, for me, the latent theme of sensitivity to injustice is no less evident. François seems compelled to seek fairness—sometimes for himself but more often for others. He attributes his identification with the marginalized in part to his strong Christian faith, but his early witnessing of systemic racial inequity also contributed. We read of his opposing apartheid as a medical student and of his standing up to senior medical colleagues as a young doctor, in defence of his patients' best interests. We learn of his discomfort with the position of the Catholic Church on contraception and his associated lapse in practice of his faith for a twenty-year period. While later reconciled, François continues to challenge aspects of present-day Catholicism, including the role of women within the church, that are not founded on core Christian values. In similar vein, he reserves some of his most trenchant criticism for his own medical specialty, identifying the sometimes-harmful influence of the pharmaceutical industry on the more recent evolution of diagnostic classification systems in psychiatry.

François celebrates his objectively illustrious medical career and his research publications that contributed to our understanding of the overlap between physical and mental illness, acknowledging his mentors, included some of the most influential figures in modern psychiatry. He is equally proud of his children's achievements and of his wife Sarie's success as a clinical art therapist; her published work has advanced this developing field, and is widely respected. However, François also recounts the pain of career disappointments, some of which were suffered during his later working life, and reflects on the "slippery slope" of the academic medical career. He particularly regrets the disruptive impacts of some of the associated geographical moves on his marriage and family life. In so doing, he will cause many of us to reflect on our own struggle to reconcile the drive for career progression and reward with the inherent desire to be a good spouse and parent.

In the later chapters, François shares his own experience of an advanced prostate cancer diagnosis. He questions the wisdom of referring to the "battle" with cancer, a term that has recently come into common parlance.

Here, he advances a cogent argument regarding the most useful attitude to adopt in the face of serious illness. Speaking with the authority of someone whose exuberance in living is unquestionable, he cautions against the relentless pursuit of heroic treatments to the point where the opportunity to meet death in a supported and dignified manner is lost. François whimsically relates how he has personally decided to "negotiate" with his cancer rather than do battle with it and underlying his playful tone is an important message.

Toward the end of the book, François, unsurprisingly, states that, notwithstanding his achievements in other areas, his most valued legacy is his children and grandchildren. He retains the hope and belief that human wisdom will prevail in preventing the tragedy and futility of another world war. The awful events currently unfolding in Ukraine seem likely to test whether this confidence is justified. Although François ruefully refers to his autobiography as an "auto-obituary," one is not at all convinced that it represents his final literary statement. We await the next product of his undiminished spirit.

Prof. Vincent Russell, MD, MSc, FRCPsych, FRCPC

Associate professor, Department of Psychiatry, RCSI University of Medicine and Health Sciences, Dublin.

Chapter One
With Hope in My Heart

The central theme of this book is hope. The Reverend Desmond Tutu, a great man in whom hope burned brightly right until his death, said of hope that it is being able to see that there is light despite all the darkness.

Over my long career I've experienced numerous setbacks and dark times in my personal life. Failures in examinations, defeats in my sporting career, death of an infant child, a brother who developed schizophrenia, unsuccessful applications for academic promotion, family conflicts, and the development of an aggressive form of prostate cancer. My initial reaction to these disappointments was depression, coupled with anger.

But as I pondered these events, I also came to realize their potential utility. The old cliché "every cloud has a silver lining" is apposite. If one examines a situation carefully, there is nearly always a positive way of viewing it, and finding hope within it. Getting a fatal illness can stimulate adjustment techniques such as exercise, meditation, and prayer. Death of a family member can help reconcile surviving members and gives one a proxy in heaven. Losses at sport can promote extra training, or they can induce an awareness of one's limitations. Failure in an examination provides an opportunity to improve one's knowledge, and to help develop a constructive approach to the examination ordeal.

My Christian faith has helped me cope with these crises. Hope is an essential tenet of Christianity and it is also an essential ingredient of health. Hopelessness, its opposite, is implicit in the act of suicide.

Psychiatry is a supplementary theme in this book. How did I become a psychiatrist and why? Who were my mentors, and how did they influence me? What out-of-the-ordinary patients did I encounter? My special interest was psychosomatic medicine—or "liaison" psychiatry—and I made leading-edge research contributions in this subspecialty area. During my training as a psychiatrist, I was fortunate to be influenced by two great men: William Sargant in London, England, and George Engel in Rochester, New York. They both had optimistic attitudes in their clinical approaches to medicine.

Although Sargant stressed strongly the key role medications played in recovery from mental illness, his whole demeanour when he was interviewing patients radiated hope and optimism. I observed first-hand how his patients assimilated his attitude, and how it promoted their recovery.

Engel used the phrases "helplessness-hopelessness" and "giving-up, given-up" to portray the crucial role these feelings play in the causation of illness. He held a weekly meeting called the "Sep-Dep conference" (abbreviation for separation and depression) to discuss the role of these situations in health and disease. Engel explicitly emphasized the role of hope in maintaining health.

In my clinical practice I have tried to emulate the positivity of these renowned psychiatrists, and transmit an attitude of hope and optimism in my patients. With compassionate and helpful care, using the full arsenal of psychiatric treatments that are available, in an appropriate manner, I believe that almost all those with mental health problems can be steered toward health and a better quality of life.

In the later pages of this memoir, I offer some musings on the future of humanity, and the use and misuse of Earth, our microscopic home in the vastness of space. Human activity is disrupting the earth's climate, endangering not only biological diversity, but mankind's life and health, as well. War is always with us, as is the threat of pandemics. Yet I remain hopeful, as we all must, that the inherent wisdom of our species will find long-term solutions to these seemingly intractable problems. As the ancient French proverb says, *"L'espoir fait vivre.* "Hope enables Life.

Chapter Two
A Moment in Time

Port Elizabeth, South Africa, June 5, 1948.

It is eight in the morning, and the Afrikaans family I live with on weekdays are huddled around the radio listening to the news broadcast. With whites only as voters, the national elections had been held the previous day, and the results are awaited with feverish frenzy. The Afrikaners in South Africa are the descendants of the original Dutch, French and German settlers who arrived during the 17th, 18th and 19th centuries. They have their own language (Afrikaans) and distinctive culture of which they are very proud.

On the crackling old radio (at that time called a wireless), the announcement quickly comes through in Afrikaans: *"The National Party has won the South African election. General Smuts has conceded defeat. Dr. Daniel Malan will be the new prime minister of South Africa."*

The du Plessis family throw up their hands and shout in unison with excitement. They then look rather sheepishly at me, the only non-Afrikaner in the group, to see how I am reacting. At thirteen years of age, and still non-politicized in my views, I have no idea what all this means, so I just smile sphinxlike, and say nothing.

General Smuts had turned seventy-eight that year, had been prime minister since 1939, and had dominated South African politics since the end of the South African War in 1902. He played a key role in the Peace Conference that ended the Anglo-Boer War, and again in writing the South Africa constitution, which led to the formation of the Union of South Africa in 1910. He was deputy prime minister to General Botha and, on the latter's death in 1919, became prime minister. A statesman and a philosopher, he was a powerful leader with international recognition. He played substantial roles in both world wars, in 1919 arguing for a strong League of Nations, as described vividly by Margaret MacMillan in her seminal work, *Paris 1919*, and in 1945, Smuts helped draft the United Nations Charter in San Francisco after World War II. Yet he was unloved by many from his own Afrikaner people. The worst epithet that an Afrikaner can level against a fellow Afrikaner is that he is a *"hands-opper,"*—a hands-upper, one who surrenders. This was the case even though Smuts had a distinguished career fighting the British in the Anglo-Boer War. Botha and Smuts together created the South Africa Party, which eventually morphed into the United Party— united because it attempted to reconcile English and Afrikaans speaking South Africans. It was also anti-Black in its political philosophy.

One of the policies that Smuts promoted in the lead-up to the 1948 election was to foster the link between South Africa, as a Commonwealth country, and the Crown. In February 1947, he invited King George VI, his queen, Elizabeth, and the royal family, including the two young princesses, Elizabeth and Margaret, to visit South Africa. A huge fanfare accompanied this trip. The royal family toured the country in a special white train—all other South African trains were a dirty, dull brown colour—and everywhere they went they were fêted and met important local dignitaries.

In Grade 7 when they came to Port Elizabeth, I was the student selected to meet the queen and the princesses, should they wish to meet young scholars. As it turned out, they did not wish to meet young scholars, so Princess Elizabeth lost her last and only chance to meet me. The royal train did, however, pass through our village of Perseverance, on the way to its next port of call. The whole local population lined up beside the tracks, all bedecked in our Sunday best, holding and vigorously waving

South African and British flags. The white train whizzed by, at high speed, with blinds firmly shut, not a soul visible on it. No wonder the royal visit did little to influence the general election sixteen months later in General Smuts' favour!

Fortunately, my father later made up for this missed royal opportunity. In 1961, Princess Elizabeth, now queen, visited Roubaix in northern France to meet with senior executives of the French textile industry, and he was one of the dignitaries who stood in line to shake her hand.

Papa with other textile firm directors, meeting the queen at her visit to Roubaix, France (c. 1961)

The announcement that Dr. Malan would lead the National Party (NP) as its prime minister became my first lesson in politics. The du Plessis' were a delightful and kind-hearted family, and I lived in their home on weekdays for two and a half years while learning to speak Afrikaans. They were very good to me. However, as members of the NP, they were totally committed to maintaining white supremacy in South Africa, and would not dream of extending the vote to Black South Africans.

During my lifetime I have lived through three remarkable periods of change in South African political history. At my birth, the country was a quasi-apartheid society: segregation of the races was quietly carried out and accepted, both within South Africa and by the international community. Between 1948 and 1994, apartheid was explicit and legislated, and the country became, in effect, a fascist dictatorship. The third and final phase began with the transfer of power to the African National Congress in 1994, after the release of Nelson Mandela, as the whole edifice of apartheid crashed, and a more democratic form of government was established. These changes had an enormous effect on me and my family.

I began my anti-apartheid activities during my middle years as a medical student. When I left South Africa in 1958 to pursue a residency in England, it was my intention to return after my studies were completed. Accelerating racial conflicts in the 1960s impelled us not to go back.

The illegalities and immorality of apartheid also had a major effect on my career plans and my philosophy. They caused me to identify strongly with the poor and the marginalized in our society, and few are more marginalized than those with chronic psychiatric illness.

My experience as an activist in the political maelstrom that was South Africa became a founding factor that influenced my decision to follow a career path in psychiatry.

Chapter Three
My Tangled, Travelled Roots

I first came into the light at Port Elizabeth, South Africa, in December 1934. It was an inauspicious year to be born. The Depression was at its height. Millions in North America and Europe were unemployed, starving or freezing to death. Hitler had become führer of Germany after murdering Röhm and over 200 others, in the infamous Night of the Long Knives. Stalin started his ghastly purges in Russia, executing foe and friend alike. Meanwhile, Japan had invaded Manchuria, and was planning an assault on China and Southeast Asia. On the positive side, 1934 was the year the Dionne quintuplets were born in Canada, and also the year that Sophia Loren, Brigitte Bardot, and Leonard Cohen came into the world; Franklin D. Roosevelt was in the second year of his presidency, and the benefits of his New Deal were beginning to kick in. Mary Pickford, Charlie Chaplin, and Maurice Chevalier were at the height of their fame, and 1934 was also the year that Flash Gordon and Donald Duck cartoons first appeared. In England, King George V was coming to the end of his twenty-five-year reign.

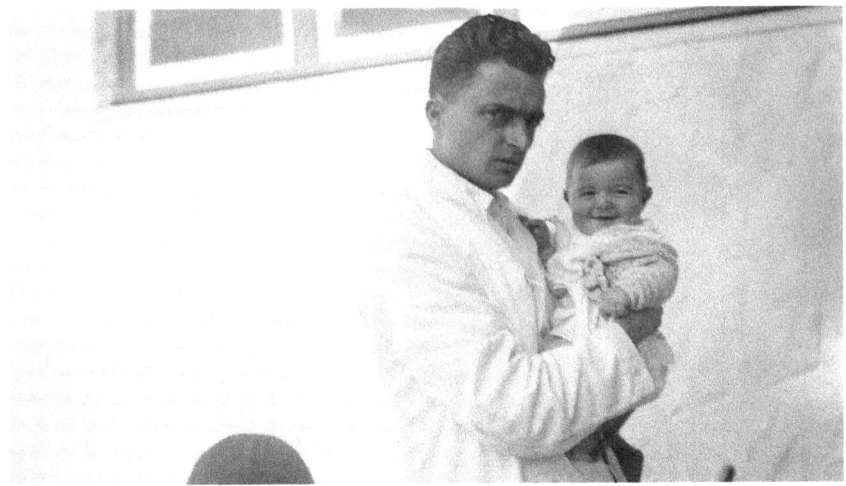

François, aged four months, cradled by Papa

Because we were born in the same year, I've had a fascination with the Dionne quints and their tumultuous lives. Part of the appeal is that I, too, am one of five children. As of 2022, of the original five only two, Annette and Cécile, remain alive. One can scarcely imagine childhoods more disrupted by publicity, government interference, and money-making than theirs.

The quints were born in a small village near North Bay in Ontario. Five identical babies had never been born from a single fertilized ovum, and survived, in recorded history before, so it is perhaps not surprising that such a worldwide hullaballoo ensued. The quints, their French-Canadian parents Oliva and Elize, together with the physician who delivered them, Dr. Dafoe, achieved instant fame. However, when the parents started charging visitors a fee for viewing the infants, the Ontario provincial government took umbrage, declared the parents unfit to care for their children, and passed a law to take over their care—and immediately began charging visitors a fee for viewing the children! Quintland (sic) became the most famous Ontario tourist attraction, even superseding Niagara Falls. The quints were nine years old before the parents regained their custody, but by this time behavioural issues were already apparent in some of them.

In their later years, the quints attempted to recoup some of the profits the provincial government made out of them. It was only in 1999 that the three survivors received a settlement for the trauma that had been inflicted on them as children.

I had two older sisters, Christiane and Denyse, born respectively seven and five years before me. Our father, something of a misogynist, and clearly unaware of the fact that the gender of a child depended on his, not the mother's genes, desperately wanted a son. He cockily promised my mother the gift of a motor car if she produced a son, or a bicycle if she produced a daughter. Although I was not, of course, aware of it, there likely was joy in the household when I appeared on the scene. My mother duly got a big, black, beautiful Buick 1934 sedan.

That car was also the scene of my earliest memory. In October 1937, just before my third birthday (I know the date exactly because mother was eight months pregnant with my younger brother, David, when the event happened; he was born November 10, 1937), she was driving home after picking up Christiane and Denyse from school. The girls were arguing on the backseat, and I was sitting in the front passenger seat, without a seatbelt, which had yet to be invented. Mother turned around to chastise my sisters, did not see a truck stopping in front of her, and rear-ended it. I crashed into the dashboard, sustaining bruises and abrasions on my face and forehead. Fortunately, she had not been going fast, so the damage was not serious. Nothing like a near-death experience, as it seemed to me at the time, to scar the brain!

Both my parents were born and raised in France—my father in 1902 in Amiens, in the Pas-de-Calais region, my mother in 1900 in Poitiers in southwest France; her family then moved south to Aix-en-Provence. They immigrated to South Africa independently in their twenties, shortly after the First World War.

My father, Martin, whom we called Papa, was too young to be drafted by the French Army in the brutal and horrific World War I. After completing his schooling, he went to Bradford in England, where he learned both English and the basics of the wool trade. He then returned to France to serve his eighteen-month compulsory military service, which included a spell in the French occupation force of the Ruhr in Western Germany. In 1922, he joined the French textile firm of Prouvost Lefebvre, which had its world headquarters at Roubaix. Within a few months, because of his proficiency in English, he was invited to represent the firm in South Africa, where he moved in 1925. Port Elizabeth was at that time the centre of the wool industry in South Africa, so that was where he located. Its population then was approximately 100,000.

In his memoirs, *Life Was Not All Wool,* published shortly before his death in 1973, Papa described his childhood, especially his traumatic relationship with his parents. He portrays his father as short-tempered and his mother as not very supportive, but also admits he was not an easy child. During World War I, and in order to teach him discipline, his mother sent him to a priest called Abbé Ledoux, vicar of a small village near Calais. Every afternoon, Abbé Ledoux took him for long walks. They discussed "interesting things like history, philosophy and geography and also my personal problems. He told me to become a practical man, and in that respect, I have not failed him." Abbé Ledoux had a large library and introduced Papa to reading. He characterized Ledoux as a maverick, and under his influence, Papa himself became one.

Papa in his Potez plane, ready to take off

Flying over the big hole of Kimberley (c. 1925)

The crashed Potez

In his little book, Papa outlines his sojourn in the French Army, and how he immigrated first to England then to South Africa. He became one of the first men in South Africa to own and fly an airplane, a small, one-prop French model called the Potez. Unfortunately, he later crashed it, amazingly without serious injury. A very strong wind was blowing when he was at a low altitude, and he lost control. Realizing he would have to land and there being no fields nearby, he flew the plane into a clump of trees. This destroyed the plane but likely saved his life and that of his passenger.

I have a theory as to why Papa was keen to go to South Africa, though he never told me the story himself. He was born in 1902, at the end of the Anglo-Boer War in which France, together with almost all European nations, supported the Boers against the British Empire. Christian De Wet was a Boer general, who, during the final guerrilla stages of the war, managed to inflict much damage on British troops, while evading capture himself. De Wet became a folk hero in France, and Papa's parents gave him the middle name of Christian, after the General. From birth therefore, he had a connection with South Africa.

The first family car: a 1910 Citroén Darracq. Papa, aged eight, is seated on the floorboard, his father is driving and his mother is behind him.

My mother, Yvonne Nadaud, whom we called Maman, came from a musical family and showed early talent. She completed her musical education as a violinist at the Paris Conservatoire during World War I, and became an accomplished professional musician. Her older sister Hélène had married an ex-officer in the British Army named Harold Watson-Smith, and they had immigrated to South Africa where their first two children were born, one of whom died in infancy. The other was John, executed by the Nazis in France in 1944. They got into financial difficulties and Yvonne was sent out from France by her family to help them. She quickly found a permanent position as a violinist in the Cape Town City Orchestra. Hélène returned to France with her family, whereas Yvonne remained in Cape Town, and became a lead violinist in the orchestra. In 1925, she became famous in the world of music for the first South African performance, as soloist, of Ralph Vaughn-Williams' beautiful tone-poem *The Lark Ascending,* which has remained a concert hall favourite ever since. We played a recording of *The Lark* at her funeral in 1995. She also played and performed publicly in a women-only professional string quartet, which might qualify as a world-first for that period.

All-women string quartet, c. 1925. From l.to r: Yvonne Nadaud, Inger Boberg, Mabel Lamb, and an unknown cellist

Maman's musical family in 1894. Her mother, aged nineteen, is playing the cello and her grandmother is standing on left.

The miracle meeting between Maman and Papa occurred in May 1927. Papa had been recalled to France by his firm for updates on its progress in South Africa. Meanwhile, Maman had a younger brother, Jacques, who had died earlier that year from tuberculosis, so she returned to France to support her family. Unknown to each other, they both reserved cabins on the *Carnarvon Castle*, one of the Union-Castle Line mail boats that provided a weekly passenger service between Cape Town and Southampton. As the only young French couple on the boat, they were quickly drawn to each other.

Papa, a raconteur in the vintage of Maurice Chevalier, with the same accent when he spoke English, and the same gestures, told us the story many times. One evening, they both were leaning on the railing of the deck of the liner, as it slowly steamed north on the Atlantic Ocean. Papa said, "Yvonne, isn't that a beautiful sunset?" To which Maman allegedly replied, "Yes, Martin, I would love to get married to you!" Maman strongly denied the accuracy of this anecdote, but never gave us her correct rendition. They duly returned to France where each family inspected the other to ensure the blood lines and ancestries were good enough for their progeny. Papa's parents, whose ancestry was part peasant, part bourgeois, were particularly impressed with Maman's ancestry. Not only were they aristocrats through her father, Fernand Nadaud, from the twelfth century, but they included two French popes in the fourteenth century, Clement VI and Gregory XI. For seventy-five years, the papacy moved from Rome to Avignon in the south of France. Clement was the pope who built the palace at Avignon, and Gregory XI was the last French pope. It was him who moved the papacy back to Rome in 1378. Maman's mother was an amateur musician and her maternal great-grandfather, Louis Roy, was an admiral in the French navy during the nineteenth century.

Perhaps Maman's family were dazzled by Papa's outgoing, entrepreneurial personality, but in their own way, the rest of his family was equally illustrious. Papa's father was a telephone engineer who had been decorated with the *Legion d'Honneur* for his spying efforts in World War I. He had been caught behind the lines in the city of Lille, when the Germans overran Northern France in 1914 from August to October, and was held there, though not imprisoned, for the duration of the war. Meanwhile, at great risk to himself, he sent secret messages across the lines to the Allies about German troop movements. His work in behind-the-lines espionage is mentioned in the biography of the famous French spy, *Louise de Bettignies,* by Renée Deruyk. Grandpère was the chief telephone operator who *"established an underground telephone cable connection between Lille and the British Army zone of occupation"* (my translation) so that de Bettignies, and others, could communicate across the trenches with Allied army leaders conducting the war. Louise led a spy group, and is one of the chief characters under the pseudonym "Lili" in Kate Quinn's page-turning novel, *The Alice Network*. The novel vividly portrays the dreadful conditions that existed in German-occupied Lille.

This meant that Papa was without his father for most of his impressionable teenage years. Papa's paternal ancestors were farmers from the tiny village of Givenchy-en-Gohelle, near Vimy, and in my novel *Father, Unknown*, I provide my theory as to how we received the family name of

"Mai." Papa's mother's family were well-known lawyers, merchants, and seamen in the city of Boulogne-Sur-Mer in the north of France.

Papa's family was quixotic, especially on his mother's side. Her first name was Thérèse, and we called her Grandmère. She was the second of seven children and the oldest daughter of Guillaume Delattre, a noted lawyer and journalist, and Marie Buron. Her next younger sister was Marguerite. The only son in the family was Joseph—oldest in the sib line—whom we all got to know as Oncle Joseph.

Our Grandpère René fell in love with Marguerite, the second sister, and asked her to marry him, but Guillaume Delattre, their father, told him that he had to marry Thérèse, not Marguerite, as Thérèse was the oldest daughter and thus had to marry first. Grandpère complied. They married, and went on to have two children, Renée and Martin, our father.

Oncle Joseph was a physician who served heroically in the French Army troops and was injured in the horrific Battle of Verdun in WW I. For this, he was awarded the *Chevalier de la Légion d'honneur* decoration. He and his wife, Adrienne, had no children and were notorious in the family as hoarders. I visited their home in 1953 and was astounded at the sight. Old newspapers were piled high on tables through the house, reaching up to the ceiling, so one walked through the house as if creeping through a narrow cave with high walls stacked with newspapers. One had to dodge boxes filled to the rim with dried peach stones as one walked around each room, and old clothes and books filled all the remaining nooks and crannies in the house. If only I'd had an iPhone handy to picture the compressed chaos in the house.

A year after my visit, Oncle Joseph died in his bedroom on the first floor. He was placed directly from his bed into the coffin. Unfortunately, the pall bearers had not allowed for the fact that a narrow spiral staircase led down from the first floor to ground level, and the casket could not be carried around its sharp corners. While standing dead in his coffin, poor Oncle Joseph had to be hopped down the steps, one at a time, as he made his final descent of the stairwell.

Maman and Papa duly married at Aix-en-Provence in July 1927. They flew to Corsica for their honeymoon, and both recount the story of travelling in a tiny one-prop seaplane without radio communication. Fortunately, the pilot had homing pigeons on board, so every thirty minutes he would open a window on the plane and release one, with message attached, which would inform the world of the plane's whereabouts. On the way back from Corsica the little plane encountered severe turbulence, and in his memoirs, Papa states that Maman and another female passenger clung onto him, fearful that they were going to crash, and all perish.

Over sixty years later, in 1991, at the invitation of my brother Vincent in New York, Maman flew from London to New York on a British Airways supersonic Concorde, in effect arriving before she had left London. Her life truly spanned a remarkable aeronautical revolution.

Maman and Papa returned to South Africa where their five children were born—Christiane in 1928, Denyse in 1929, François in 1934, David in 1937, and Vincent in 1940. Maman and Papa always spoke French to each other, and Maman always spoke French to us, her children. We were in an anglophone environment so we children always spoke English with each other. Our schooling was all in English, but there was sufficient French at home for us all to be almost fluent in conversational French by the time we completed our high school education.

Papa, carrying four of his five children—David, François, Denyse, and Christiane—on the beach near Port Elizabeth, 1938

In his entertaining autobiography, *Dear Me*, Peter Ustinov, the British actor, narrates the immense odds against his being born. Had it not been for World War I, his parents would never have met and he would not have been conceived. He extends these unlikely odds back to his ancestors and adds, "I can never hope to repay the huge war debt which I personally owe to millions of people whose concerted egotism, self-sacrifice, stupidity, wisdom, bravery, cowardice, honour, and dishonour made it possible for my parents to meet under the least likely of circumstances and with the most far-fetched of pretexts." The single event that predetermined the meeting between Papa and Maman was the unfortunate death of Jacques, Maman's younger brother, at age twenty from tuberculosis. If he had not died, Maman would not have taken the *Carnarvon Castle* to Europe, and my parents would never have met. As with Ustinov, I will never be able to repay the huge debt I owe my dear Oncle Jacques, whom I never knew, for my existence.

Three things—two affecting Papa, one affecting Maman—had a major impact on our early childhood.

Papa continued working for Prouvost Lefebvre and rose steadily up the corporate ladder, eventually becoming director of the firm's branch in South Africa. During the worldwide economic Depression in the 1930s, he was able to use his position, and his steady employment income, to buy into real estate and amass a small fortune. Our family was thus one of the few who became prosperous during those difficult economic times, and in the early 1930s he built a beautiful Art-Deco style house in an affluent suburb of Port Elizabeth. I, David, and Vincent were born there.

When World War II broke out in 1939, Papa was still a French citizen. France was overrun by the German army in 1940 and suffered a disastrous defeat, leading to the establishment of the Vichy regime under Marshall Pétain. Vichy governed France even while Germany occupied the country. Pétain was under the thumb of the Nazis, even to the extent of rounding up French Jews to be sent east to extermination camps. Meanwhile, General Charles De Gaulle had fled to England to continue the battle against Nazi Germany, the highest-ranking French politician to do so. Like Churchill, De Gaulle foresaw that this was not a local battle between

Britain and France on one side, and Germany on the other, but that it would rapidly escalate into a world war. De Gaulle, supported by Churchill and the British government, attempted to foster an armed French resistance to Nazism. French citizens throughout Britain and the colonial Empire were required to swear an oath of allegiance to the Free French under De Gaulle. Papa refused to do so, following the lead of his company superiors in France, all of whom acknowledged the Vichy regime as the legitimate government of France. This got him into immense difficulties in wartime South Africa, which, under Prime Minister Jan Smuts, had declared war on Germany in support of Britain and its Empire. Poor Papa was hounded by his business competitors and the police, and was eventually arrested and carted off to the internment camp at Koffiefontein, in the Orange Free State, where he was incarcerated for three months. One of his fellow inmates was Johan Vorster, later prime minister of South Africa. A large section of Afrikaans South Africans, with bitter memories of the Anglo-Boer War just forty years earlier, had formed an organization called the *"Broederbond"* (Brotherhood), which opposed the South African war effort against Germany. Vorster was a leader in this organization. It was only through the legal intervention of his friend and lawyer in Port Elizabeth, Ben Smulian, that Papa was released from the camp. Because of these difficulties, Papa retained a lifelong bitterness toward De Gaulle.

In 1941, Papa went to the United States to spend six months at the company branch in Boston. He recounts the story of meeting a group of Free French officers in New York who accosted him as to why he was not in the French army fighting Nazi Germany. Papa replied that he had five children, and as such was not required to fight. He then asked them why they were not fighting. They replied by confiscating his passport, and it was only through the intervention of the American government, which at that time was supporting the Vichy regime and not De Gaulle's Free French movement, that it was returned. He was henceforth blacklisted by the Free French, and his life "became full of misery."

Papa's wartime misadventures and allegiances later caused difficulties between me and him. As I grew up, I developed an admiration for De Gaulle, who, through his courage and foresight on two occasions, in 1940 and again in 1958, saved the honour and integrity of France under immensely difficult circumstances. After the liberation of France in 1944, the Free French morphed into the first government of the Fourth Republic, with De Gaulle as prime minister. In 1958, with the war of Algerian independence against France now at its height, and France in chaos, De Gaulle was recalled from retirement to resolve the crisis. This he did, winding down the Algerian war and extricating France from that brutal conflict. He secured the decolonization and independence of Algeria in 1963, but it earned him the hatred of the one million French-Algerians, the so-called *colons* or "pieds noirs." The *colons* subsequently engineered at least two assassination attempts against De Gaulle, one of which nearly succeeded. The French are a fiercely individualistic people, epitomized by De Gaulle's famous line in 1962, "How can anyone govern a nation that has 246 different kinds of cheese?" I respected Papa's decision not to support De Gaulle and the Free French movement, and understand him, given the special personal conditions he faced in wartime South Africa.

Tuberculosis was a common disease. In the early twentieth century, one in seven North Americans was dying of the condition. In 1927, Maman's younger brother Jacques died from it, and after the birth of Denyse in 1929, Maman developed the disease and was sent to a sanatorium in the mountains of Switzerland for eighteen months, the accepted best treatment at that time. She eventually recovered and returned to South Africa, but the doctors told her to have no more children. Thank goodness she had no recurrence in 1934 when I appeared on the scene, nor in 1937 when David was born. However, following Vincent's birth in 1940, at the age of forty, she developed a severe recurrence and went into a deep coma. I remember—I was five—our family doctor, Dr. de Villiers, coming into the living room where we were all seated, and saying to Papa, *"Martin, she is hemorrhaging badly. I'm afraid she is gone,"* and Papa then bursting into tears. I had never seen Papa crying before, as men, including boys, were not supposed to cry, so this made a big impression on my childish mind.

At five years old I did not know what *she is gone* meant, had no conception of death and its permanence; no one explained its meaning to me. At that stage I was not close to her, because, from an early age I had been raised by a full-time nanny called Eileen Hurley, who became like a mother to me. So I cannot say I was wounded by her brush with death. I was hurt more by Papa's reaction and by the consequences, for me, of her illness.

Maman did not die. Dr. de Villiers had made a premature diagnosis; she likely was in a coma due to the haemorrhage and the tuberculosis. Perhaps miraculously, the haemorrhage stopped spontaneously, and her immune system overcame the *tubercle bacillus*. While she slowly recovered her health, we children were farmed out to various friends in Port Elizabeth. I was sent to a French family, the Leblancs, who lived on the edge of a ravine. They delighted in telling me that, if I misbehaved, werewolves living in the ravine would come out at night, especially during a full moon, and capture me. I did not know what werewolves were, but they sounded scary and I did nothing to encourage their attack. David, aged two, was sent to family friends who lived in the small village of Redhouse, on the Swartkops River, about twenty kilometres from Port Elizabeth.

Once Maman was recovered, the doctor's orders for her were that she move to the dry Karroo region of South Africa. Streptomycin and other medication treatments for tuberculosis had not yet been invented; living in a dry climate was considered the best way to prevent a recurrence of the disease. So, in late 1940 the family home in Port Elizabeth was sold, and our great trek into the interior took place. The chosen town was Cradock, about three hundred kilometres north of Port Elizabeth. In wartime South Africa, with rusty old 1930s cars, along dusty, unpaved, corrugated roads, this was not an easy relocation. Papa purchased a sheep farm in a small rural community called Halesowen, about twenty kilometres south of Cradock. There the family spent the next six years until we returned to Port Elizabeth in 1946. Both Cradock and Halesowen are in the Great Fish River valley, as it flows south to the Indian Ocean. For most of the year the river is a small stream, but when the rains come, it becomes a raging torrent, carrying much of South Africa's precious topsoil to the sea.

It is remarkable that neither I nor any of my siblings developed tuberculosis. Not only did Maman have the condition but two of our Black carers died from it. One was our nanny, called Sabena, on the farm in Halesowen; the other was Bloemfontein, the milkman. I recall watching Bloemfontein milking the cows, and dipping his fingers in the milk pail to moisten them, so that they would slip more easily over the teat. Not only did none of us develop the condition, but I am sure we all developed strong immunity to it.

In the northern summer of 1939, while still living in Port Elizabeth, the family visited our extended relatives in France. We were stranded in Dover, England, when war broke out in September 1939, with Maman, three months pregnant with Vincent, desperately trying to find a ship to take us back to South Africa before it was too late. At just under five years old, I was blasé about both the war and the difficulty of finding a ship. Far more exciting for me was watching the soldiers marching in formation up and down the promenade on the Dover waterfront. Along with many other local children, we marched alongside the soldiers, making sure we swung our arms and moved our legs as vigorously as did the soldiers, and in synchrony with them. It was great fun!

Practising navigation skills on Summerstrand beach, Port Elizabeth, 1940.

Maman did eventually find a ship going to South Africa, a mail-boat called the *Dunbar Castle*, and we quickly headed to the London docks for boarding. Because of the fear of being sunk by U-boats, our ship could not take a direct route from London to Cape Town, and we criss-crossed the Atlantic Ocean, taking three weeks in place of the usual two. This trip included a stop at St. Helena Island, and we visited Longwood, the mansion where Napoleon lived out the last six years of his life after the defeat at Waterloo. More impressive for me, however, were the huge, ancient tortoises that reside on the island. I likely saw Jonathan, a Seychelles terrestrial tortoise who is estimated now, in 2021, to be at least 186 years of age, the oldest living creature on earth, although when I saw him, he was *only* 105. We arrived safely and happily back in Cape Town, but the doomed *Dunbar Castle* sank on its next trip when it hit a mine near Dover in the English Channel.

Encounters with serious illness and death were relatively frequent for me as a young child. Maman's illness was the first, but during my early schooling in Cradock, three of my fellow students died, one from polio, another from osteogenic sarcoma in her leg, an unpleasant form of cancer in young people that affects the long bones of the limbs. It's the same condition that affected and killed twenty-three-year-old Terry Fox in Canada in 1981. (Terry became a folk hero when, with a leg prosthesis, he set out to raise money for cancer research by running 5,000 kilometres across Canada. He had to quit at just over the halfway mark because of a recurrence of his disease, and died six months later. Since then, hundreds of millions of dollars have been raised for cancer research by Terry Fox runs across the world.)

The third of my fellow students to die was a young boy who developed fatal pneumonia after inhaling a tooth that had been extracted, an accident that should never be allowed to happen. I doubt that any action was taken against the dentist; from his perspective, it was just one of those unavoidable "accidents." In present-day Canada, he would likely have been disbarred from dentistry and faced a huge civil suit. Several nuns in the convent school also died while we were there, most often from tuberculosis.

Perhaps these early encounters with illness and death prepared me for what I had to face later in life. At that early age it made me realize that death was part of life. I also had the attitude, so often described by soldiers in wartime, that it was not going to happen to me. Somehow, always hopeful and optimistic, I knew I would escape that bullet or that bug!

I did have two narrow escapes from potentially serious illnesses during my childhood. One was recurring tonsillitis for which I eventually had a tonsillectomy at the local hospital. The anaesthetic used was chloroform. I can still see, before I lost consciousness, the general practitioner surgeon, with his aggressive-looking sharp instruments poised over my masked face. The other was an attack of jaundice, which, in retrospect, was likely infectious hepatitis A, for which I happily missed three weeks of school.

As I write of my childhood, revisiting it from the other end of my life, I see my parents more clearly. Every family is flawed in some way, and I see now the flaws in mine. Papa was a traditional disciplinarian, and although he never used the words "To spare the rod is to spoil the child," this pretty much summarized his philosophy of childhood upbringing. He could be affectionate and loving toward us but we had to toe the line in both behaviour and academic merit, and there was trouble if we did not. His philosophy also was misogynistic, and both my sisters, and, to a lesser extent, my brothers and I, were hurt by this attitude. Boys were men, even supermen, and as such were not allowed to show emotion, or cry.

Maman, on the other hand, did what she could to preserve the peace, but would absent herself if there was conflict between Papa and one or more of the children. In a situation of conflict, she tried to take the simple and easy way out. She also had a stubborn streak and when she wanted something, nothing, not even Papa, could stop her.

Chapter Four
Bombs, Beethoven, and Backstroke

The farm Papa bought at Halesowen, near Cradock, was called Riverview, though all we could see of the river was a row of low-lying bushes in the distance that luxuriated and lined its banks. The Great Fish River formed the eastern boundary of the farm, with our home, perhaps a thousand metres from it. Why the river was called "Great" or "Fish," I am not sure, since the water flow was that of a small Canadian stream, and I never saw any fish in it. But it did gouge a great cavity in the earth. The area around the farmhouse was bare, and Papa's first job was to plant trees, shrubs, and gardens.

I revisited Riverview in 2016, nearly eighty years later. Its name has been changed to "Kraantz Plaas." The sheep have gone and it is now an ostrich farm. The area around the farmhouse is overgrown with the trees and gardens that Papa planted, unrecognizably different from our time, but the house is the same.

On our property were the ruins of one of the homes of Olive Schreiner, the great South African feminist and authoress. Schreiner wrote the acclaimed novel, *The Story of an African Farm*, first published under the pseudonym Ralph Iron, in 1888. She lived in or near Cradock during the 1860s and was buried, at her request, atop a mountain called Buffelskop, just west of our property. My siblings and I used the ruins of her broken-down home as a playground, with little thought for its august history.

With tennis racquet, aged nine

With siblings on steps of home at Riverview, Cradock

François on the same steps, nearly eighty years later

Schreiner was a remarkable woman. Of German ancestry, she spent her life taking up the causes of the oppressed in the world, especially Boers, Blacks, and women, and wrote numerous polemical articles on these topics, depicting these issues vividly in *The Story of an African Farm*. The book was an instant success, despite describing issues of feminism, premarital sex, and religion that were asynchronous with the times. She became a thorn in the side of Cecil Rhodes, Alfred Milner, and Lord Roberts, the men who were masterminding the Anglo-Boer War for England. She also became friendly with Emily Hobhouse, the English anti-war activist, who did so much to improve the appalling conditions in the concentration camps set up around South Africa to house Boer women and children who had been ejected from their farms by British troops.

Cradock's other, more nefarious claim to fame is that it was the home of four Black activists—Goniwe, Calata, Mkhonto, and Mhlauli—all teachers or trade unionists, who were abducted in 1985 while driving from Cradock to Port Elizabeth to take part in a conference. They were murdered and burnt in their car. Fourteen years later, at Truth and Reconciliation hearings in 1999, six government security police were denied amnesty and imprisoned for the crime.

(A word here about the *Truth and Reconciliation Commission*. It was a remarkable policy and plan of action. Established in 1995 after Mandela came to power, its objective was to encourage both the victims and the perpetrators of political violence during the Apartheid era, to tell their stories in a public and legal forum, without necessitating the threat of legal action, thereby enabling South Africa's white and Black tribes to come together. Archbishop Tutu was chair of the commission, and Alex Boraine, a noted white, liberal activist and politician, the vice-chair. Perpetrators could request amnesty for their crimes, but in fact the great majority were denied.

Noble and idealistic in intent, the commission probably did not achieve its stated goals. Many perpetrators refused to give evidence, and many victims and families were left unsatisfied and frustrated.)

On a beautifully warm, clear day in October 1940, my family witnessed a total eclipse of the sun, the first in South Africa in sixty years. Armed with special glasses, we watched the moon glide slowly over the sun's disc as the world turned as dark as night. Stars became visible in the sky, cattle and fowl fell asleep, and we all oohed and ahhed at this amazing and rare spectacle. It was all over far too quickly. I was able to re-experience this eclipse about fifty years later, when I read Barbara Mutch's epic novel *The Housemaid's Daughter*. Set in Cradock in the 1930s and 1940s, the storyline vividly incorporates the eclipse into one of its settings. Though the book is fiction, I was able to say, "I was there!"

In 1940, Cradock, a small country town of about 8,000 people, had one Afrikaans school for boys, an Afrikaans school for girls, and one English-language girls' convent run by mostly German Dominican nuns. There was no high school for Blacks. Even in those pre-Apartheid days all these schools admitted whites only, and at that early age I did not question the ethical legalities of this separation. I just assumed this was the way the whole world functioned. My two sisters and I, and later my younger brothers, were all sent to the convent as weekly boarders, taking the steam-train from Halesowen to Cradock early on a Monday morning and returning home Friday afternoon. I skipped kindergarten, became the youngest child in Standard (Grade) 1, and made good progress academically. (This situation, of being the youngest in the grade, persisted throughout the ten years of my primary and high school education, and then continued on into university and medical school training, where I graduated in medicine, at the early age of twenty-one years and six months.)

Between 1939 and 1945, South Africa was at war with Germany, but in my childish mind I never thought it weird that we were being taught by German teachers, our enemies. They were stern, but also kindly. I am sure they were being monitored closely by the ubiquitous South African police. The unfortunate nuns must have found their lives difficult, though they never showed it.

The nuns had some strange ideas about what children needed for health. Every Saturday morning, we were lined up on a bench to receive our weekly dose of a tablespoonful of castor oil. I loathed both the castor oil and its effects—abdominal pain and diarrhea. This belief in the so-called health benefits of castor oil for children was not confined to our school. There must have been plenty of castor oil spilt in many schools globally.

The war touched us in several other ways. Papa, as already mentioned, was carted off to the Koffiefontein internment camp in 1942, allegedly because he refused to swear the oath of allegiance to the Free French, but more likely because of business jealousies from the small French community in Port Elizabeth. I recall going to the station at Halesowen, and him waving goodbye to us from the window of the train as he was whisked off to the camp, and my feeling numbed by the experience. In his memoirs, Papa describes how he was nicknamed "the wild man of Borneo" by his business competitors for his risk-taking business practices. He described the three months he spent in the camp as the "most miserable in my life" and added, "it is useless for me to speak after so many years of the danger and humiliation while in that camp." The camp also housed many German and Italian prisoners of war. After his return, he admitted he was threatened and nearly killed by some of his fellow inmates for his political beliefs.

Even after he returned to the farm, the police would on occasion burst into our home to check whether we were listening to German radio (we never were). To my young mind, these examples of the power of government and police were both shocking and scary. After 1943, we were assigned Italian prisoners of war captured in the North African campaign, who came to live and work on our farm, as with many other farming communities in South Africa. Two of the POWs, Ricardo and Botta, were charming individuals who fitted in well with farm life and taught me many things, such as how to make wooden and wire toys. Toys were very hard to come by during the war years, so having home-made ones, even though primitive by today's sophisticated electronic standards, was a real joy. Once the police stopped their intrusions into our existence, I grew to love our home and life of freedom at Riverview. Papa would take us for long walks on the farm, through the drifts (dry river beds), or up to the top of the local hill. There, one could savour the distinctive, warm aromas of the acacia bush, the rooibos and the sparse fynbos vegetation. Wondrous times.

Once one has lived there, the spectacular mountains, the red earth and endless blue skies, the scrub-land, the dry eroded drifts, the magnificent night-skies dominated by the Southern Cross and the Milky Way, the emptiness and stillness, the glorious sunrises and sunsets, become built into one's brain. Papa, in describing his first train trip from Cape Town to

Port Elizabeth through the Karoo, said, "the reader can imagine my joy at discovering, with my own eyes, this wonderful country."

My brother Vincent has had the same experience. After leaving South Africa following his graduation in commerce at the University of Cape Town, he immigrated first to London, then to New York, where he became a businessman and philanthropist. About ten years ago, he purchased a farm, The Plains of Camdeboo, over 8,000 hectares, near Pearston, about fifty kilometres west of Cradock. With the help of the South African Wildlife Association, he has turned the farm into a private nature reserve where only indigenous fauna and flora are allowed. The farm is criss-crossed by trails. With "karoo-buggies"—in fact, large, battery-operated golf carts—one can drive around quietly viewing the wildlife, and the property also includes a 500-metre-high mountain from which one can see spectacular sunsets.

Not far from the Plains of Camdeboo, on the far side of the historic town of Graaff Reinet, lies the village of Nieu Bethesda, a small, dusty Karoo town that has become famous as the location of The Owl House, which we visited in 2012 on our way to see Sarie's family. The Owl House is the creation of Helen Martins, who died in 1976, at the age of seventy-nine, and is one of the world's premier examples of Outsider Art—spectacular art created by artists who have had no formal training.

The Owl House is a small structure. The four walls in each room are covered with crushed glass of strikingly different colours and patterns. The garden, called the Camel Yard, is stacked with hundreds of animals, beautifully sculpted out of concrete, wire, and crushed glass of different hues. Most animals are pointing east, a symbol of Martins' religious leanings, derived from both Christianity and Islam. Owls and camels predominate in this menagerie. Scattered throughout the garden are human figures in weird non-anatomic positions, couples reminiscent of ancient pharaohs and their wives, or those on Easter Island. There are human figures with hands upward in gestures of pleading and hope, owls with huge glass eyes, wings high as if ready to take flight, pyramids on the Giza model, all packed tightly together in a veritable maze. One of the most striking is a large, muscular, male-looking sculpture, but showing prominent breasts, accepting in their mouth an apple-like fruit from the beak of a huge swan-like bird, while they gently stroke the underside of the neck of the bird. One can view some of these remarkable works of art on the Owl House website.

Martins was born in the village, completed her education as a teacher at Graaff Reinet, got married, and as a young woman, taught at various schools in South Africa. In her thirties, she left her husband, returned to Nieu Bethesda, and started her artistic career. She was helped in her creations by a mixed-race South African named Koos Malgas. Neighbours suspected their relationship was more than that of an artist and her helper. But neighbours can sometimes be consumed by malice or jealousy.

As she aged, Martins became increasingly reclusive and depressed. She also developed eye problems, likely the result of damage to the cornea caused by the crushing of glass, and the resulting dust particles, necessary to create her masterpieces. She eventually decided to end her life and took one of the most unpleasant methods possible – swallowing a bottle of lye. She was taken to the hospital in Graaff Reinet where she died an agonizing death three days later.

Music was one area where I progressed rapidly at school. In 1942, there was a serious polio epidemic and the school closed down for three weeks. All children were sent home. Maman happened to own a complete set of Beethoven's Piano Sonatas in sheet music and one day, while practising the piano, I hit upon the *Appassionata*, Beethoven's well-known Sonata #23 opus 57, and started sight-reading the opening bars, very badly, I am sure. I still remember Maman's excitement at her child prodigy playing such a complex piece of music! After I staggered to a stop, she got on the piano and performed the rest of the movement. A student in our class, Mavis, died during this epidemic and, even now, when I hear the *Appassionata* being played, I think of Mavis with her sweet little face, penetrating eyes, smile, and short-cut dark hair. Ever since this, my first meeting with Beethoven, I have had a full-fledged affinity for his music.

Music was also the cause of my first love. At the age of eight I heard Laura, one of the girls in our class, performing beautifully on the piano and immediately fell in love with her. I can still see her, her pretty face, long dark hair, playing with verve and charm. I never spoke to her, and she never knew about my feelings, so that is as far as it went.

Papa bought me some books to read. Among them were all ten volumes of *The Children's Encyclopedia* by Arthur Mee, and a world atlas. The latter stimulated my interest in geography and I would gaze at the maps for hours. Papa would give me little problems to solve, such as finding a certain city, or working out the exact latitude and longitude of a given place.

But it was really Mrs. Watson who taught me to love books and reading. Mrs. Watson was a plump, motherly woman, with greying hair, who lacked some teeth, and wore half-rimmed spectacles over which she would peer at me. She was a seamstress from Port Elizabeth, who, for a few months in 1943, came to the farm to help Maman with sewing issues. I would lie on the floor on my stomach in her sewing room, feet waving and swinging above and behind me, surrounded by her equipment and materials, one of Mee's Encyclopedia volumes under my nose, and we would discuss all the fascinating wonders of the world revealed therein. Mrs. Watson also introduced me to the William books by Richmal Crompton, and the wondrous world of Jules Verne, and I quickly mowed them all down. Perhaps because I was totally the opposite, with a desire to avoid trouble like the plague, I identified completely with William, and all the antics and mischief he got into. I have never forgotten Mrs. Watson; my contact with her was brief, and she had a life-long impact on me. Wherever you are, dear lady, thank you.

Boys were not permitted to continue past Grade 4 at the convent, so in 1945, at the age of eleven, a decision was made to send me as a boarder to the newly opened Marist Brothers College, at Inanda in Johannesburg, now called St. David's College. Both my sisters had been sent to Roedean, a well-known girls' school in the city, so it was thought appropriate to send me to school in Johannesburg as well. Maman accompanied me on the train due north from Cradock, a thirty-six-hour, 1,000-kilometre train ride up steep inclines to Johannesburg, far above sea level. There she introduced me to the school and the brothers.

The two years I spent in Johannesburg were the unhappiest in my life. It took me a year to adjust and recover from homesickness. No doubt, I had a form of childhood depression, but in those days, there were no therapists or counselors, so I had to make the best of it myself. Hope seemed to have abandoned me. I held on to the resentments for many years thereafter.

When I accosted my mother about it in later life, she would say, simply, *"What else could we have done? I was sick, your father was away, we could not send you to an Afrikaans secular school in Cradock."* She might also have added, a horrific world war was going on and we were stuck in that isolated place in the middle of nowhere. I am sure she was right; there was nothing much else she could have done.

One of many unpleasant memories of my time with the Marist Brothers was trudging to the movies on Saturday afternoons. The whole school would march, in crocodile formation, to the local bioscope,[1] the Odeon, to watch the latest American horror movie. I have retained an aversion to this genre ever since.

Boys slept forty to a dormitory, four rows of ten, each dormitory monitored by a brother. At one-mile-high elevation, Johannesburg gets cold in the winter and there was no heating in the school buildings. In the mornings I would wake up with my feet like blocks of ice. I wrote to my mother, who suggested I wear socks in bed at night. On the first morning after I did so, Brother Bartholomew accosted me. "Come and see me in my office tonight," he said sternly. I was given six cuts on the backside with the leather strap for wearing socks in bed! I was never, thank goodness, abused sexually, and as far as I know none of the other boys was either. Sex abuse of boys has been reported in Marist Brothers Colleges in Australia, New Zealand, Spain, and Chile, but not in South Africa. Most of the brothers were caring and dedicated men.

I am sure that the general sexual abuse of minors was as prevalent then as it became later in the twentieth century, especially in boarding (residential) schools. If one heard about a man who was a sexual predator, one gave him a wide berth, cracked snide jokes about him, and left it at that. Nothing was said aloud. It was never the huge public health and criminal issue it became in the 1980s and 1990s. The tragedy is that many young boys and girls who were abused then were scarred for life, and the perpetrators died before being brought to justice.

Curiously, my unhappiness at Marist Brothers did not come through in the letters I wrote home. Maman diligently kept nearly all the letters I

---

1 A South African term for cinema.

wrote from 1943 until shortly before she died in 1995. I only discovered them after her death. From this I can only conclude that I suppressed my feelings, keeping them from my parents, not wanting to disappoint them. Another possibility is that she discarded the letters in which I complained about my miseries. In none of the letters do I mention the horror movies I so hated. Instead, I told them how much I enjoyed Laurel and Hardy, and *Son of Flicker*. On another occasion I state, with thinly disguised sarcasm, "Yesterday at the bioscope we saw 'Three is a family'. It was not bad, not any <u>love</u>" (three underlinings of love in original).

Bullying was endemic at Marist Brothers, as it likely was in all schools. Although not bullied myself, I was on one occasion, to my eternal regret, a perpetrator. My victim was an unfortunate boy called Lucas, who used the locker adjacent to mine, forcing us to interact daily. I took a dislike to Lucas. He was unattractive, had body odour, was non-communicative and a grouch. I knew he was unpopular with others, as well, so one day I challenged him to a boxing match. I am not much of a boxer, but egged on by a group of fellow students, I gave him a sound physical beating.

Looking back on these events, I now have deep remorse about my behaviour. I have no doubt that Lucas came from a deprived family and social background, and I only added to his woes. I don't know what happened to him subsequently, but hope his life improved after me.

I was myself the victim of bullying later, as a first-year medical student. A fellow student called Jan, an Afrikaner, took a dislike to me and my French ancestry. He was much bigger and stronger than me, and he teased me mercilessly about my background, short stature, and rounded facial features. A popular form of bullying was to shave off the victim's hair, and I had a horror-filled fear of this being done to me. Of course, Jan noted my fear and this stoked his bullying behaviour, making my life a misery. In those days there was no official denunciation of bullying, so victims had to cope with it alone, as best they could.

Boxing was the rage in South Africa during my childhood. In 1946, while at Marist Brothers, the whole school was rivetted by the world heavyweight championship between Joe Louis and Billy Conn. Louis had knocked out Conn at their only previous meeting in 1942, in the thirteenth round of a fifteen-round contest, even though Conn had been leading until that point. Conn was a light heavyweight and was hoping to become the first in that category to become the world heavyweight champion. The whole school, of course, was united in the hope that Conn, an Irish-American, would defeat Louis, a Black, but Conn was knocked out in the eighth round, much to the school's chagrin.

As an adult I have a total aversion to boxing, so it may seem puzzling that I was into boxing as a child. It is an example of how one can be swayed by crowd-power into supporting a sport or a political policy, even on a subject contrary to one's inner being.

My spell at Marist Brothers ended on a high note. I made four good friends there—a German boy called Binder, an Italian boy named Rudolph, a Jewish boy called Harry, and an English boy named Robert who lived in a one-bed apartment with his single mom. Lonely rejects all, and a bit like I felt myself to be. I lost touch with them all after I left the college. One of my classmates there, Peter Cazalet, has become a world-renowned ballet dancer, and an expert on stage design. In retrospect, it is curious that German, Italian, and Jewish émigrés in South Africa sent their children to Catholic schools during the war years. Perhaps they sensed less prejudice there. I also finished Marist Brothers on a high note academically, coming second in Grade 6 in a class of thirty-two boys.

The war ended, finally, in 1945. I remember the joy and excitement at school when this happened, scarcely a thought given to the tens of millions whose lives had been lost or wrecked in Europe, Asia, and Africa by carpet and atomic bombing and other assorted lethal weaponry.

Maman's health had gradually improved, so in 1946, Papa sold Riverview and the family returned to Port Elizabeth. My schooling in Johannesburg ended, and from 1947 until completing high school matriculation in 1950, I attended Grey High School in Port Elizabeth.

Grey High was named after the liberal governor of the Cape Colony, Sir George Grey, who founded the school in 1856. An explorer as a young man in Australia, he was British governor of the Cape Colony from 1854 until 1861. He is far better known in New Zealand, where he was governor both before and after his sojourn at the Cape. He even became one of the earliest prime ministers of New Zealand, after it became a self-governing colony. He played a big part in attempting to settle the Maori question, and also in creating the New Zealand constitution.

In South Africa, despite a relatively short stay as governor, he opened schools and libraries, often with books that he, as a life-long collector, donated himself. A man with a knack for saving colonies from economic ruin, he was ahead of his time, and proposed that the four provinces—the Cape Colony, Natal, Orange Free State, and Transvaal—join and become a unitary federation on the Canadian model. As this was contrary to colonial policy at the time, he was dismissed and recalled to London. His policies toward Indigenous people were liberal for that period in history, though would certainly be regarded as reactionary now. He died in London, in 1898, two years after reconciling with his wife after forty years of separation.

David, François, and Vincent in Grey High School uniform, c. 1948

Grey High School was, and still is, a boys-only school with approximately one third of its pupils living in residences as boarders. It was the poshest school in Port Elizabeth, modeled on the British public school, with strong discipline and regimentation. The school is on spacious grounds, surrounded by playing fields and trees. All buildings are whitewashed, with a spark of the old Dutch gables visible in their facade. The central edifice is crowned by an impressive clock-tower that chimes the time every fifteen minutes. The headmaster's office is directly under the clock tower.

The teachers and teaching were mostly of high calibre. At that time, each grade was streamed into four categories: A, B, C, and D. A was for the academically gifted, B for the less gifted, C for commercial students, and D for students with technical aptitudes. For Grades 7 and 8, I was in the A stream, and for Grades 9 and 10, in the D stream. The change came about because I did not do well in the Grade 8 examinations, and because I wished to drop Latin and take geography instead.

For three months in mid-1947, our schooling was interrupted by a family visit to France, when all of us, with the exception of Christiane, who was studying radiography, took the mail boat to Europe to visit our grandparents. Between 1940 and 1944, there had been no communication between my parents and their parents, and their respective families, who were all isolated in German-occupied France. Maman discovered that her father was ill, and he died in 1945, but her mother was still alive, as were Papa's parents. I have just one vivid memory of my maternal grandfather. In the summer of 1939, he took me, aged four and a half, for a ride on the pinion of his motorbike and we went to watch the Tour-de-France cyclists whizzing through Aix-en-Provence at high speed.

The visit to both sets of families in 1947, Maman's in Aix-en-Provence and Papa's at Wimereux, near Boulogne-Sur-Mer, was very enjoyable. Our teachers had given us set-work to do while we were away, and our older sister Denyse acted as tutor to her three younger brothers. Fortunately, she was not strict and my brothers and I got away with much mischief. We played cricket wherever we went, and young French boys who watched us were drop-jawed at this astonishing game. At Wimereux, with the white cliffs of Dover visible in the distance, we played war games in the blockhouses overlooking the Channel that had just recently been vacated by their German army builders. I teased Grandpère about the little red ribbon he had in the lapel of his jacket; he had been awarded a *Légion d'honneur* for the services he rendered France as a spy in Lille during World War I. He responded, very indulgently, at the ignorance of what he must have regarded his hillbilly South African grandchildren.

We discovered we had a cousin, John Watson-Smith, oldest son of my mother's sister Hélène. John had joined the French Resistance under Charles De Gaulle. He was captured by the Nazis shortly after D-Day, then tortured and executed on July 8, 1944, at the age of twenty-two. I have a haunting photo of him taken shortly before his death, surrounded by English airmen he had rescued and hidden, and have been told by several people I resembled him when I was his age.

My first cousin, John Watson-Smith (centre) surrounded by four un-named Allied airmen in 1944, shortly before his capture, torture, and execution by the Nazis.

We had previously visited France in 1939, just before the outbreak of war, and, aged four and a half, I learned to swim in the Aix-en-Provence municipal pool during that visit. Our coach's teaching technique was to hurl me into the water at the deep end and force me to swim to the side to survive, rendering me panic-stricken. When we returned in 1947, I discovered that this man had been shot by the French after the war for collaboration with the Nazis. *Rough justice*, I thought!

Getting back to South Africa in late 1947, I found I had missed out on much schoolwork, and only achieved a second-class pass in the Grade 8 examinations the following year. However, I changed one of my courses, studied more consistently, and was able to upgrade this to a first-class pass in the matriculation and final examinations at the end of Grade 10.

During my final two years of high school, I took strongly to English and Afrikaans, and also to mathematics, physics, and chemistry. I became fascinated by the chemical elements and the Periodic Table, and amassed a collection of forty of the ninety-two known elements by the time I completed high school. I was particularly enthralled by sodium and potassium, which flared when touched by water, and had a small jar of mercury, with a high density and weight. I loved its silvery liquidity. At our home at Totteridge there was a small shed close to the farmhouse that acted as my laboratory. Regretfully, it all disappeared when the farm was sold.

Our physics teacher was something of a sadist. On one occasion, to illustrate the electrical difference between voltage and amperage, he made the class stand in a circle holding hands, and threw a high-voltage, low-amperage current through us. We all screamed in pain at the shock intensity. We survived, but it was a grossly unpleasant event, to say the least. A good learning experience though; I have never forgotten that it is high amperage, not high voltage, that kills! I doubt that a modern-day physics teacher would escape serious discipline charges for inflicting this on pupils.

We had a boy in our class called Myron Sandwick. During our school years we were not especially friendly. After matriculation he went to Johannesburg to do dentistry and I went to Cape Town to do medicine, and we had nothing to do with each other for the next sixty-seven years. He returned to Port Elizabeth to practise, and I travelled the world. In 2017, now both well into our eighties, we re-met on the internet, re-introduced by my brother Vincent, and since then, have become close, though distant pen-friends. Shared childhood experiences have great meaning in later life.

The year 1948 was a huge turning point in the South African political landscape, when General Jan Smuts, prime minister and part of the political scene for fifty years, was defeated by the National Party under Dr. Daniel Malan. Smuts had been prime minister off and on for almost thirty years. Although little explicit anti-Black legislation had been passed during the many years that the United Party was in power, it made sure that any calls to liberalize the vote to include Blacks were knocked down. The only exception were three white representatives of all Blacks, in a House of more than 150 members. Even this limited degree of liberalism was too much for the National Party (NP), who abolished this representation shortly after they came to power. During the thirties and forties, the NP progressively increased their share of the vote amongst Afrikaner people by appealing to the "Swart Gevaar," the Black Danger, the fear that the Blacks, who far outnumbered the whites in population, would swamp and eventually take over the country. Their reward came in 1948, and the NP dominated South African politics for the next forty-six years, until 1994, when the African National Congress (ANC), under the leadership of Nelson Mandela, won the election and he became the first Black president of South Africa.

Unwritten apartheid had existed in South Africa since the Act of Union in 1910, when, ironically, the four provinces—the Cape, Natal, Transvaal, and the Orange Free State—united to form one country. Apartheid had been covertly promoted by General Smuts as prime minister or senior minister during most of that time, and it was the National Party that introduced and enforced all the offensive racial legislative measures over the forty-six years they were in power. Although I was unaware of it at the time, the election of the National Party was to have a huge impact on all South Africans, including my family.

At the time, that drama passed me by, as I was not yet sensitive to the pervading injustices of apartheid. My politicization appeared only in the 1950s, when I became a medical student. Living with an Afrikaans-speaking family was of great assistance academically, as it helped me obtain a first-class pass in my matriculation exams, and I was pretty-well functionally trilingual when I entered medical school in 1951.

Papa bought the farm, called Totteridge Park, near the village of Redhouse, in 1946, when we moved from Cradock, and kept it until 1962, when he retired from his job as director of the firm's operations in South Africa. He was essentially a gentleman farmer and at various times he had chickens, sheep, and cattle. The farmhouse was a magnificent structure with arched porticoes on the lower-floor balcony, beautiful, solid, dark stinkwood beams on the ceiling in large sitting and dining rooms, pegged wooden floors, and a large kitchen with a sturdy wood stove. It was built around the year 1900 by descendants of the 1820 settlers from Britain who founded Port Elizabeth in the nineteenth century. The house was declared a national monument in 1985, and there were plans to make it a tourist attraction. It came to a sad end.

In 1988, the then-owner, Gerhardus Gouws, shot and killed his wife, set fire to the house, and killed himself. It was never rebuilt. I visited the farm in 1996, and gazed with grief at the ruined, black, derelict building that had been our beautiful home for sixteen years. Sometimes it is preferable to retain the memory than see the present-day reality.

Our home at Totteridge Park, with family lined up on entrance stoep c. 1950.
The house burned down in the 1988 and was never rebuilt.

While at Totteridge I joined a Sea-Scout troop, and one year the troop travelled by train to camp at the Victoria Falls on the Zambezi River, 3,000 kilometres north of Port Elizabeth. We hiked to the bottom of the gorge to be sprayed by the falls, and went boating on the river above the falls, sharing it with crocodiles and hippopotamuses. On the train back we stopped off at Kimberley, where we saw the Big Hole, at that time the largest cavity on earth, gouged by muscle power alone. Billions worth of diamonds were dug out of the ground, and hundreds of workers lost their lives following accidents in the effort.

In Kimberley, we were billeted at the Red Cross office building and I had the misfortune to sleep alongside a human skeleton, housed in a vertical, coffin-like structure. I did not get much sleep that night!

We had many good teachers at Grey High School, and it was our English teacher Dudley Clear (whom we mischievously and rather unfairly nicknamed Clearly Dud) who taught me to write, and to appreciate literature and poetry. Once a month we had to write and hand in an essay, and he, slowly, somewhat painfully, taught me the elements of spelling, syntax, and sentence and paragraph structure. Through him I retain a love for the English classic novelists and poets such as Shakespeare, Hardy, Austen, the Brontës, Dickens, Coleridge, Wordsworth, Keats, and others. I can still see him pacing up and down the aisles of our classroom, reading Coleridge's epic poem *The Rime of the Ancient Mariner*, reciting it with all its onomatopoeic and alliterative intensity:

"God save thee ancient Mariner!

From the fiends that plague thee thus! —

Why look'st thou so? – With my cross bow

I shot the ALBATROSS.

All in a hot and copper sky,

The bloody sun at noon,

Right up above the mast did stand,

No bigger than the moon.

Day after day, day after day,

We stuck, nor breath nor motion;

As idle as a painted ship

Upon a painted ocean.

Water, water, everywhere,

And all the boards did shrink;

Water, water everywhere,

Nor any drop to drink."

I have a wonderful edition of the *Rime*, with dramatic paintings by Gustave Doré, that I often leaf through and recite. Mr. Clear also took us for long hikes to the wilderness beaches around Port Elizabeth, where we would socialize and play games. I cherish these memories.

Mr. Waring (nicknamed Cocky), our mathematics teacher, was another who made a big impression. He would tell us, his "brilliant" class of A students, using a mock serious tone of voice while tapping the back of his right hand on to the palm of his left, "Last Sunday I went down to the harbour [in Port Elizabeth] and I saw the jellyfish flopping up and down helplessly against the pier, doing nothing, thinking nothing, just floating around and I said to myself, *there goes 7A*." Yet one felt that underneath this facetious manner, he retained a warm regard for us, his jellyfish students.

Mr. Ferguson (nicknamed "Gussie"), our history teacher, was bright, articulate, and knowledgeable. He would speak uninterruptedly for the forty-five-minute duration of the class, sending some students to sleep, though personally I was entranced by his anecdotes. My friend Desmond ffolliott and I noticed that, while speaking, he salivated profusely, sending spittle flying through the air onto the floor. So, we mischievously stole some elemental sodium from the chemistry laboratory, cut it into tiny pieces, and distributed them on the floor in front of the teacher's desk before Gussie entered the classroom. Sodium is element 11 on the Periodic Table, and reacts strongly when it comes into contact with water. We would watch, and struggle to stifle our smiles as the sodium would flare up in tiny sparks on the floor as the spittle and element connected, while Gussie continued his didactic monologue on ancient Roman or Egyptian history, perhaps pretending not to see the sparks. Gussie aroused my lifelong interest in history.

Standard 7A Grey High School, 1947.

François, seated, front row at left; Myron Sandwick, back row, second from left; "Gussie" Ferguson, our history teacher, seated, in centre; Denis Pudifin, my friend and roommate while we were medical students together in Cape Town, who later became a well-known academic internist in Durban, is standing second from the right in the second row from the back.

Our headmaster was Mr. Gordon (nicknamed "Flash"), a pleasant enough man but also a strict disciplinarian. He did not teach any classes, and my only contact with him was being sent down to his office for cuts on the backside when I failed to do my homework.

My classmate Desmond and I shared a fascination with chemistry and we decided to make a bomb. Desmond and his family had immigrated to South Africa from Northern Ireland in 1948 because his father, a family physician, objected to the introduction of the National Health Service in the United

Kingdom. Desmond was proud of having an ancestor who was one of the four soldiers who assassinated Thomas Becket, archbishop of Canterbury, at the orders of King Henry II, in 1170. Desmond took the initiative in making the bomb, perhaps influenced by his experiences in the Northern Ireland political maelstrom. We collected and put together the ingredients and, to avoid police detection, took them to a remote area in the bush outside Port Elizabeth. The resulting explosion was successful, and now, seventy years later, I still have a perforated eardrum to commemorate it. Desmond and I charted separate careers when we left Grey after matriculating. He completed training as an accountant, but by remarkable coincidence, we reconnected in London, Ontario, when we moved there in 1972, twenty-two years later.

Of course, I was teased relentlessly about by French ethnic origins, especially by the sons of British migrants, who quickly nicknamed me "Froggie." This led me to try to conceal my ethnic origins—not very easy when my name is "François" and one of my middle names is "Marie." A Welsh boy named Glyn appeared the leader of this group. Each time he saw me it was, "Hi, Froggie!" with just that element of disdain that made him, and others with him, giggle or roar with laughter, with pictures in their heads of our family guzzling down dozens of these unfortunate amphibians at every meal. I consulted with Maman, who, knowing of the Welsh love of leeks, suggested I call Glyn "Leeky" in return. I did, and the Froggie epithet quickly vanished.

I was also training hard as a swimmer, with backstroke as my specialty, following in the footsteps of Christiane, my older sister, a champion backstroker. Christiane won the South African women's backstroke championship, and narrowly missed out representing the country at the London Olympics of 1948 and Helsinki in 1952. I was rewarded in 1950, at age fifteen, by winning the South African Junior 100-yard backstroke championship held in Pietermaritzburg. A year later, I won the bronze medal in the Redhouse River Mile, an annual long-distance event featuring over 100 competitors from the Eastern Cape Province.

I continued competitive swimming throughout my years as a medical student and represented the University of Cape Town at the annual intervarsity tournaments, winning several key races for the university, and earned a swimming "blue." However, I never again succeeded at the national level. Successful swimmers have to be tall and long-boned, and have large paddles for hands and feet, and I stopped growing at around sixteen. Perhaps my short stature spurred my academic studies.

Grey High School swimming team wearing ultra-modern, stylish swimsuits, c. 1949. François, front row second from right. Peter Ponsonby, our coach, in centre.

University of Cape Town swim team, c. 1954. François, seated on right. Bill Ritchie, later a well-known architect in South Africa, in white jacket, seated third from right.

All sports were encouraged at Grey, but cricket and rugby were the centrepieces. David excelled at cricket and Vincent at rugby, and both achieved major success.

There is a fascinating sequel to the school's sponsorship of sports. In October 2019, sixty-nine years after I matriculated from Grey, and twenty-five years after the end of Apartheid, South Africa won the World Cup finals rugby match against England in Tokyo, Japan, to the great jubilation of South Africans of all colours. The captain of the South African team was Siya Kolisi, from Port Elizabeth, the first Black South African ever to lead the national team.

After the final game in Tokyo, the English journal *The Guardian* had the following item in its report of the game, "Siya Kolisi (the team captain) grew up in deep poverty but was spotted by scouts and won a sports scholarship to a prestigious school with a record of producing sports stars." The prestigious school was Grey, and the sponsor of the scholarship was Vincent, my brother!

Vincent, himself well over six feet tall, in centre, dwarfed by Siya Kolisi at left, and Eben Etzebeth, at right, respectively captain and lock of the Springbok South African rugby team.

Chapter Five
Moving into Medicine

With high school behind me, the big question arose: What was I to do with the rest of my life? I had turned sixteen in December 1950, and was quite undecided about what career to choose. Once a month, Papa would take me out for lunch at the posh restaurant in the King Edward Hotel in Port Elizabeth for fatherly chats, and he gently but firmly suggested I go into medicine.

Maman kept the results of a vocational guidance test I took at the end of my matriculation, and I have it front of me now. It is not detailed, but it gives my twelve fields of interests in order of preference. The top three were social intercourse, conversation (individual), science/laboratory work. The bottom three were public speaking, working with machines and mechanical devices, and business buying and selling. The report ended by stating, "Francois' decision to become a doctor is a wise one." I have no regrets about that decision, but even now, seventy years later, business, buying and selling remain at the bottom of my list of fields of interest. The guidance counsellor quickly spotted that, unlike my father and my brother Vincent, I was no entrepreneur, and I remain so.

I knew that Papa had wanted to be a doctor, but for various reasons, this never happened. Getting a first-class matriculation pass that included mathematics rendered me eligible for medicine, and as I did not have a better idea, that is what happened. I enrolled in the faculty of medicine at the University of Cape Town, starting February 1951. I had not much of a clue what I was undertaking, struggled with studying, and promptly failed the mid-term examinations in June.

Then something happened. I am not sure where or how the idea got into my head, but I decided I wanted to be a pediatrician, wanted it really badly. I knew that to be a pediatrician one had to be a physician first, so for the rest of the academic year, with that incredible incentive to stimulate me, I studied like a miner working under a hard-driving master, and passed the year-end examinations with flying colours. The pediatrics idea died almost as swiftly as it had arrived—I'm not sure why, but it likely just petered out. I lost my fervour about caring for children. But by then I was launched into my medical career.

South Africa follows the British, not the North American, model in medical education. Hence, the first year consisted of basic sciences—chemistry, physics, zoology, and botany. Year Two was anatomy and physiology; Year Three: pathology and pharmacology. The final three years were the clinical years—medicine, surgery, and obstetrics and gynecology. Psychiatry occupied a tiny portion of Year Five. On qualifying at the end of six years, one is awarded a bachelor of medicine and a bachelor of surgery. Year One was the sorting-out year. There were 250 aspiring doctors in first year, and a maximum of 120 passed into the second year. Thereafter, one had to do really poorly to be thrown out of medical school.

I was not a top medical student. In both second and third years, I got involved in playing bridge every evening with my fellow students in the boarding house where we lived. I became a better bridge player but a poorer student. As a result, I failed physiology in Year Two, and pathology in Year Three, but on both occasions managed to pass the supplemental examinations; thus, I did not lose a year.

I became quite depressed after the failure in pathology. To encourage me, Papa gave me a small car, a grey-blue Morris Mini-Minor. He also wrote me a sympathetic and supportive letter that included the Latin words, derived from the Catholic Mass, *"Sursum corda"* (Lift up your hearts). I replied, again following the Mass, *"Habemus ad Dominum"*

(We have lifted them up to the Lord). These were gracious and generous gestures from him, because I was largely to blame for my failures. Perhaps totally.

On one memorable, moonlit summer Saturday night, after completing our bridge at around eleven at night, someone said, "Let's climb Table Mountain." So, off the four of us trundled, firstly around the mountain to get to its front, then 3,500 feet up the steep and stony Platteklip Gorge, watching the lights of Cape Town get dimmer and smaller as we climbed. We arrived at the top in time to see a glorious sunrise. We returned down the back of the mountain through the beautiful Kirstenbosch Gardens, exhausted but exhilarated. The dreaminess continued for days thereafter.

While a medical student I joyfully continued playing and practising the piano, without taking lessons. I also learnt how to play the pipe organ, and was back-up organist at St. Michael's church at Rondebosch, a suburb of Cape Town. When at home at Port Elizabeth on holidays, Maman would give me pieces to practise, and I would return to Cape Town to work on them on pianos at the Conservatorium of Music at the university. The practice area was in a small prefabricated hut, divided into twelve tiny cubicles, without sound-proofing, each containing an upright piano. As I practised, one was deafened by the din of eleven other students practising simultaneously on surrounding pianos, and I could barely hear my own sound. It was like working in a machine shop.

On my return home for vacations, Maman and I would play together, she on her violin, me on the piano, and we would perform sonatas by Beethoven, Mozart, Schubert, and Dvorak. There was no audience and the quality, at least on my side, was modest, but I treasure those memories. Later in life, in both London and Ottawa, I was able to repeat this experience of playing in small musical ensembles with violinists, cellists, clarinetists, and flutists, and this gave me great pleasure. I frequently attended concerts given by the Cape Town City Orchestra, in which Maman had performed as a violinist twenty-five years earlier, and thus became familiar with the symphonies, concertos, and sonatas of Beethoven, Mozart, Brahms, and other great composers.

Performing a Mozart piano-violin sonata with Maman, c. 1973

Papa visited me briefly in September 1953, and in a letter to Maman and Denyse, I mention my pleasure at his gift of a series of long-playing records that he gave me, which included the opera *The Barber of Seville,* sung by Victoria de los Ángeles, Beethoven's 9th and 1st Symphonies, and Grieg's Piano Concerto. This letter was written just prior to Denyse's wedding with Richard, and I requested they send me photos of the wedding, adding, "I've come to the conclusion that I'll have to wait at least six years before I get married, and it's a very long time when you look into the future." In fact, I got married in December 1959, so the prediction was remarkably prescient!

As a third-year medical student, I visited France in the summer of 1953. This turned out to be the last time I would see Grandpère, because a year later he developed prostate cancer, for which he had a prostatectomy and castration. This was shortly after Huggins had discovered the value of testosterone suppression in the treatment of the disease. However, Grandpère died within a year of diagnosis, at the age of eighty-four.

During this visit to France, I spent time with my father's cousin, Dr. Guy Delpierre, who was a family doctor in Fauquembergues, a small country town not far from Boulogne. He had played his part during World War II, concealing British soldiers and airmen fleeing from the Germans. He later became a psychoanalyst, but his interest in the psychological aspects of medicine was obvious to me even then. He would take me on his housecalls, and while examining a patient he would give me a running commentary on the patient's attitudes and behaviour, even while diagnosing various physical health ailments. Medicine runs in the Delpierre family; Guy's middle son, Stéphane, also became a doctor, then a respirologist, and is now retired and living in Marseilles.

As part of this trip, the family, including David, Vincent, and me, went to London and dined with Mr. and Mrs. Anstey, Denyse's future parents-in-law. Their home was in a posh neighbourhood of London's West End, and their indoor servant arrangements were on a par with those found in *Downton Abbey*. My brothers and I were used to drinking wine. From a young age, in the French manner, we were given diluted wine at all evening meals. At the Anstey dinner that night, therefore, it was no problem offering wine to Vincent, aged thirteen, David, fifteen, and me, eighteen. The wine was good, so the three of us quickly drained our glasses, thinking it was diluted, like at home. The butler was trained to fill a glass that was empty. By the end of the meal, the three of us were quite sozzled, greatly embarrassing Denyse, Maman, and Papa, who were trying hard to impress the aristocratic Ansteys with how cultured the Mai family from the colonies was.

These comings-and-goings between South Africa and France have caused me much ethnic identity confusion. Like Pierre Trudeau, I could describe myself as a "citizen of the world." Displacement, of course, is a common occurrence in North America, Europe, and elsewhere, as tens of millions have been transposed, either voluntarily or otherwise. Fortunately, I remained in English-speaking Commonwealth countries, so was able to adapt easily.

An accent is like a rubber stamp on one's character, displaying one's ethnic or geographic origins as soon as one opens one's mouth. A few years ago, I was in Florida, and walked into a citrus fruit shop and asked the manager, "Please can I have some oranges?" His reply was, "Do you come from Cape Town or Johannesburg?"

Having lived in Canada now for nearly fifty years, and becoming a citizen in 1978, I am proud of my Canadian-ness and always root for Canadians in international sport competitions. However, if there are no Canadians performing, I retain a soft spot for both South African and French athletes.

I found my clinical years extraordinarily complex and confusing, most likely because of my youth and immaturity. I could not assimilate the huge mass of medical information thrown at us, and in Year Five, I seriously considered dropping out of medical school. Likely, it was associated with being clinically depressed, although I was not aware of this at the time. In those days there were no counsellors or even clinics to assist troubled students. Now it is the reverse; counsellors are everywhere, in schools and universities, and they appear out of the woodwork whenever there is a major disaster. There being no professionals, I consulted a fellow student, David Ferguson, who suggested it would be best for me to plod along, finish my course, and then perhaps take a year off. I did plod on, with difficulty, and in my final year failed surgery. I thus had to spend an extra six months to complete the supplemental, finally graduating in June of 1957.

In our fourth year we did our obstetrics and gynecology rotation and I witnessed my first childbirth. I wrote home to my family, "I was so amazed and enthralled that I could hardly believe my eyes. I just couldn't believe that it was actually a real human being who was coming out . . . to think it has happened to all of us!! We have to watch at least three deliveries before we're allowed to 'catch' one ourselves."

I retain a darker memory to do with the miracle of childbirth. I was assisting a resident, who was an Afrikaner—hence, presumably a member of the National Party—who was carrying out a caesarean section on a woman of colour. After removing the child, he immediately sterilized the mother by sectioning and tying the fallopian tubes, without having obtained prior written consent from her. He must have known about my sensitivities on this issue, because he tried to get me to do the dirty work of tying the tubes, but I refused. Apartheid reared its ugly head in all sorts of unexpected places.

The psychiatry program in Year Five was singularly uninspiring. In groups of fifteen students, we visited Valkenburg Hospital, the big psychiatric institution on the outskirts of Cape Town, to witness a psychiatrist interviewing a few patients. In addition, we had about ten didactic lectures, and the recommended text for study was *A Textbook of Psychiatry* by Henderson and Gillespie. The parts of the book I found most absorbing were the detailed case histories of individual patients, which sometimes continued on for many pages. It is fascinating to re-read these old narratives now, in the light of the huge changes that have occurred in psychiatry in the last sixty years. In those days, the mid-fifties, there were few treatments for psychiatric illness. Electric convulsion therapy, insulin shock treatment, and psychosurgery had been introduced in the previous twenty years. They were thought to be effective, although no one quite knew how, when, or why, so their use was grossly abused. Barbiturates, bromides, and paraldehyde were the main sedating agents, and they were used for agitated patients. Somehow, despite my lack of engagement, I managed to pass the oral examination that followed. At the time I had no special interest in psychiatry, and this exposure did little to stoke my enthusiasm.

Curiously, during my six years as a medical student, I developed no relationship with any of my teachers that could be regarded as mentoring. This could, of course, be because of my introspective character. However, the teachers at the University of Cape Town were high-powered academics with the publish-or-perish mentality, and I suspect they only showed interest in the top students, from which category I was definitely absent. My loss, because we had excellent faculty at the University of Cape Town: Professors John Brock (an old Grey boy) and Frank Forman headed the department of medicine, Jannie Louw, the department of surgery, and James Louw, obstetrics and gynecology. All were individuals with international reputations. The university continues to rank high in the world for its academic programs, and is still rated the top university in Africa.

The mid-1950s were the years of Elvis Presley and the birth of rock and roll and the beat poets. Young people would spend weekend nights acting out at dance halls and coffee bars. I say this now a little ruefully, for the joys of jazz and rock and roll completely passed me by, immersed and struggling as I was in my studies. I was socially reserved, and kept myself apart from social fads.

During my student years I played a part in developing a medical clinic, called SHAWCO—the Student Health and Welfare Centres Organization—in one of the shanty towns near Cape Town. A group of us would go there once a week with Dr. Golda Selzer, one of our pathology professors, to provide medical care to poverty-stricken residents. Selzer, together with a medical student, Andrew Kinnear, had founded SHAWCO several years earlier. The medical problems we witnessed were immense, and I suspect it was a little like trying to plug a leaking dyke with one's finger. Nevertheless, SHAWCO has now expanded into a huge enterprise with medical clinics and educational facilities in rural areas, in both the Western and Eastern Cape.

Clinical medical student group, 1955, François, seated on left.
Joce Kane-Berman, centre, the only woman in the group, later chief executive officer at Groot Schuur Hospital in Cape Town

With parents and brothers at medical school graduation—June 1957

Through my membership of the Kolbe Society, the students' Catholic group, I became involved with student politics, and, in July 1956, was elected president of the National Catholic Federation of Students (NCFS), a position I held for one year. This election came as quite a shock to me as I had not canvassed for it. I suspect it happened by default, because the two favoured candidates both faced strong opposition, and, like a dark horse, I came up the middle. When offered this position, I was in my last year of medicine, and knew I had heavy study responsibilities to prepare for my final examinations four months later, so I sent a telegram to Papa: "Have been offered NCFS presidency for one year. Advantages good for career. Disadvantage may fail my final exams." Papa replied, "Take it. A bird in the hand is worth two in the bush." I did take it and, as predicted, failed my final examinations. In my acceptance speech, I quoted Shakespeare's character Malvolio, in *Twelfth Night*, where he states, "Some are born great, some achieve greatness, and others have greatness thrust upon them." Being elected president of the NCFS was not exactly a great position, but I was proclaiming it was not a position I had actively sought.

During my year as president, I became friendly with the vice-president, Noel Burns. The friendship has continued through our lifetimes, and included our wives and children. Noel moved to Hamilton, Ontario, where he became an authority on Lake Erie, and wrote an excellent book, *Erie: The Lake that Survived,* on the pollution and eventual cleanup of the lake in the 1980s. With his family, he then moved to New Zealand, where he obtained a position cleaning up the inland waterways of that country. Unfortunately, Lyn, his lovely wife, died there in 1988 from breast cancer. The friendship between our families has endured for over sixty years.

In the mid-1950s, all mixed-race social activities were banned by legislation. On one occasion, while I was president, the NCFS held a mixed-race party on a beach near Durban, and next day it became headline news in newspapers throughout South Africa, complete with photographs of Black and white students actually socializing together around a fire and enjoying themselves. The extent to which the government blocked attempts to reconcile Black and white South Africa was outrageous, as was how it managed to get the entire South African press onside in its efforts. Even then, I had the feeling that our opposition to apartheid was akin to pinpricking an elephant.

On another occasion, the NCFS had an executive meeting at Pius XII University College, now the National University of Lesotho, in Maseru, Lesotho, then called Basutoland. One evening we heard some gunshots, rushed to the scene, and found a young Black man unconscious, lying on the ground, with wounds in his stomach. We placed him in a *bakkie*[2] to take him to the local hospital, and as the unofficial "doctor" in the group, I cared for him, cradling his head on my lap, while sitting in the van. There was little else I could do. I could feel his whole body going limp as he died from internal blood loss in my arms, the first death I ever witnessed.

In the early to mid-1950s, I and South Africans of all colours were riveted by the wedding of Seretse Khama, heir to the throne of Bechuanaland (now Botswana), and Ruth Williams, a white woman from London. They returned to Bechuanaland, but were exiled back to London through the political machinations of the South African government. It only emerged

---

2 A bakkie is the South African expression for a small pick-up truck

much later the extent to which the British government, behind the scenes, aided and abetted the South African government in its effort to prevent the Khamas from returning to their country. These egregious intrigues are strikingly portrayed in the movie *A Marriage of Inconvenience,* produced in 1990 and based on a book of the same name.

What was I to do after graduation? I decided to forego the competitive atmosphere of Groote Schuur Hospital, my teaching hospital alma mater. Instead, I chose Victoria Hospital, the small, 120-bed provincial institution in the suburb of Wynberg, on the eastern outskirts of Cape Town, behind Table Mountain. The hands-on clinical experience there was incredible. Every second night I was on emergency call and dealt with remarkable clinical problems. One night a young man was brought in with a six-inch dagger in his back, right up to the hilt. It had penetrated his lung but somehow had missed the heart and all major arteries, so he was alive. I had to pull the knife out by placing my foot on his back to get the leverage required. On another occasion, a family brought in a three-year-old Caucasian boy, his face blue from lack of oxygen, not breathing and without a pulse. He had been found at the bottom of the home garden swimming pool. On the floor in the corridor, just inside the front entrance of the hospital, I applied artificial respiration, compressing his chest rhythmically, lifting his little body, while letting his head hang down to allow all the water to drain out of his lungs. All this surrounded by his grief-stricken family and a group of nurses, looking on. (This was before the days of mouth-to-mouth resuscitation). After about five minutes, he started breathing spontaneously, his pulse returned, and his colour quickly changed from blue to pink, giving me a secret thrill, followed by grateful oohs and aahs from his family. He was admitted to the ward for one night and discharged next day with no permanent after-effects.

We saw endless young children with kwashiorkor, a form of malnourishment caused by severe protein deficiency in their diet. It was so common, and the hospital so crowded, we could not admit the children to the ward, and treated many as daily out-patients, where many died. I must admit that these experiences hardened my sensitivities to human distress.

It was the only way one could cope with the mass of human suffering one encountered.

The downside of working in the outpatient department was becoming infested with fleas. In the evening I would peel off my clothes in an empty bathtub. As the fleas sprang off my body they would land in the tub and could easily be seen against its white background. I would then spray them with ethyl chloride, a local anaesthetic normally used to freeze the skin in minor surgery. This would stun the fleas, following which they could easily be caught and crushed. My maximum number caught in one night was twenty-six.

I had the opportunity to perform minor surgery while at Victoria Hospital under the supervision of the resident. My first case was a young man requiring a circumcision because of phimosis. This is a condition affecting some young men, in which the foreskin of the penis is tight and cannot be pulled back. Circumcision is its appropriate treatment. After I scrubbed for the procedure, feeling a combination of excitement and apprehension, the resident saw my hands trembling and immediately decided that cutting off a foreskin was not the opportune way to start my surgical career, so he performed the procedure himself. Subsequently, I did carry out some appendectomy and herniorrhaphy operations without mishap, but to my relief, was never again considered for a circumcision.

Another unusual case, also involving the male sex organ, was a man in his twenties who came to the emergency department suffering from the rare condition of a fractured penis. The organ was visibly hemorrhagic, swollen, blue, and flaccid. The fracture had occurred during extra-vigorous sexual intercourse with his wife, though it can also be caused by violent masturbation. Because of the complexity and delicacy of the case, I had to involve the consultant surgeon in the treatment. He was so fascinated that he took over the care of this man, and transferred him to Groote Schuur Hospital for surgery, so I never saw him again. Even with surgical repair, a majority of men with this condition develop long-term complications such as erectile dysfunction. Let that be a lesson: moderation in all things.

Shortly after starting work at the Victoria Hospital, I wrote home, *"I am getting myself registered on the South African Medical and Dental Council as a medical practitioner, which will open up new and better jobs. The cost of registration, however, is fifteen pounds, which brings my already meagre savings to freezing point. It's surprising how money disappears—it's not stolen, it's not spent (much), it's not given away, it just disappears! But I'm not the first to realize this fact. On the whole I am thrifty, but it doesn't seem to help much. But at least I have been more or less self-supporting for the last year, which I have never been until now."* I wisely failed to mention in this letter that *argent* has a habit of slipping even through closed fingers.

At that time there was a shortage of laboratory and X-ray technicians, and at night we interns had to work the X-ray machines and carry out blood and urine analyses to make the emergency diagnoses. We also had to match blood for transfusions. One night a man was in surgery for treatment of a gastro-intestinal haemorrhage, and it was my task to ensure that the transfused blood matched the blood of the patient on the operating table. The lab was close to the surgical theatre, and the surgeon started shouting loudly and endlessly at me, within hearing of the theatre staff, "Mai, hurry up and complete the matching or the patient will die on the table!" He did not seem to care about the fact that if incompatible blood was transfused, the patient would also die. I was, after all, not a professional laboratory technician. I felt abused by the surgeon's public maltreatment of me—no hospital would tolerate that treatment of interns by a staff-man these days. In retrospect, it is remarkable that neither that patient, nor any others, died from an incompatible transfusion.

During my year as an intern, I was heavily committed to my clinical training, but had not forgotten my interest in South African history, or my political affiliations. I maintained my membership with the Liberal Party, lobbied parliamentarians on political matters, and subscribed to *Contact*, the party newsletter, published by Patrick Duncan, the well-known author and son of Sir Patrick Duncan, governor-general of South Africa from 1937 until his death in 1943.

Chapter Six
Tempestuous Times

South Africa is a country with a long and bloody narrative of colonization and the repression of its native peoples, a repression that, around the world, goes hand in hand with the 500-year history of European expansionism and exploitation. For a quarter of twentieth-century history, as momentous events unfolded, I was there. I was thirteen when the Duplessis family cheered the arrival of Apartheid, nineteen when I began to recognize Apartheid for what it was, and twenty-four when I left the country of my birth.

Knowledge of the history of one's land of birth and schooling arrives gradually, and many years of study have brought me an understanding of the effect that the colonization of South Africa had on the country, and on me. So, before I continue with my ambitions in medicine, allow me to summarize that history until my political awakening.

In 1497, a Portuguese ship skippered by Vasco da Gama became the first to round the southern point of Africa; he named it the Cape of Storms, on its way to the treasures of India and the Spice Islands. However, when he returned to Portugal, King Joao renamed it the Cape of Good Hope, a wonderfully symbolic and perhaps, now, ironic name. As a child, I read stories about the concept of Hope flying over South Africa during its early days, benignly predicting a wonderful future for that beautiful and empty country.

It was not until 1652, over 150 years later, that the Dutch decided to establish a permanent settlement in what is now Cape Town. A handful of settlers followed, including about 250 French Huguenot refugees, cruelly thrown out of France by the revocation of the Edict of Nantes by King Louis XIV in 1685. The Edict shattered the hundred years of religious tolerance practised under the influence of the great philosopher Michel de Montaigne in the sixteenth century.

Thousands of French Protestants fled to neighbouring countries, and some of those who went to Holland were sent to South Africa. They brought with them many skills including, joyfully, those of wine-making. Many settled in or near the town of Franschhoek (Afrikaans for French Corner). Other than their family names, little of French language or culture survived more than a generation or two. But there are traces: Franschhoek boasts a Huguenot Museum, French flags flutter in the wind, and one can even hear French being spoken, mostly by visitors from France. Around 20 percent of Afrikaners have French-origin surnames, such as du Toit, de Villiers, du Plessis, and Michaud, and most are proud of their ancestry.

The only representatives of the human race the Dutch found after their arrival in South Africa were the hunter-gatherers now called the San, also known as the Khoisan people. Conflicts quickly began, and it was not long before the Dutch governor placed a bounty on the heads of any San who refused employment or slavery. Another example of genocide, the saddest word in language.

The Dutch farmers slowly expanded eastward, and, in the late eighteenth century, they encountered the Bantu people, who had been slowly moving south and west from their origins in east Africa. The momentous encounter occurred at or near the Great Fish River, and it was not long before endless bloody battles began between the frontier Boers (as the Dutch farmers called themselves) and the Bantu peoples on the opposite side of the Fish River. The Bantu tribes were organized and powerful, and not as easily subjugated as the San.

During the Napoleonic Wars, the British took over the Cape from the Dutch, an action confirmed by the Council of Vienna in 1815. This became the setting for strife between the British government and the Boers, the British exerting far tighter control over the country than their Dutch forerunners. For the farmers, the last straw was the British Parliament enacting the release of all slaves in the Empire in 1833. The Boers, whose farms were mainly in the interior part of the eastern Cape Colony, decided to uproot and move, *en masse,* into the northern interior part of South Africa. This mass movement became known as *Die Groot Trek* and it has assumed mythological proportions in the culture and minds of Afrikanerdom. There, in the north, they were sure they would be out of range of nefarious British government control.

Initially they moved into the territory now known as Natal, but this led to struggles with the Zulus, so they retreated back to the area between the Orange River in the south, and Limpopo River in the north, an area relatively free of human habitation. Two Boer republics were established: in 1852, the Orange Free State—between the Orange and the Vaal Rivers—and, in 1854, the Transvaal—between the Vaal and the Limpopo Rivers.

An uneasy truce was established between the Boer republics and the British Cape Colony and this might have become permanent but for the discovery of diamonds in the Orange Free State in the 1870s, and gold in the Transvaal in the 1880s. A huge influx of prospectors followed, especially in the Transvaal, including entrepreneurs such as Cecil Rhodes and Alfred Beit. They became a substantial and powerful minority known as "Uitlanders" (those from elsewhere, foreigners) and pawns in the Anglo-Boer wars that followed. The Orange Free State was not affected to the same extent as Transvaal, mainly because the British government had hived off the diamond deposits to ensure they came under control of the Cape Colony.

Tensions between the two Boer republics and the British government continued throughout the 1880s and 1890s. Paul Kruger, who, as a boy, had emigrated north with the *Groot Trek*, was elected president of the Transvaal, and represented its interests with verve and expedience. He quickly became the big bug-bear of the British government. It became clear the British wanted to take over the republics, by force-of-arms if necessary. This was exemplified in the Jameson Raid in 1895, when Leander Jameson, a physician and friend of Cecil Rhodes, invaded the Transvaal with an armed commando, hoping to provoke an insurrection by the Uitlanders. The insurrection never arose, and the commando was quickly disarmed, its members arrested. The raid was a huge embarrassment to Rhodes, who was forced to resign his premiership of the Cape Colony.

In subsequent negotiations it became clear that the British government had lost none of its resolve to control the republics and the mines, using their support for the Uitlanders as a pretext. Following one set of bitter negotiations, Kruger concluded sadly, "You English just want to take over my country."

In October 1899, Kruger decided to declare war on Britain. His reasoning was that he would catch Britain by surprise and secure quick victories by capturing Natal and Durban, thereby securing a port to the sea, from which support and supplies from European allies could be replenished. In retrospect, this was a huge strategic error, because it galvanized Britain and its huge Empire resources into action. Under the Boer general, Louis Botha, who, eleven years later, became the first prime minister of a united South Africa, they invaded northern Natal and won some important victories in late 1899 and early 1900, though they never reached Durban.

The tide turned in February 1900, when British forces encircled and defeated a large Boer force under General Pieter Cronje at the battle of Paardeberg, and by mid-1900, both Bloemfontein and Pretoria were occupied. Kruger fled by train to the Mozambique coast and then to Holland, where he lived out his life.

With Bloemfontein and Pretoria occupied, and Kruger gone, many thought the war over, but it was not. For the next two years, the Boers conducted a guerilla campaign, living in the countryside, which of course they knew well, planning the capture of supplies from British troops to replenish their own depleted stores, and destroying telegraphic and rail communications. Some of the Boer generals, men such as de Wet, Botha, and Smuts, became household names in Europe because of their ability to inflict damage on the British, while evading capture themselves. At this point the histories of Canada and South Africa overlapped.

Canada, along with Australia and New Zealand, responded to the British government's call for armed support. This did not occur without great controversy, as Quebec strongly opposed providing aid and Wilfred

Laurier, the prime minister, himself from Quebec, had to tread a fine line between French and English Canadians. Eventually, Laurier agreed to supply an army of approximately 2,000 volunteers. The first contingent left in October 1899, and the second in January 1900. The great majority were British expatriates, but amongst them were a handful of French Quebecers and non-British Canadians.

As someone who has lived in both Canada and South Africa, this period of South African history is of especial interest to me, and it was while researching it that I came across a character in the Boer War, as amateur historians often do, whose life is one of abiding fascination.

John McCrae was a member of the second contingent that left Halifax for South Africa, arriving as the British were celebrating the victory at Paardeberg. He was a copious letter-writer, and the originals are held in the Library and Archives in Ottawa. I have transcribed all the letters he wrote to his family during the year he spent in South Africa, and also the official journal he kept as an officer in the army. McCrae spent the calendar year 1900 fighting for the British Empire against the Boers. Later, during World War I, McCrae became famous as the author of the poem *In Flanders Fields*, where he urged his countrymen to

> "Take up the quarrel with the foe
>
> To you from failing hands we throw
>
> The torch, be yours to hold [it] high.
>
> If ye break faith with us who die
>
> We shall not sleep, though poppies grow
>
> In Flanders fields."

I've had a lifelong fascination with McCrae because he, like me, was an academic, physician, and writer. In 1914, he co-authored, with John Adami, his department head, *A Textbook on Pathology for Students of Medicine*, which became a classic. He died four years later in 1918, from pneumococcal meningitis, in Boulogne, where my paternal family is from. Also, he is buried in the military cemetery in the small town of Wimereux, ten kilometres north of Boulogne, where our family visited our grandparents in 1947 and 1953.

McCrae was born in Guelph, Ontario, in 1872, and trained from an early age in the army reserves, in which his father also was a prominent figure. He attended medical school in Toronto, whence he graduated with honours in 1898, followed by a lectureship in pathology in the medical faculty at McGill University in Montreal. There, he became a popular figure and was well-known as a teacher, writer, poet, and researcher. Despite his Scottish ancestral background, he was an ardent British Empire loyalist and agitated to join the Canadian volunteers. With the support of his father and the faculty of medicine at McGill University, he was accepted into the second contingent, and arrived in Cape Town in mid-February 1900. His role was that of an artillery gunner, not a physician, but as he recounts in letters home to his family, he was not only an unofficial physician, but also an unofficial veterinary surgeon to his section. Cavalry was an essential part of both the British and the Boer generals masterminding the war. The death and destruction of these unfortunate horses were even harsher than those of the army personnel. Over 10 percent of them died *en route* from Canada before reaching Cape Town, and had to be thrown overboard.

Much to his chagrin, McCrae was assigned to protect the lines of communication—rail and telegraph —between the Cape and the republics, and to seek out Cape rebels, Afrikaners who were supporting the Boers against the Empire. His letters reveal he became increasingly bored and frustrated during this period. Eventually, after a four-month period, he was transferred to the eastern Transvaal, where he saw action at the battles of Pienaarspoort, Belfast, and Machadodorp. By this time, it had become British policy to invade Boer farm houses, eject the women and children, and send them to concentration camps. The purpose of this policy was to make it difficult for the Boers, fighting in the veld, to replenish their stores. In a letter to his mother from Machadodorp dated October 5, 1900, McCrae describes an expedition to destroy a farm:

> *[W]e had an action last week. On Tues. a.m. we went out as far as Gen. Grobler's farm—and took a good deal of the loot. At a place where we camped, some sniping was done, but there were no casualties. In one case firing from a house*

occurred. There were women, in the house, so we could not shell it. But next morning, we went out, and I took up a position covering the mounted infantry who went to the house. The night was a miserably wet one: heavy rain & hailstorms all through it. In the morning a regular scotch mist hung over everything so we could not see clearly for any distance. Otherwise, I daresay we would have a chance for some shells. The M.S. went to the house, gave the women ½ hour to get necessaries out, and burnt it. We got back in a very uncomfortable, cold drizzle, and got to camp in time to avoid a very heavy 2 hours rain which came on. The weather rather spoiled our expedition, as our plans had been rather more extensive."

McCrae gives no thought to the family of women and children they had ejected from their home, whom they left to cope with the heavy rain without shelter. One can dismiss this as collateral damage done to civilians during the course of pursuing a war, despite it being British policy to destroy Boer farms. Yet it is difficult to square this with McCrae's professional mission as a physician. His pugnacious attitude is reflected later in the same letter where he writes, "*I am sorry to see in the Globe and other Canadian newspapers—letters from grousing Tommies, on all sorts of grounds—that they will never volunteer under British officers again, etc. It makes me sick: I wonder if they are soldiers or babies.*" It appears that, to avoid internal conflict, McCrae was able to place his dual roles as a physician and a soldier in separate compartments in his brain. When manning his artillery guns, his responsibility as a caring and compassionate physician and human being was suppressed.

By the end of 1900, McCrae had become sick, likely with enteric fever, and decided to return to Canada, where he arrived in January 1901, and lived another seventeen years. Upon his return he was appointed professor of pathology at the University of Vermont, where he taught until 1911, also resuming his duties at McGill.

While McCrae was putting down his gun and taking up the stethoscope, the guerilla warfare that the Boers were executing against the British continued for another eighteen months and became increasingly brutal.

Both sides had the unofficial policy of take no prisoners, and prisoners were indeed shot. Breaker Morant, an Australian soldier who had allegedly shot a prisoner, was tried, found guilty, and executed, much to the fury of the Australian government and troops. On the Boer side, a well-known and liked Canadian, Gat Howard, a friend of McCrae's, was captured and shot by them. In a letter to his mother dated June 10, 1901, after returning to Canada, McCrae writes, "I was sorry to read Gen. Alderson's acct. of Gat Howard's death: it is likely to be true, and it seems like murder, sure enough."

Set up during the guerilla phase of the war, concentration camps became a huge blot on the British conduct of the war. The Boers were using their homes and farms to replenish equipment and supplies, so Lord Milner decided to burn Boer farms, destroy crops and farm animals, and herd the women and children into the camps, termed "Concentration." Blacks involved in the war were sent to separate camps. Conditions, especially hygiene and nutrition, were deplorable in the camps and over 25,000 whites, and almost as many Blacks, died during the nearly two-year period they were operative.

Emily Hobhouse, an English anti-war activist, supported by Olive Schreiner, played a large part in exposing and improving conditions in the camps. Hobhouse, an English woman from a family of activists, was invited by a radical British politician to investigate the plight of women and children in the war camps. Hobhouse visited several camps in South Africa between December 1900 and February 1901, and was appalled by the overcrowding, abysmal hygiene, sickness, and especially the pathetic condition of the children, who were dying at the rate of fifty a day. She returned to England, met politicians and others, and, in a harrowing report, described and decried what she had seen. This led to an improvement in the camp conditions, in particular the food and water quality, and the provision of better bedding and clothing. Hobhouse returned to South Africa in October 1901, but the governor refused permission for her to land in Cape Town, and she was obliged to return to England. After the war she became a heroine in South Africa, and was granted honorary citizenship in the country. Her ashes were placed in the National Women's Monument in Bloemfontein.

Another young person who rose to prominence during the war was Winston Churchill. Late in 1899, he went to South Africa as a journalist for the *Morning Post* in London. In an engagement with the Boers in Natal shortly after his arrival, he was captured. Churchill habitually carried a Mauser pistol with him, but on this occasion, he had left it in his tent. As he was wearing a military uniform at the time of his capture, the Boer commanders, Piet Joubert and Jan Smuts, spent much time debating whether he was a military man or a civilian. They eventually decided on the former, and he was placed on a train and imprisoned in Pretoria. He had barely arrived there when he began planning his escape. After carefully surveying the camp, the sentries, and surroundings, one evening he climbed over the fence and casually sauntered toward the Pretoria station, and walked east along the tracks, aiming for Lorenço Marques (now Maputo) in Portuguese East Africa. His escape was discovered the next day, and the Transvaal government immediately issued a proclamation: CHURCHILL: WANTED DEAD OR ALIVE.

Along the train tracks Churchill, by good fortune, encountered a friendly English family who sheltered, fed, and cleaned him up, and from there he managed to make his way back to the coast, buried in the cargo of a freight train. He returned to Durban by boat, then to the frontlines, from where he continued his reporting of the war. By this time, because of his incarceration and escape, he had become famous, both in England and South Africa.

There is a fascinating sequel to Churchill's story. He was an ardent British Empire loyalist, with no doubts that Britain was fighting a just war in South Africa, and this remained his opinion for many years thereafter. However, nearly fifty years later, in a short story entitled *The Dream*, Churchill recounts an imagined conversation with his (long-dead) father about the Anglo-Boer War. In the imagined discussion, his father tells him, "England should not have done that." It seems that, with the passage of time, and his leadership role in two mighty world wars, he had changed his mind about England's justification in fighting the South African war.

By early 1902, it became increasingly clear to the Boers they were fighting a losing battle. The British government generously allowed sixty Boer leaders and generals peaceful passage to come, from wherever they were in the veldt, to the town of Vereeniging in the Transvaal. There, peace negotiations were haggled out. In the end, the Boers lost suzerainty of their republics, but were able to eke out some compensation in the form of a £3-million grant to repair the destruction suffered in the war.

It is incredible that only eight years later, in 1910, a conference was held that led to the Act of Union of the four provinces—Cape Colony, Natal, Orange Free State and Transvaal. At the all-white elections held later that year, a Boer general, Louis Botha, who led the South Africa Party, became the first prime minister of a united South Africa. It seemed that Hope was at last smiling on this beautiful but blighted country!

Sidelined by both the British and the Boers, during the war and the peace negotiations that followed, were Black South Africans. Officially, they were not part of the war; unofficially both sides used and abused them for menial tasks, and tens of thousands lost their lives. Black leaders knew this, and after the Act of Union they gathered in Bloemfontein in 1912, and founded the African National Congress (ANC) to protect and further their interests.

During the middle years of my medical studentship, from 1954 on, I became politicized to the injustices and immorality of Apartheid. The National Party government was introducing increasingly tough anti-Black legislation, and Black South Africans were becoming increasingly strident in opposing it. I was influenced by my Catholic faith, which taught the equality of all men and women of any colour in the eyes of God.

Two illustrious men influenced my developing political convictions. The first was Father Peter Paul Feeney, chaplain to our Kolbe (Catholic students) Society. Tall, lithe, and handsome in his Dominican order white robes, he was an articulate and engaging man who helped me found an organization called *Quo Vadis* which arranged on-campus meetings to discuss political and ethical issues. The second was Martin Versfeld, professor of Philosophy at the University of Cape Town, who had an international reputation as an authority on Descartes, Aristotle and St. Augustine, and had published many books on these and other topics. The one I enjoyed most is *Food for Thought: A Philosopher's Cookbook*, an entertaining tome in which he reconciles the history of philosophy on the one hand, with cooking, eating, and recipes on the other. The book includes many recipes in which a key feature is the need for the chef to be creative, and never cook the same dish twice. Both Feeney and Versfeld were strongly liberal in their philosophic and political orientations, and I imbibed their imaginative ideas.

Fr. Peter Paul Feeney officiating at the wedding of my niece Marie-Louise, Christiane's daughter, with Brian Hancock, in St Michael's Church, Rondebosch, September 1973.

Through the ministrations of the chaplain and the teaching and written words of the philosopher I became an anti-apartheid activist, writing letters to the editor, taking part in demonstrations outside Parliament in Cape Town, often locked within a sandwich board stridently announcing to the world, END APARTHEID NOW, and organizing presentations at the university. As they were entering the House of Assembly, I got to see, though not to meet, National Party leaders such as Johannes Strydom (prime minister at the time), Eric Louw, who was foreign minister, and the noted future prime minister Hendrik Verwoerd, who was assassinated on the floor of the House of Assembly in 1966.

We had ten or twelve non-white students in our class, out of a total of 120. The term "non-white" was the official word used in South Africa to describe anyone whose ethnic origin was not Caucasian. Almost all the non-whites in our class were East Indian or "coloured" (mixed race) in origin. There were no Black Africans as they tended not to migrate to the Western Cape, from which area the university drew most of its students. The non-whites in the class were not allowed to examine white patients, or even watch an autopsy on a white individual. There were separate wards in the hospital for whites and non-whites, and quality and efficiency of care were not as good on the non-white wards. I remember being asked by a white woman, as I was about to examine her, whether I had used my stethoscope on a Black individual. She made me wipe it "clean" before she would allow me to examine her.

During the Apartheid era, all South Africans had to carry a card indicating their racial category: White, Black, "Coloured,"[3] or Indian. This led to appalling complications. If there was doubt as to whether a particular individual was white or "coloured", not only skin colour, but hair, eyes, nails, and even skin creases would be examined by a bureaucrat to help define the category. Many siblings from the same family would be classified into different races. Patients would be admitted to hospital in the white ward, where it would be deemed that they were, in fact, "coloured," so they would be transferred to the non-white ward. These legal and personal machinations caused untold misery to individuals and families.

We liberals were aware that the Nationalist government dubbed all its opponents, irrespective of their political affiliations, as Communist. As a practising Catholic, I was nothing of the sort. Years later, during the 1960s, I wrote a reference letter for my friend and medical colleague George Parsons. When I saw him subsequently, he told me the committee that interviewed him for the job asked him, "How come one of your reference letter-writers is a Communist?" Only then did I realize that the government had been collecting a file on my anti-apartheid activities. Although I have never seen the file, it probably still lies, gathering dust, in the archives somewhere in Pretoria.

---

3 "Coloured" was the official term used by the Apartheid regime to denote people of mixed-race origin. It now has offensive connotations. For this reason, when I use the word, I will place it in quotes.

My political activities were relatively tame. I did not risk limb and life, as did many other activists. In 1963, Albie Sachs, a lawyer with whom I had been friendly during our days as students, was arrested and placed in solitary confinement for ninety days with only the Bible to keep him company. When he was released, he was immediately re-arrested and placed in solitary for a further ninety days. In his book, *The Jail Diary of Albie Sachs*, he describes how he coped with the solitude, monotony, and intensive interrogations. He felt guilt and sorrow for what he knew was the much worse treatment meted out to Blacks when arrested. In 1988, by which time he had moved to Lorenço Marques (now Maputo), to distance himself from the violence, his right arm was blown off when he opened a letter bomb addressed to him. At the end of the Apartheid era, this remarkable individual helped draft the new South African Constitution, modeled on the Canadian, and subsequently was selected by Nelson Mandela to serve on the Supreme Court of South Africa. He remained a judge until his retirement in 2009. I met him again in Ottawa when he toured Canada in 2008 and he signed, rather unsteadily, a copy of his book I had bought many years previously—using his remaining left hand. The famous Black Consciousness leader and activist, Steve Biko, died in custody from beatings and torture after his arrest. Donald Woods, a journalist friend of Biko, has written a fascinating account of Biko's life and death, and of Woods' own dramatic escape from the South African police. Thousands of others were similarly harmed and died in the battle for justice in the country. Blacks who were suspected by their comrades of collaborating or snitching to the police were subjected to a ghastly death by "necklacing": a tire doused with gasoline was placed over their necks and set alight.

The prisons were filled with Black political activists, some of whom were incarcerated because of their violent opposition to Apartheid. Every year hundreds were executed by hanging for this reason. Many died after being tortured, or when they "jumped" or were pushed out of high police buildings. In his book *The Sharpeville Six*, Prakash Diar, a lawyer now living in Ottawa, describes his defense of a group of five men and one woman who were wrongly convicted of murdering a Black man during a riot in 1984. They were sentenced to death. This caused a huge international outcry and this, together with the finding that there had been coercion of state witnesses, eventually led to the verdict being reversed. The six were released, just days before the scheduled hangings in 1988. What they believed were to be their last few days on earth on Death Row, are described in dramatic detail in Diar's book.

Yet political activism continued in prison. In his autobiography *Long Walk To Freedom*, Mandela describes how he, together with many other prisoners on Robben Island, off the coast of Cape Town, were able to continue their education clandestinely, while imprisoned. Music, especially singing, played a huge part in buoying up the spirits of those under lock-and-key, a point also mentioned by Albie Sachs in his book. Hope is never far from the surface in South Africa, even in the most depressing circumstances. That hope was rewarded in 1994. Eighty-two long years after it was founded, after much conflict and suffering, the ANC finally took power in South Africa, following its first national and democratic elections.

Regretfully, violence continues in South Africa to this day, although it is now less racially tinged. An exception is the number of white farmers killed by Blacks on their isolated farms. The Baragwanath Hospital in Johannesburg, one of the biggest hospitals in the world, is internationally famous for its emergency department, and its management of trauma resulting from a vast array of weaponry. The human inventiveness for harming one another knows no bounds.

During my intern year, being associated with such dreadful events affecting the physical heart did not stop me from getting involved in other *affaires du coeur*.

Chapter Seven
Love at Second Sight

An event occurred during my twelve-month spell at Victoria Hospital that had a life-long impact on me. I met Sarie, my future wife. She was a staff nurse in the hospital and we had had some casual professional face-to-face dealings with each other over patients during my first six months in the hospital, without any spark alighting.

The small-miracle meeting occurred on New Year's Eve 1957. Sarie had planned to go out dancing with her boyfriend at the time, but at the last minute he stood her up. So, beautifully dressed in a new white outfit, looking like an angel, she came to the hospital to visit her girlfriend, and met me unexpectedly at the front door, just adjacent to the spot where I had resuscitated the young, half-drowned boy a few weeks earlier. It was not quite love at first sight, but something pretty close, so I invited her for a drive later in the evening when I had an hour or so to spare. We went up to Rhodes Memorial, a commonly used meeting spot in Cape Town for lovers.

Sarie loves telling the story of what we discussed that evening. A year or so previously, a young married couple with whom I was friendly invited me to lunch, and during the meal they made a written list, perhaps with a little of my help, on the qualities that my future wife would require. These were: she had to be petite, have long dark hair, speak French, be an active sportswoman, a lover of music, and be able to perform on the piano. She also had to be Catholic, be comfortably off, to dress well, and to love children. The arithmetic was simple: Sarie had only two—the final two—of these ten qualities, so she immediately dismissed herself as a candidate for being my wife.

Nevertheless, something clicked in both of us that night and we continued going for drives to the beaches, mountains, and gardens around Cape Town, becoming increasingly fond of each other. By the end of May, when Sarie left Cape Town to go to Provincial Hospital in Port Elizabeth to do her midwifery, I happily abandoned the remaining eight of the wifely requirements on that feckless list.

Sarie and François at our informal engagement, July 1958.

Sarie, née Roelofse, was born in the small, lovely town of George, on the Garden Route midway between Cape Town and Port Elizabeth. George and nearby Knysna are also the location of descendants of George Rex, an alleged illegitimate son of King George III, who settled there early in the nineteenth century, and himself fathered numerous children in the area.

Sarie's ancestors had come to South Africa during the seventeenth century from the Low Countries, France, and Denmark. Her mother's maiden name was Barnard, and Sarie's maternal grandfather, Koos, was brother to Chris Barnard's father, Adam. Chris Barnard was the surgeon who performed the world's first heart transplant operation in 1967 at Groote Schuur Hospital. In his book *One Life*, Barnard vividly describes his penurious childhood, very similar to that of Sarie, and also mentions his uncle Koos, who was a fisherman. As a resident, before he became famous, Barnard was one of my tutors when I did my surgical rotation, but we did not make much of an impression on each other.

Barnard's autobiography is a thoughtful analysis of his life and training leading up to his heart transplant operation. He emerges as a man who is driven by work and ambition, but also sensitive to the many medical, technical, and ethical problems raised by this enormously complex procedure. He describes in detail the surgery in the donor, the removal of the beating, living heart, from a young woman of twenty-five who had received major brain trauma in an auto crash. Then the immediate **anastomosing**[4] of all the great vessels of that heart, to those of the recipient, whose failing heart had been removed. The thrill and excitement in the operating room when the new heart started beating was palpable.

The recipient's name was Louis Washkansky, and Barnard details the five days following recovery, and the happiness Louis felt after surgery, before he succumbed to pneumonia eighteen days after the transplant. By the twelfth day following surgery it was becoming clear that pneumonia was going to kill him, yet instead of receiving palliative care, he was subjected to endless tests, antibiotics, naso-gastric feeding, and electrolyte infusions, in a desperate effort to keep him alive. This torturous treatment

---

4 **Note**: Words written in bold in the text are defined in the glossary on page 195

rendered him miserable for his final five days. Barnard was so involved emotionally with Washkansky's survival that it impaired his clinical judgement. It reminded me of the old adage:

> *Thou Shalt Not Kill*
>
> *but do not strive,*
>
> *Officiously,*
>
> *To keep alive.*

During World War II, when Sarie was around four years old, her family moved to the small town of Dewetsdorp in the Orange Free State, named after Christian de Wet's father. There, her father got a job in a reformatory school where he enrolled in upgrading courses in Bloemfontein, at the University of the Orange Free State. He eventually passed his matriculation examinations, and completed courses in construction and architecture. Subsequently he built some lovely homes in George. He had particular expertise in stone work, and I witnessed a beautiful living room hearth he built, in which fossil remains could be seen in the cut stone.

As a child, Sarie would follow her father around on his building projects and be his helpmate, and thus she imbibed a huge amount of information about building and construction. This has been very helpful to us in our married life. She can speak the language of builders, so when we have renovations or improvements, she is the one to manage the workers. Often, they would be shocked that it was the woman of the house giving orders as to what had to be done; they would turn their gaze to me as if to say, *"What do you say, man-of-the-house?"* I would say nothing, then look at Sarie indicating that in this home, it was the woman, not the man of the house, who made decisions about construction. Workers were singularly unimpressed with my incompetence and ignorance.

When Sarie was young her family was not well-to-do and, it being the war years, she recounts stories of going to one-room school-houses, barefoot on cold winter mornings, and being dressed up in old flour sacks, softened and prettied-up by her mother, who was a superlative seamstress. Sarie identifies with many of the anecdotes recounted by her cousin, Chris Barnard, in his autobiography *One Life,* about his childhood in the George and Knysna area. After the war, the family moved to Constantia, near Cape Town, where her father obtained another teaching job at the local reformatory school. She loved the area around Constantia, with its mountains, forests and streams and this gave her a love of nature, the outdoors and the freedom of exploration. Later Sarie's family moved back to George where she completed high school education. She did not relish the idea of spending the rest of her days in a small country town, so quickly made the decision, against the wishes of her parents, to move to Cape Town and take up nursing. She studied hard and passed all the examinations required to become a registered nurse, ending up at Victoria Hospital in Wynberg.

Sarie had an older brother, Boetie, and a younger sister, Rita. Their father was a strict disciplinarian and Boetie especially was affected by this. Yet both her father and Boetie had a tender side to their personalities. When Boetie got married he carried over the parenting technique to the way he raised his son, Martin. As a result, the latter, as an adult, had endless problems in personal relationships and holding down jobs. Boetie died following a stroke at the age of fifty-three.

During our visit to South Africa in April 2016, Sarie and I met Martin for lunch in Cape Town. Then in his late fifties, he was essentially destitute, with no job and no income. His parents were dead and he was abandoned by surviving members of his family, living on a pittance in a back-pack residence, doing odd jobs for older people. When his mother became ill following a stroke, he walked over 150 kilometres to be at her side (he could not afford transport) and provided total care for her until she died.

When we got back to Canada, I decided to send Martin a small monthly donation, to contribute to essential expenses. He was greatly appreciative of these gifts, and each time thanked me lavishly, calling me his "Star." I fully expected to continue these donations for the rest of my life and, after I died, to pass on this responsibility to one of my sons, his cousins.

A year later, after sending him that month's cash, he replied in his usual way, thanking me, his Star, profusely. In his email, he said, *"I've not been feeling well, François. I have a pulled muscle in my back and have a pain in my leg."* Before replying, I deliberated; *"Shall I tell him,"* I wondered, *"to go and see a doctor, and send him extra money to do so, or shall I just tell him to take a pain killer?"* Knowing of his limited circumstances I decided on the latter, and suggested he take some Tylenol. Twenty-four hours later, his sister wrote us to say Martin had died from a ruptured aortic aneurysm the day before. In other words, the symptoms he was describing to me in his email were the symptoms of the aneurysm that killed him; he was in the process of dying whilst we were in email communication with each other. I felt bad that I had not told him to go to a doctor or a hospital, although, because of the seriousness of a ruptured aortic aneurysm, it is doubtful that anything could have been done to save him. Perhaps, however, I did help ease his last few months of life on this earth.

I was coming to the end of my internship and now had to decide what to do next. In the 1950s, training programs for specialization in medicine were limited in South Africa, so I decided to go to England to seek a residency, though wasn't sure in what area. My vague plan was to get the necessary training and experience to become a general practitioner, then return to South Africa. For this, I needed more clinical experience in general medicine, obstetrics and gynecology, and psychiatry, so I briefly returned home to Port Elizabeth, said a sad farewell to family and to Sarie, and flew off to London. I spent six weeks living with my sister Denyse and Richard, her husband, at their beautiful home near Westerham, Kent trying, without success, to get a residency in obstetrics and gynecology.

Westerham is famous as the birthplace of James Wolfe, the victor of the Battle of Québec in 1759, and also as the home of Winston Churchill. His country home was at Chartwell, nearby. There are statues of both these great Englishmen in the town square.

Trying to get a job tested my patience to the extreme. "I am still waiting," I wrote home, "for letters to arrive telling me that my services are urgently required for a job here, or there, but none has arrived yet! But I'm waiting patiently. I've now decided to apply for a house-job in medicine as well, because they are easier to obtain than Obstetrics. I need more experience in medicine and it may give me an opening in obstetrics later on." Re-reading these letters home reminds me how keen I was then to go into obstetrics and gynecology. To me, now, it's a mystery, and a hidden blessing I was never offered a residency in ob-gyn. I likely would have made a very poor consultant in those specialties.

While waiting in Westerham I read, and was enthralled by the six volumes of Winston Churchill's history of the Second World War. Westerham is not far from Biggin Hill, one of the airfields used during the Battle of Britain. With Denyse and her family, we visited Biggin Hill during an air display of period Spitfires and Hurricanes. It seemed incredible that these small, slow-going planes were the instruments that sabotaged Hitler's efforts to dominate the globe. It was a lofty event.

Finally, I was offered an internship in medicine and neurology at St. Margaret's Hospital, Epping, Essex. The clinical experience I gained there was excellent, though both the consultant and resident were harsh teachers. Shortly after starting I wrote home, "I'm gradually beginning to understand the system at this hospital. At a ward-round last week I was given absolute h--- by my chief for not doing something properly, and he then began firing all sorts of questions at me, none of which I could answer. It wasn't a very impressive performance, in front of patients, nurses, and doctors, but he actually apologized afterward, and said it was all for my own good, with which I heartily agreed. I'm determined not to let this happen again!" I would not be so tolerant now of this abusive treatment by my seniors. As I discovered then and at Victoria Hospital in Cape Town, in those days, specialist-consultants could be very humiliating publicly toward their underlings.

While at St. Margaret's Hospital, I spent much of my time in dreamland, thinking about Sarie. It was the only time in my life I briefly contemplated suicide. I was depressed, lonely, and felt at sea in a foreign country, together with all the uncertainties about my future. These thoughts were short-lived and clearly never acted upon. Hope springs eternal.

Maman and Papa were opposed to my relationship with Sarie, because of ethnic and social status differences, and they hoped my going to London would help break it up, but it was too late for that. However, once we got married, they came not only to accept her, but also to respect and love her, for her initiative and practical common sense, and for the effect she had on me and my career plans. And for producing many grandsons for them.

During the ensuing ten months we were apart we corresponded almost daily by snail-mail. Remember, this was 1958-59—no email, no texting, no Skyping. Even telephoning long distance was horrendously expensive for a poor medical intern. We still have a box containing hundreds of love letters we exchanged. They will be opened another day.

In April 1959 Sarie completed her midwifery training and immediately got on the mail boat and sailed to England. I went to meet her in Southampton and it was shortly after that we became engaged. By that time, we already had a wordless commitment to each other, but to confirm it I asked her, *"My Darlingk* [my nickname for her], *will you be the mother of my children?"* She replied with a very firm hug!

The next problem was getting an engagement ring. My monthly stipend was around twenty-five pounds, and when I gazed into the windows of jewellery shops, I noted even the smallest rings were at least that amount. So, I delayed the decision as long as possible. I was thrown headlong into the purchase by a big family event in Boulogne, a few months later; the elaborate *Communion Solennelle* of my cousin, Jean-Eric de Prat. My family informed me, in no uncertain terms, it would be quite unacceptable socially for me to take Sarie to the event, unless I had tangible evidence we were betrothed. On the way to the airport, we stopped, and passed a jewellery shop, I pushed Sarie through the shop door, and said to the attendant, "This lady wants a ring!" It cost me the whole of my previous month's income, but though small and simple in design, it is a beautiful work of art we both treasure. At Jean-Eric's event, Sarie was happily accepted as a full-fledged member of the family.

It was not an easy engagement. For nine months, from April to December 1959, I was studying hard for the Part I segment of the diploma in psychological medicine examination. What Sarie mostly saw of me was the back of my head while studying at my desk. Fortunately, she worked as a nurse in the children's ward of the local hospital in Brentwood, at a fulfilling and time-consuming job. She was raised as a member of the Dutch Reformed Church in South Africa, and was now taking instruction in the Catholic faith. During our engagement she was baptized and received into the church, a moment that was gratifying to us both.

It was in May 1959 that I started my job as an intern at Warley Psychiatric Hospital at Brentwood, Essex. A bit of psychiatric knowledge, I thought, would be good for a general practitioner. Within two weeks of starting the job, however, I decided, almost by inspiration, that this was it:

I wanted to be, I *had* to be, a psychiatrist. So, two major decisions about my future, namely my lifetime's companion, and my career and occupational identity, were made within a few weeks of each other. I duly registered for a correspondence course in neuro-anatomy, neuro-physiology, and psychology, all prerequisites for obtaining the diploma in psychological medicine (DPM) and for the required examinations that had to be passed to specialize.

I wrote, and passed, my Part I examinations in early December, and the only convenient wedding date we could find after that was December 26, Boxing Day! Although pugilism had nothing to do with the origin of this sobriquet, it seemed an inauspicious day to start something as complex as a marriage.

Sarie and François: departure for honeymoon. The event coincided with an electric thunderstorm, Nature's *Son et Lumière* tribute.

We married at a Nuptial Mass conducted by the parish priest, Fr. Donnelly, in the Catholic Church in nearby Sevenoaks, and retired to Denyse and Richard's house for the reception. I had selected beautiful music for the ceremony, including the well-known wedding march by Felix Mendelsohn. I was at the altar as Sarie entered the church, on the arm of Richard, her about-to-be brother-in-law. She wore a lovely white wedding dress, and I was struck by her angelic beauty. Denyse's daughter, Charlotte, aged five, was the flower girl, and her son, Christopher, three, was the ring-bearer. During the ceremony he held tightly onto it in his pocket, as if reluctant to part with it. I had to pry it out of his hand to place it on Sarie's finger during the ceremony. Sadly, for Sarie, none of her family from South Africa was able to be there.

The reception was a sedate family affair, with an excellent *menu* and *gâteau de mariage* provided by Denyse. The heavens must have approved because there was a loud thunderclap from above as we departed the home in a limo to a hotel in London, where we were to spend our wedding night.

As a wedding gift Papa had offered us a two-week honeymoon vacation in Rome. I contacted Father Joseph Fitzgerald, who was student chaplain to our NCFS organization in South Africa when I was president, and who had relocated to Rome. (He later became bishop of Bloemfontein, and then archbishop of Johannesburg). Fitz, as we called him, helped us enjoy several wonderful honeymoon adventures. He arranged a semi-private audience with Pope John XXIII (now a saint), during which he blessed our wedding rings and gave us a delightfully animated homily about love, none of which we understood because he was speaking Italian, though a neighbouring nun translated the outlines to us. His gestures said it all. The other was a visit to the Catacomb of St. Priscilla, within which are the earliest known mural representations of the Virgin Mary, dating from the second century. Alone in the catacomb, surrounded by ancient tombs, just Fitz, Sarie, and me, was an eerie experience, especially when we got locked underground, and had to rattle the exit gate loudly before the priest who had let us in remembered we were there.

A year later we received a letter from Fitz congratulating us on the birth of Martin, our first son. He enclosed some photos of the Catacomb of St Priscilla, then added, "You remember how narrowly we escaped spending a night in the catacombs. Fr. Drouart and I still have a laugh about it." Fitz died in 1986.

On our return to England, we went straight to Brentwood where I had to complete my senior internship at Warley Psychiatric Hospital. I realize now I did not know what I was letting myself in for by becoming a psychiatrist. Psychiatry then was a backwater medical specialty, largely carried out in big mental hospitals located on the fringes of cities, far from academic medical centres. There was a strong societal prejudice against psychiatry, both within and without the medical profession, as evidenced by my parents' opposition to my making it my career.

I was often asked, especially at interviews when applying for a job, "Doctor, why did you take up psychiatry?" In those days, I gave a standard reply, "Because I am interested in people, rather than in diseases. I want to know what makes them tick, what makes them do the things they do. I enjoy listening to people; I'm more of a listener than a talker, and I know the ability to listen is important for a psychiatrist." These responses were accepted by selection committees, but they were also a bit simplistic. I know now there exist deeper, what one would call unconscious, personal reasons related to childhood and family relationship issues, that influenced me in the decision. During my years at boarding school, again during my fifth year of medicine, and when I first moved to England, I had what now would be called a clinical depression, but had no treatment because in those days psychological therapies were not widely available. So, I stumbled through on my own. At the time I started psychiatry, no one in my family had had psychiatric therapy, as far as I knew.

Through my reading I developed an interest in a psychotherapeutic, though not a psychoanalytic, approach to the treatment of mental conditions. I was especially interested in the writings of Carl Jung, originally a disciple of Freud, who later separated from Freud to establish his own school of therapy. I quickly became disillusioned with psychoanalysis. During my second year of residency, while working at Belmont Hospital with Dr. William Sargant, I registered at the Tavistock Clinic in London, for a two-year weekly course to learn the elements of the **psychoanalytic** approach to **psychotherapy**. My tutor was a Dr. E.H. I would present my cases to him, he would interpret psychopathology, and then recommend a psychotherapeutic treatment. An exemplary Freudian, he saw everything in a sexual context, even when it was clear, in my mind, that other, non-sexual processes were contributing to the patient's problems. Eventually this attitude became so inappropriate and irritating that I withdrew from this course, after only six months into the two-year program. Dr. E.H. was very distressed by this; he said I was full of defenses and resistance, and needed to be psychoanalyzed myself to be cured. I politely declined his offer.

My ambivalence about psychoanalysis was amusingly demonstrated a few years later. During a **Grand Rounds** presentation I was giving to residents and psychiatrists on psychopathology, I inadvertently said "Sigmoid" Freud, instead of Sigmund Freud. My audience roared with laughter at my highly Freudian slip-of-the-tongue. The sigmoid colon is part of the large intestine, just above the rectum.

During the 1950s psychoanalysis was at its height in the United States, and almost all the academic departments and heads of department were analysts. In the United Kingdom, psychoanalysis never reached that level of ascendancy, the British being more skeptical about its place in psychiatric therapy. Perhaps not all psychiatrists at the Tavistock Clinic were as rigid as Dr. E.H., but my experience there explains the gradual fall from grace experienced in the psychoanalytic movement, even in the US during the 1960s and 1970s.

Though rejecting Freud, I retained my sympathy toward the Jungian approach to psychotherapy, although by no stretch of the imagination would I call myself a Jungian. However, I found his concepts of the collective unconscious, his classification of people as extraverts or introverts, the animus and anima, made sense. Jung also stressed the substantial role of spirituality in human life and experience.

During my medical student and intern years, I had plenty of experiences with cancer, suffering, and with death. Like many physicians, I dealt with the suffering of others by distancing myself emotionally, as a way of not getting too involved with the anguish that accompanies human illness, existence, and dying. I now regret this attitude. I have friends, both medical and non-medical, and I myself at times, who have been distressed by the cold and detached manner with which physicians sometimes manage serious medical problems. Evidence of a caring attitude, I truly believe, may be the most important medicine a doctor can provide the sick. Palliative care physicians are the only group about whom one can say, collectively, truly feel for their patients, and have compassion for them. A friend of mine, a psychiatrist, died a painful death from pancreatic cancer, partly because of unfeeling medical care. He was undertreated with **narcotic analgesics** during the terminal, **metastatic** stages of his illness. In some ways, the current push to allow so-called Medical Assistance in Dying (MAiD) can be regarded as due to the failure of the health-care system to provide adequate symptomatic support, palliative care, and relief to dying patients.

The death of my brother David, in December 2006, gave insight into the difficulties caregivers have managing terminal illness in those with chronic psychiatric conditions. Some of the events described in the next chapter occurred later, following our relocation first to Australia in 1964, then to Canada in 1972.

Chapter Eight
My Brother's Keeper

During our childhood, David was my chief playmate on the farm in Cradock. I remember him then as a quiet, undemonstrative and undemanding child, always anxious to please. He clashed with Papa over eating meat, which David hated, and which Papa considered essential to our childhood health. This led David to keep meat in his cheek at meals, without swallowing. Later, he would spit it out into the toilet.

The farm was criss-crossed with dams and water channels to promote irrigation of the crops, and our favourite game was to make miniature dams and water channels, using underground water pumped from a solitary windmill near the farmhouse. Our water-engineering efforts ended up muddying our hands, faces, and clothes, but it was great fun. The windmill also provided water for an above-ground circular reservoir, perhaps twenty metres in diameter and two metres deep, where we swam daily during the summer.

In 1946, Dade (my nickname for David) joined me for my second year at Marist Brothers' College in Johannesburg. I was meant to care for him, be my brother's keeper, but was ineffective in this role. I suspect he suffered as much loneliness and homesickness as I did in my first year at the school, but he kept this within, and rarely called on me for help. He experienced headaches and, in a letter home, I made a tart comment about the nursing care he received when he was ill. I wrote, "I suppose Dade told you he was sick yesterday with a bad headache and Matron gave him castor oil. Fancy, giving castor oil for a headache!" It appears my critical medical opinions were apparent even at that young age! Poor David! With his gentle, unassuming nature, he was ill-equipped to deal with the rigours of the world.

I had much less to do with him after 1947 because we were at separate schools, so our contact was limited to vacations. I was aware of his increasing success in sports, but he had academic difficulties. Papa put pressure on his sons to succeed in our school work. David did not meet these expectations, which caused further conflict between them.

Vincent was closer to him than I was, both in age and in school levels. He remembers David as a gentle boy, always thoughtful and considerate, who never teased or bullied him or anyone else. This was unique to him because Papa himself was a big tease, and both Vincent and I aped this trait to a certain extent.

David, though a good swimmer, had his biggest success in cricket. In Grade 8, he played for Eastern Province[5] in the Nuffield national tournament, an accomplishment equalled by no one before or since, and in Grade 10 he became captain of the school cricket team. He was both the top bowler and the top batsman on the team. George Cox, the school cricket coach, himself a highly successful English county cricket player, invited David to go to England with him and was certain David would crack the professional level in English county cricket. Papa refused to allow David to go, believing, I suspect, that being a sports professional was *déclassée,* and not worthy of our fine family traditions. David was deeply disappointed by this. How differently his life might have played out had he gone to England, and become a professional cricket player.

---

5 the eastern part of the Cape Province centered on Port Elizabeth.

The Grey High School cricket team, 1955. David, the team captain, is in the seated row second from left. George Cox, the coach, is on his left. Cox was a well-known English county cricketer.

In 1955, David's matriculation year at Grey High School in Port Elizabeth, he wrote me a letter. I was then a fifth-year medical student in Cape Town. Unfortunately, I have not retained a copy of this letter but I recall some of its contents. He was seeking my help and advice because of feelings of insecurity, anxiety, and embarrassment because he blushed easily and lacked confidence. At the time I was but a naïve medical student, and responded with vague words of comfort and reassurance. In retrospect, I missed the boat in not being firmer by advising him to get professional advice or counselling.

During their time together at Grey High School, Vincent looked up to David as his successful older brother, proud of what he had accomplished. He saw David as modest and distinguished, someone who had no enemies. No one had a bad word to say about him. Vincent knows of no incident or character defect that signalled the psychiatric storm that was to follow. David, he says, was an "incredibly successful ladies' man, with several very attractive girlfriends who adored him. He was charming and good-looking. He also had close relationships with his male peers."

In his final year at Grey, David was selected to be a prefect, an honour that neither Vincent nor I achieved. Prefects were selected by their character, to set an example to other students. They alone wore white blazers, in stark contrast to other students who wore blue blazers. David possessed quiet leadership skills that were appreciated by both teachers and his fellow students. Because of his difficulty with mathematics, in Grade 10 he dropped mathematics for French, and this enabled him to pass his matriculation examinations at the second-class level.

Papa wanted David to help him on the farm at Totteridge Park, so he left to complete a two-year diploma course at Cedara Agricultural College near the town of Pietermaritzberg in Natal, the leading farming school in South Africa. Possibly as a result of a personality conflict with teachers, rather than for academic reasons, David failed this course and was bitterly disappointed. This may have been the first sign, the trigger that foreshadowed his oncoming psychiatric illness.

Despite his failure, Papa went ahead and bought David a farm at Thornhill near Port Elizabeth, with the intention of integrating the functions of this farm with those of Totteridge Park. David worked the farm alone, and it was not long thereafter that his psychiatric problems became manifest. He developed paranoid symptoms, believing that Papa had stolen certain articles of his, including a hat. He became uncharacteristically agitated, angry, and belligerent, and incapable of managing the business and financial affairs on the farm. Dr. Maurice Robertson, our family physician in Port Elizabeth, drove David to Cape Town where he saw Dr. McGregor, a neuropsychiatrist. David was admitted to the psychiatric unit at Groote Schuur Hospital where he had a course of **electro-convulsive therapy**. Vincent, in Cape Town at the time, recalls taking David out for a day. During the outing, David began adopting bizarre postures in the middle of the street, which left Vincent bewildered. It seems probable that this performance was a **catatonic** side-effect of a phenothiazine drug David was taking, suggesting that Dr. McGregor may have made a diagnosis of **schizophrenia**. We are not certain about this as we do not have access to McGregor's records. David never used street drugs such as "dagga", as cannabis was called in South Africa, and which was widely, though illicitly, available.

David recovered from this episode but never returned to the farm at Thornhill. In late 1959 he visited the United Kingdom and served as my best man when Sarie and I got married in December that year. He gave a warm and animated address, welcoming Sarie into our family, and even developed a shine for Brigitte, Sarie's bridesmaid.

Returning to South Africa, David went on to Rhodesia (now Zimbabwe) and joined the army. Our sister Christiane lived in Salisbury (now Harare) where David was based, so she could keep an eye on him. For a while, the situation seemed to stabilize, but early in 1963 things began to fall apart. Christiane told us that the army staff had reported David as being belligerent and insubordinate, and said they intended to discharge him dishonourably if he did not resign his commission.

At that time, I was in Edinburgh studying for my membership of the Royal College of Physicians (MRCP) examination, while working as a senior resident at Stratheden Psychiatric Hospital at the ancient castle town of Cupar, Fife. As the psychiatric expert in the family, and with the help of Denyse and Richard, her husband, I was designated to fly to Salisbury to help resolve the situation.

In Salisbury I could see that David was in a state of denial. Other than being low-keyed and withdrawn, he did not appear to be overtly disturbed. He reported no delusions or hallucinations and refused to admit any difficulties in the army. Amongst other activities we played some tennis together. He refused also to go and see a psychiatrist. Because of time constraints, I was unable to see army officials to ascertain details of the difficulties, so returned to the United Kingdom, having accomplished little. A short time later David was let go from the army, a devastating blow to his self-esteem, his third after his failures at Cedara College and the farm at Thornhill. It seemed to me he had immense difficulties adjusting to the structured surroundings of a work or educational setting.

He moved to London, England, where he was admitted to Guy's Hospital under the care of a well-known psychiatrist, Dr. J.J. Fleminger, who now diagnosed schizophrenia. David was placed on phenothiazines and given yet another course of electro-convulsive therapy. He remained an in-patient for three to four months, then was discharged on **Stelazine**, an anti-psychotic drug, which he continued taking until the mid-1970s, when the drug was changed to intramuscular **Modecate**, which he continued taking for the rest of his life. He was almost religious about keeping his two-weekly appointments for the injection.

For the first few years after his discharge from Guy's Hospital, David lived with Denyse and Richard and their four children, Charlotte, Christopher, Alexander, and Arabella in their spacious home at Westerham in Kent. They all, in particular Denyse, were very supportive of him. He managed to get a menial job on a mushroom farm, buy a small car, and even find a girlfriend called Sue, whom he would visit in London on weekends. He had an active social life and played cricket successfully for the Sevenoaks Vine team, a level just below county cricket. These good-tidings were not to last, as the negative symptoms of his schizophrenia became increasingly prominent. These included **flattened and inappropriate emotional responses**, **poverty of ideation** and speech, **anhedonia**, lack of motivation, **perseveration**, and severely limited social function. He also displayed **cognitive dysfunction** in his everyday behaviour. For the last twenty-five years of his life, David lived in a small bachelor apartment in Sevenoaks, Kent, paid for by Vincent, within walking distance of the apartment where Maman lived. He would visit her daily, and she became his main social support.

Denyse and her children saw him regularly during this period. In due course he lost his job, stopped playing tennis and cricket, and Sue let him go. He was unable to manage money and would spend his stipend on useless articles of food and clothing as soon as he received it. Arrangement had to be made, therefore, for him to receive smaller amounts of cash more frequently. His repetitive complaints were sad, almost tragic. If asked how he was feeling he had two or three standard replies, such as, *"I've got aches and pains in my teeth"* or, *"My life is hell."* His teeth were indeed in poor condition, but dentists were never able to help him. He smoked cigarettes endlessly, drank large amounts of coffee, and spent most of his day pacing up and down his apartment. At precisely 3.15 p.m., every day, he would phone his nephew Christopher with the same opening statement, *"I'm still struggling with my aches and pains"*.

During one of my visits to Maman in Sevenoaks, I remember him berating her in an angry, loud voice, trying to force her to give him some money. She held her ground, but I was fearful that he was going to strike her. David was still big and strong, and I am not sure I could have out-muscled him. There must have been other occasions when he threatened her, when there was no one else around, which she never talked about. In fact, he never seems to have harmed her. Maman died on December 18, 1995. When I told David about this, he showed no emotional reaction, nor did he show any at her funeral.

At that same visit to Sevenoaks, I went to his apartment and knocked at the door. He came to the entrance, stood on the threshold - but did not let me in. We had a brief conversation, and I glimpsed and smelt the chaos within. As I left his apartment, I wept at the abject state of his living conditions.

Yet he also showed endearing quirks of character. Every month or two he would send almost every member of the family a birthday card, even though he knew well enough the date of each person's birthday. Moreover, the narrative in each birthday card or letter was identical to the previous one, part English, part French. In company, he cracked little jokes, the same ones each time, as if he had no memory of the fact he had told them before. The rather forced laughter from his listeners, after telling the joke, was pretty well the only thing that ever brought a smile to David's face. This suggested he retained some courage in dealing with his inner demons.

In December 2006, at the onset of his final illness, David phoned Christopher complaining of a lot of pain. The paramedics came, but he would not let them into his flat until Christopher came. He had a scrotal infection and a testicle had to be removed. During his recovery he got into trouble with the hospital authorities for smoking on the ward. He was transferred to a psychiatric ward but his agitation increased. He refused treatment for both his physical and psychiatric conditions, and shortly thereafter developed a stroke from which he died several days later. If he had been compelled to have medication treatment, against his wishes, it would not likely have extended his life. In any event, death was a relief for him.

Eleven years after Maman died, David passed on the same day, December eighteenth. He is buried in the graveyard at Westerham, behind its ancient church, together with Maman and Papa. I was touched that our son Nicolas flew from his home in Victoria, BC, to attend the funeral, as he had done also for Maman's funeral in 1996.

The following was a poem I wrote and recited at the family commemoration of his life in January 2007:

<u>DEAREST DAVID</u>

NOW, YOU ARE GONE FROM THIS WORLD

BUT NOT FROM OUR HEARTS, OUR MEMORIES.

IN YOUR CHEERY CHILDHOOD;

YOU WERE MY PRIME PLAYMATE

AT HOME, AT SCHOOL.

AH, YOUR SPORT, YOUR SCHOOL SUCCESSES.

SUCH PROMISE, SUCH HOPE,

FELLED IN THE PRIME OF YOUTH.

WE

WITNESSED YOUR STRUGGLES TO CONQUER

WITH COURAGE, FAITH AND HOPE

WITH A SPIRIT OF FIERCE INDEPENDENCE,

AN ILLNESS THAT SCARED YOU, ENGULFED YOU.

WE

CHERISHED YOUR MONTHLY HAPPY BIRTHDAY LETTERS.

YOUR MEMORY FOR LONG-FORGOTTEN DETAIL

ASTONISHED US.

WE

ASK FORGIVENESS FOR HURTS COMMITTED.

NOW YOU ARE AWAY

FROM THIS WORLD OF SORROWS,

WITH GOD, WITH ANCESTORS.

DAVID, DEAREST DEPARTED

PRAY FOR US

INTERCEDE FOR US

SO WE MAY ACCOMPLISH OUR EARTHLY GOALS.

GOODBYE … FOR NOW.

FRANÇOIS

January 3, 2007

After his death, Christopher and his wife Tamsin went to clean up David's apartment. They described it as being in a "pitiful" state, laden with hundreds of boxes of matches, empty packets of cigarettes, dirty clothes everywhere, and cheap plastic pens, and stinking of cigarette smoke. Coffee stains covered the kitchen and bedroom.

In retrospect, I regret my lamentable absence of involvement in David's care during most of his lifetime. Perhaps in part because I lived in a different country, I was able to box his illness into a different compartment of my brain, but I am sure part of my problem was that I did not want to be tainted by the stigma of his mental illness. Whereas in my professional life I was preaching the necessity of destigmatizing mental illness, in my personal life I was doing just the opposite. It was only in my early sixties that I realized my hypocrisy and short-sightedness and joined the Schizophrenia

Society of Ontario (SSO), of which I eventually became a board member. When I told the society president why I was joining, she replied, "So, you've come out of the closet, at last." In its family support groups I spoke openly about my own family's experience of mental illness, realizing that by publicly denying David's illness, I had missed a golden opportunity to help break down the barriers that force sufferers to hide their illness from society. The provincial schizophrenia societies are important players in public education and their worthy programs help reduce the stigma.

Western society is now, thank goodness, more open about psychiatric illness. Post-traumatic stress disorder receives considerable publicity, and workers are less embarrassed about requesting leave for conditions such as depression and drug-dependency. Treatments in psychiatry are also more effective, and in recent decades there have been major developments in our understanding of schizophrenia and its treatment. If David's illness had begun now, in 2021, its treatment would likely have been more effective, and he would have had a much better prognosis. Yet the stigma persists, and that affects both the motivation to receive treatment and the recruitment of professionals to mental health programs. There remains a widespread tendency to regard a psychiatric illness as different from a physical one. Having had a hip replacement or a coronary bypass is a badge of honour at a cocktail party, but few boast about having had a nervous breakdown.

At an international conference on stigma organized by the Mental Health Commission of Canada (MHCC) in Ottawa in 2012, it was recommended that "any effort to reduce stigma must involve those who know it best: the individual who has experienced mental illness." The MHCC has played a major role in raising awareness of mental illness in Canada, and its huge economic costs. It also outlined methods of dealing with stigma. Family members can play a crucial role in this regard. Amongst its many recommendations, the commission emphasised that education efforts should be directed especially toward young people and First Nations groups.

With my siblings' involvement—along with, belatedly, my own—in schizophrenia support groups and publicity about mental illness, some good may yet emerge from David's tragic life.

I have often wondered if there was evidence of formal psychiatric illness in our family background. Was David's illness inherited? Papa's paternal grandfather, Jules, was a wine merchant in Paris during the nineteenth century, and he had had difficulty managing his business affairs. His death in 1889, at the age of forty-eight, when he was run down and killed by a horse carriage while under the influence of liquor, may even have been suicidal, as my cousin Eugéne de Prat believed. Papa himself was strongly self-sufficient during his youth and manhood, but after his retirement he became heavily dependent on alcohol, which undoubtedly hastened his death. One of Christiane's children, Keith, has also developed schizophrenia. These facts suggest there was an underlying genetic element to David's illness.

Without my awareness of it at the time, I now believe these subterranean family dynamics strongly influenced my choice of psychiatry as a career.

Chapter Nine
Highs and Lows

It seems paradoxical that, as a medical student, I had trouble studying and passing examinations, yet never failed a postgraduate examination. I attribute this to the confidence and commitment that came from getting married, and the awareness I now had a designated career goal as a psychiatrist. As a medical student, I felt overwhelmed by the amount of knowledge and detail I was obliged to assimilate; as a physician, now, with a specialist identity, I knew I just had to know everything there was to know in my domain. Once again, as in my first year of medicine, I studied and worked like a beaver building its dam. In December 1959, I passed Part I of the diploma in psychological medicine (DPM) examinations in the University of London, and in June 1961, I passed Part II, consisting of neurology and psychiatry, giving me the designation of a fully fledged psychiatric specialist. On passing the latter examination, I sent the following telegram to my parents in South Africa: "Very shocked. DPM successful." To which they replied, "Neither shocked nor surprised. Have wonderful holiday, fond love, Papa and Maman."

My first year in a psychiatric setting, prior to getting my diploma, I spent as a senior house officer at Warley Hospital in Brentwood, Essex. Warley was a huge traditional psychiatric hospital, built during the Victorian era to house long-term patients, and it included a short-term admissions unit in a separate building. The grounds were spacious and well-treed, with lovely gardens, and I enjoyed my daily walk from one end to the other, inhaling the fresh floral odours and listening to the cuckoos singing their two-note call, reminding me of Beethoven's simulation of the call in the soaring lyrics of the second movement in his 6th (Pastorale) Symphony. I learnt later that cuckoos are parasites, laying their eggs in the nests of other birds after ejecting the eggs. The foster-parent birds did not recognize the cuckoo's eggs as not being their own. They incubated, then hatched and reared the cuckoo chick, even if it was much larger than they were. How on earth, I wonder, did this beautiful, gentle-looking bird, with a lovely, two-note song, develop this rapacious reproductive technique? I suspect Beethoven did not know the bird's nature, or we may never have heard the Andante molto mosso movement of his symphony.

Most of my day was spent in the Admissions Unit following my consultant around, although he would not let me sit in on his private interview sessions. I also carried out electric convulsive treatments (ECT) on patients he recommended, which were the great majority. On some days I performed twenty or more ECTs in one morning. Not only was this use excessive, I now realize our procedures were grossly disrespectful to the patients. All patients scheduled for ECT would be lined up in the dormitory, with their heads facing the centre aisle, separated only by linen screens. I would give the patient an intravenous anesthetic, followed, as soon as they were asleep, by a muscle relaxant. When they were asleep and relaxed, I would apply the two electrodes to each temporal region of the head, then press the button on the machine that produced the convulsion. The nurse would then give the patient oxygen, and as soon as they started breathing spontaneously, we would go on to the next patient.

I knew at the time this was gross over-usage of the treatment, and that my consultant was prescribing ECT to patients who were not depressed and not psychotic, but as the most junior member of the staff, there was little I could do about it. I just had to follow the consultant's orders, even when I saw some who reacted badly to the treatment. Strangely enough, even though I disagreed with his clinical approach, he gave me an excellent reference when I left the hospital.

On one occasion, I accompanied the senior resident on his rounds. We went to the padded cell, still used in those days to control the behaviour of some difficult patients. He unlocked the door of the cell and the young patient emerged, with a fierce look on her face. She glared at the resident, her therapist, and then took a vicious swipe at his head, sending him sprawling on the floor, breaking his spectacles, though he was otherwise uninjured. He got up, picked up his shattered spectacles, replaced them on his nose, cocked his head sideways, turned to the patient, and asked her quizzically, "Now, why did you do that?" Her face contorted with anger, and she screamed, "You're a bloody bastard locking me up in this hole!"

At Warley Hospital, I was also the physician responsible for one of the back wards that housed patients who had been there many years, even decades. The atmosphere there was depressing; most of the patients had chronic schizophrenia, a few had dementia. They would just hang around all day, lost in their personal worlds. The ward had a stale, stuffy, airless smell, and there was a strict daily routine of rising, meals, bedtime, and lights out. Patients rarely left the ward, had no stimulating social or recreational activities, and led an increasingly vegetative lifestyle. However, I did have one good success. A woman, likely in her fifties though looking at least a decade older, had been incarcerated for over ten years, and was assumed to have schizophrenia. After examination, I re-diagnosed her with chronic agitated depression, gave her a course of ECT, and she recovered sufficiently to be able to be discharged home to her devoted husband.

I had a sense of helplessness and hopelessness about these back wards. They were the final holdover from the eighteenth and nineteenth centuries, when the main function of a psychiatric institution was to warehouse the patient until they died. Thankfully, a huge change in the philosophy of the psychiatric institution came a few years later, in the 1960s, when more powerful pharmacological and psychosocial treatments became available. The old Victorian hospitals were emptied, perhaps too rapidly. When one sees the large number of unfortunate street dwellers in our societies, many of whom have serious psychiatric issues, one wonders if the psychiatric hospitals were not closed too radically, throwing out the baby with the bathwater, as it were. Group homes run by foster parents, and religiously based movements such as l'Arche, founded by Jean Vanier, are part of the answer to homelessness. In l'Arche, Vanier, who died in 2019, emphasized the need for belonging, inclusion, and forgiveness in caring for severely handicapped and homeless people. Governments need to give far more thought to this issue, which is a blight on our affluent western society. I do not believe the excellence of the l'Arche movement will be affected by recent detrimental revelations of the sexually predatory actions of Vanier himself.

A favourite expression at Warley was to call the doctor-on-duty, and let them know that a particular patient in a back ward had "collapsed." To collapse was a serious provisional diagnosis, so I would rush to the ward and examine the patient, who often was not able to give me a history because of the serious nature of their psychiatric condition. By the time I got there, the patient had often recovered from their state of collapse, and nothing further needed to be done. On one occasion, however, when I got to the patient, a woman with chronic schizophrenia in her mid-forties, I found her unconscious, coughing, and she had difficulty breathing. She expired a few minutes later. At autopsy the next day a small acorn she must have inhaled was found in her bronchial tubes. She had died from suffocation resulting from blocking of her breathing apparatus. This event made me take a referral nurse's diagnosis of a collapsed patient more seriously.

I cannot say I learned much clinical psychiatry at Warley. Most of the psychiatrists worked in their own little cocoons and had little interest in the career of a young, budding colleague. Some seemed a little crazy themselves, fitting the image society has of psychiatrists. One staff member was extraordinarily voluble, and visibly and almost constantly euphoric. He told me once, "I know I'm manic-depressive; everyone has been waiting for years for me to go into a depression, but I'm happier like this." My chief was a more traditional Freudian; he smoked a pipe, had long, flowing white hair and beard, and no disaster fazed him.

I entered psychiatry just at the tail end of the use of insulin coma therapy for schizophrenia. Introduced by Manfred Sakel in 1933 in Vienna, it became the treatment of choice for schizophrenia until it was superseded by the neuroleptic drugs in the mid to late 1950s. The patient was given a subcutaneous injection of twenty units of soluble insulin a day, and the dose increased until coma was induced. After thirty minutes the coma was interrupted by administering glucose, either by naso-gastric tube or intravenous infusion. Although I did not personally work in the insulin therapy wards at Warley Hospital, I remember seeing and hearing the ten or twelve patients with schizophrenia, all of whom were receiving insulin shock treatment simultaneously in a dormitory-style ward. There would be loud moans or screams as they were going into, or emerging from, their coma. Although it seemed to help some patients, it was not an edifying treatment approach. Insulin therapy of schizophrenia rapidly disappeared shortly thereafter, once the phenothiazine group of drugs such as chlorpromazine (Largactil) became widely available. A Canadian psychiatrist called Heinz Lehmann played a key role in the early development of chlorpromazine. Although I never met Lehmann, I heard him speaking at Canadian Psychiatric Association meetings after we moved to Canada in 1972. He appeared fit and lithe, continued riding his bicycle in Montréal until his mid-eighties, and died in 1999 at the age of eighty-seven. He came through as a caring man who shared the sufferings of his patients. He was one of the greats in Canadian psychiatry.

At the time, I speculated whether schizophrenic patients given insulin coma therapy improved because they were given a temporary physical illness—namely, the hypoglycaemic coma. The idea for this hypothesis came from the Austrian psychiatrist Julius Wagner-Jauregg. In the mid-1920s, Wagner-Jauregg found that administering malaria parasites to patients who had general paresis of the insane, a form of tertiary syphilis, was often beneficial in the latter condition. This was the first treatment ever found to help these unfortunate patients, and the world was so excited by this discovery that Wagner-Jauregg was awarded the 1927 Nobel Prize in Physiology and Medicine. He remains the only psychiatrist to be so honoured in the 120 years of the prize's history.

After a year at Warley Hospital, I obtained a position as a resident at Belmont Hospital in Sutton, Surrey. Belmont was an acute-care psychiatric facility with no long-term beds. During World War II it became famous as the treatment centre for soldiers with PTSD, at that time simply called war neurosis or "shell-shock," and other war-induced psychiatric conditions.

Sarie and I had major problems finding suitable accommodation while I was working at Belmont. Martin and Nicolas, our first two sons, were born during this period—Martin, on January 10, 1961, and Nicolas, 365 days, minus a few hours, later, on January 9, 1962. Papa, true to form, was thrilled with his first grandsons who carried the Mai family name, as were Sarie and I. The landlords and landladies in the Sutton area of south London were less impressed. Many had signs on their property indicating that "NO CHILDREN, BLACKS, IRISH, AND THOSE WITH PETS ACCEPTED. We had to change our place of abode four times during this two-year period. Rent took over a third of my salary, and because Sarie had to stop working to care for the boys, times were not easy. Unlike the landlords, my sister Denyse and her husband Richard were very helpful; they sold us their old Austin car at a very reasonable price, and were generous with old baby clothes and other material necessities. Denyse did not even ask for the return of the baby clothes when, shortly after, she found she was pregnant with Arabella, her youngest daughter.

For my first year at Belmont, I was fortunate to be assigned as resident to Dr. William Sargant, author of a standard textbook *An Introduction to Physical Methods of Treatment in Psychiatry*, first published in 1944, with numerous subsequent editions and translations into many languages. Sargant was a wonderful mentor and I owe him a huge debt of gratitude. Curiously, though, it is not because he taught me a great deal about pharmaceuticals, though he certainly did that too. Sargant had a powerful personality, a huge presence; he was eternally optimistic and hopeful about the capacity of his patients to recover, and this they mostly did. He never refused a patient referral, no matter how chronic and complex their condition, and they came to him from all over Britain. Sargant transmitted his therapeutic optimism to me. His colleagues would tease him by saying it was his strong personality that caused their recovery. He would laugh this off, while continuing to believe it was the pills that made the difference. I have to say, now, that I agree with his critical colleagues.

Once, he went away for a three-week lecture tour of North America, leaving me in charge of his thirty or so patients. Even though I prescribed the same medications he did, few of the patients got better while he was away. When he returned, they had an almost immediate recovery. He taught me to always be positive about a patient's capacity for growth and change, and this became a key part of my psychiatric practice and teaching thereafter. I think I impressed him too. I told him the story of how, while working at the Warley Psychiatric Hospital, I had discovered a middle-aged woman who had languished in a back ward for ten years with undiagnosed agitated depression, and recovered with a course of ECT therapy I carried out. Sargant recounted this story to many of his senior colleagues. In the reference he wrote me after I stopped working with him, he stated, *"Dr. Mai seems more interested in the social aspects of psychiatry, but he carried out my treatments to my satisfaction."* Damning with faint praise?

Sargant later became a controversial figure for his use (or perhaps misuse) of continuous narcosis therapy in certain conditions, sometimes without the consent of the patient. However, he did not carry out any narcosis therapy for the year that I worked with him at Belmont. He also never recommended daily ECT treatments, as did other psychiatrists, such as Ewen Cameron in Montréal, at that time. Sargant never prescribed ECT more than twice weekly, up to a total of eight or ten, and he regarded this number and frequency as sufficient. He did not misuse electro-convulsive therapy, as has been alleged.

Neuroleptic (anti-psychotic) medication, as well as the **antidepressant drugs** such as the tricyclic and mono-amine-oxidase inhibitor group of drugs, were coming on the market, and Sargant was very excited about these developments. He and his colleagues at St Thomas' Hospital in London carried out many of the early studies in the use of imipramine and phenelzine. Clinical depression is thought to be caused, at least in part, by changes in the concentration of mono-amines, a chemical active at microscopic nerve endings in the brain. Antidepressant medications correct these changes. Sargant taught me much about the use of antidepressant and antipsychotic drugs.

War produces both physical and mental casualties, and Sargant believed in the usefulness of abreaction therapy in PTSD. He would use one of several techniques, either the inhalation of nitrous oxide, ether, or carbon dioxide, or a small dose of amylo-barbitone sodium given intravenously, enough to release inhibitions but not so much as to sedate the patient. Seated beside the patient, with me just behind him, he would administer the drug, then encourage them to relive their traumatic experience, even if this involved shouting or screaming in anger or fear. He believed that best results came if the patient expressed anger. During World War II, Sargant had worked at Belmont Hospital treating the psychiatric war wounded, and now, fifteen years later, he still had veterans returning to him for periodic refresher abreactive treatments.

Sargant also had a large private practice on Wimpole Street in London, and he would visit Belmont Hospital once a week to interview each of his thirty-odd patients across a table, with me sitting next to him. I never heard him utter the word "psychotherapy," although without knowing it, I believe he was practising psychotherapy. One interesting patient, a young man I'll call Steven, was preoccupied with what he regarded as an abnormal gait, although it was not visibly abnormal to an observer. I suspect he had a type of obsessional disorder, or possibly was in a mono-symptomatic delusional state. Sargant realized that this young man's problem did not lend itself to medications, ECT or leucotomy, so during one interview with the patient, he turned to me and, out of the corner of his mouth he whispered, "Are you talking to this man?" He meant, of course, are you giving him psychotherapy. In fact, I did give him a lot of my time in psychotherapy, seeing him daily throughout his admission, but did not get very far. He eventually discharged himself, having made little progress with his gait preoccupation. He might have done well with cognitive-behavioural psychotherapy, but in those days, it was not available.

By the end of World War II, Sargant had become one of the best-known British psychiatrists, and he would recount to me his war experiences with pride. Belmont Hospital was situated on a slight geographic incline near Sutton, Surrey, on the southern fringe of London. One can just see the silhouette of St. Paul's Cathedral in the distance, in downtown London. Every morning, during the London Blitzes in 1940 and again in 1944-5, he and the staff would gaze toward the city to see if the dome of St. Paul's was still standing.

Sargant was also famous as the prefrontal leucotomy expert in Great Britain, and patients were referred to him from all over the country. **Prefrontal leucotomy** (sometimes called lobotomy) was introduced into medicine by the Portuguese neurologist Egas Moniz, who died in 1955. For this he was awarded the Nobel Prize for Medicine in 1949, the first Portuguese citizen to be given the award. With hindsight it is easy to aver that it was a gross blunder to award the Nobel to Moniz for developing a treatment that is now reviled. It must be remembered that during the thirties and forties and earlier, there were virtually no treatments for serious mental illness, and any procedure, no matter how radical, that caused some improvement, had to be considered. Now very few, if any, leucotomies are performed; there is even a society-led prejudice against it. However, during the fifties and early sixties it was still an operation performed on certain psychiatric conditions, particularly those with intractable obsessional neuroses, and certain forms of difficult-to-treat depression. During the year I worked with Sargant, he recommended a leucotomy at least once a week. He was not, of course, the surgeon, but advised the surgeon to bilaterally section only the medial-frontal fibres linking the frontal lobes to the rest of the brain, the minimal number of white matter fibres sectioned. This was much less radical than what had been cut in the early days of prefrontal leucotomy. It seemed to help most of the patients we saw, at least in the short term. I did, it must be said, see a number who went on to develop adverse personality changes such as insensitivity and impulsivity. The permanency of these changes, the lack of long-term benefits, and the availability of other treatments, is the reason prefrontal leucotomy is no longer a recommended treatment in psychiatry.

In a fascinating interview published in the *Bulletin of the Royal College of Psychiatrists* in 1987, the year before he died, Sargant recounted details of his childhood as the son of a Methodist minister, including his battles with penury as an intern, and bouts of tuberculosis as a young man. At the end of the interview, he stated, "[Psychiatric] patients are not getting treatment as much as they should; many are just being talked to . . . to go back and just use 'talking treatment' is going to mean that psychiatry's going to be a long time putting itself right again." With his avoidance of the word "psychotherapy," Sargant was true to form right until the end.

It has been alleged that during his youth, Sargant had some depressive breakdowns, in addition to tuberculosis, but this was not alluded to in the interview.

I spent another year at Belmont Hospital, while working with some of the other eminent psychiatrists who were based there, people such as Louis Minski, Eliot Slater, and David Shaw, and this mentoring experience was highly beneficial for me clinically. Regretfully, the hospital was closed and demolished in the 1980s.

The Cries of my Beloved Country

It was whilst working at Belmont that Sarie and I decided we were not returning to South Africa. In 1960 the infamous Sharpeville massacre occurred, with more than sixty unarmed black South Africans shot in the back and killed as they fled police during an anti-Apartheid demonstration. This led to huge national and international protests. In a referendum, South African whites had decided in favour of a republic, and Hendrik Verwoerd, the prime minister, requested continued South African membership of the British Commonwealth, but this was denied. South Africa was duly ejected from the Commonwealth, and became a republic. As residents of England, we applied for British citizenship, which was accepted with little fanfare. To our astonishment, within a week we received a letter from the South African Embassy demanding that we surrender our South African passports, thereby abandoning our citizenship! In other words, the British government, without our permission, knowledge, or authority, had notified the South African Embassy in London of our application for British citizenship. We had no choice but to comply.

I felt and still feel guilt about that decision. We were born and raised in South Africa, and I had all my pre-doctorate education there. We loved the country passionately, its beauty, its free-flowing spirit, and the energy of its people. All Sarie's family lived there, and as Afrikaners, had no intention of leaving. So, we were among the hundreds of thousands who fled the country, part of the huge South African diaspora living in the United Kingdom, the United States, Canada, Australia, New Zealand, and elsewhere.

As white liberals we felt we had no role in the country, as if caught in a trap; to be shot by the Blacks because we were white, or shot by the Whites because we were liberal. We were certain the increasingly tense South African political situation would lead inevitably to a major racial conflict, out of which there would be no winners. With our growing young family of boys, we did not really want to be part of that scenario.

I was also influenced by the futuristic and dystopic novel *When Smuts Goes*, by the historian Arthur Keppel-Jones, published in 1947. Keppel-Jones foresaw the Afrikaner Nationalists taking over the country, establishing a fascist dictatorship in which the Blacks are increasingly marginalized. Eventually, a Black-white civil war breaks out, which leads to international intervention and defeat of the Nationalists, who are all deported to Argentina and other countries. The novel presaged a future for South Africa that was far more dystopic than what in fact happened. However, to me, in 1960, the future that Keppel-Jones portrayed seemed all too probable.

I remain full of admiration for the countless South Africans who decided to continue the fight from within the country, and risked health and life to do so—men such as Alan Paton, Albie Sachs, Nelson Mandela, Steve Biko, and innumerable others. Alan Paton developed an international reputation after the publication of his novel *Cry, the Beloved Country*, in 1948. The storyline is based on his headship of a reformatory school in the Transvaal, and the tragic effects of Apartheid on the residents. It includes many memorable quotations. "These hills [near Ixopo] are grass-covered and rolling, and are lovely beyond any singing of it." Later, describing the anticipated results of Apartheid, a character says, "I have one fear in my heart . . . they will all turn to hating." In the 1950s, Paton became leader of the Liberal Party of South Africa. In 1955 I heard him speak at an election rally in Cape Town, and was inspired by his passion and eloquence. Both he and the party were subsequently banned and his passport was confiscated. Another well-known novel, *The Power of One* by Bryce Courtenay, describes the racial and tribal tensions in South Africa. Both the Black versus white and the English versus Afrikaans conflicts are vividly portrayed.

While in Britain I continued my anti-apartheid activities on a reduced scale, mainly writing letters-to-the-Editor. The following appeared in *The Scotsman,* in April 1963, and was written in response to an op-ed by a journalist who had supported the nationalist regime in South Africa.

> "As a born-and-bred South African, and perhaps therefore in a better position to assess the situation than Mr. J. W. Kinnear in "The Scotsman" of April 9, I should like to

point out that apart from the "distortion and bias" of his own letter, it contained several inaccuracies.

It may be true to say that the present main opposition party is not "muzzled"—its racialist policy differs little from the government. However, a large number of prominent Liberals—usually called "Communists" by the government – are imprisoned because of their political activities, and innumerable "native" leaders are in prison, or house-confined—irrespective as to whether or not they preach violence or non-violence. And what is the recent government order preventing newspapers from any mention of a "banned' individual, or his activities, if not press "muzzling?" This apart from the unofficial policy of "self-censorship" enforced on non-government newspapers.

Can one call a country "bulging with prosperity" when the price of property has fallen 20-25% of the level five years ago? Or when the rate of emigration of its university staff is so high that senior staff positions cannot be filled with men of adequate calibre?

My own experience of South Africa is that it is a desperately unhappy country. The whole policy of apartheid is founded on fear of the Black man—which in many instances reaches preposterous proportions. No country, or individual, can be happy when behaviour and attitudes can only be maintained by force and fear.

Nevertheless, I agree that there is little basic understanding outside of South Africa of the enormity—perhaps insolubility—of her problems, which extend back deep in her history, and an adequate appreciation of these should undoubtedly exist before indiscriminate criticism is leveled at South Africans. This said, however, one feels that present policies fall far short of the ideal by every standard—moral, humanitarian, political, economic, and psychological—by which they can be measured.

The BBC film commentator did have an anti-South African bias, but all shades of opinion were allowed their say, and the intelligent uncommitted individual can assess these on their merits, without reference to producer bias. I was as impressed with Chief Albert Luthuli's persistent confidence in humanity, and his rejection of violence, as I was appalled at the minister of justice's pallid defence of widespread corporal punishment in the courts. Which of these is to be regarded as the most "civilized"?

Much to the fury of the South African government, Albert Luthuli was awarded the Nobel Peace Prize in 1960, for his leadership in the non-violent struggle against Apartheid, the first person of African descent to be given such an honour. With the country in turmoil, I fully anticipated a civil war would take place. Although dreadful events happened in the subsequent thirty years until the fall of Apartheid, to me, it is astonishing that no formal civil war occurred. This is likely due to the fact that during this thirty-year period, the Nationalists essentially had total control of the country, with the tacit support of the United States and Britain, making any Black insurrection doomed to failure. I am sure this is also due to the good sense and perspicacity of both Nelson Mandela and Frederik de Klerk, who led the Black and white tribes respectively, in the negotiations to abandon apartheid in the early 1990s. Their joint award of the Nobel Peace Prize in 1993 was richly deserved. I suspect that the fall of the Berlin Wall in 1989, with the accompanying collapse of Communism and the Soviet Union, also played a part. Prior to this event the United States, the United Kingdom and the West implicitly supported Apartheid-South Africa, because of its strong anti-communist policies. With the fall of the Wall, this support evaporated, and de Klerk realized the game was up. We can also thank the wisdom of Judge de Wet who, at the widely-reported Rivonia Trial in 1963, did not impose the death penalty on Mandela, as demanded by the Prosecution, but rather sent him to life imprisonment. After twenty-seven years in prison, often in degrading circumstances especially at the outset, he was thus available from 1990 onward, to lead South Africa out of the Apartheid era with magnanimous good sense.

Regretfully, the wonderful future for South Africa the world predicted when Mandela came to power, has not come to pass. In his great little book, *What's Gone Wrong: On the Brink of a Failed State*, published in 2014, Alex Boraine, previously deputy-chair of the Truth and Reconciliation Commission, expressed his belief that South Africa was becoming a failed state. What has gone wrong in Alan Paton's "beloved country?" he asked. Boraine answered his question by pointing the finger at the African National Congress, which, after many years in political exile, under the successive presidencies of Thabo Mbeki and Jacob Zuma, following Mandela, had shown signs of "party chauvinism, poor leadership, a climate of entitlement, jettisoning of moral compass, bad judgement, and incompetence." Mandela himself was a beacon of tolerance and magnanimity, but subsequently, intolerance, corruption, and violence have become endemic in the country. Cyril Ramaphosa succeeded Zuma as president in 2018. He is a wealthy businessman who has been critical of corruption, and the sense of entitlement that pervaded the African National Congress leadership, and corruption is less than previously. He has some well-qualified ministers in his cabinet, but there are leftovers from Zuma's regime who will be intent on displacing him and turning the clock back.

Matters of Life and Death

After completing my stint at Belmont Hospital and obtaining my diploma in psychological medicine, I decided I wanted to be an academic psychiatrist, not a psychiatric consultant working in a mental hospital or in a private-practice setting. In other words, I wanted a university appointment. I had no university contacts in South Africa or the United Kingdom, nor had I carried out research that might have led to getting an academic position. The only road to academia that appeared possible was to pass the MRCP examination—that is, the Membership of the Royal College of Physicians. This is a specialty qualification in general medicine offered in the United Kingdom by medical colleges in London and Edinburgh. It is notoriously difficult to obtain, with many aspiring internists and training physicians trying repeatedly and unsuccessfully to pass the examination. I undertook this objective with much trepidation, and even asked a psychologist at Belmont Hospital to carry out an IQ test on me to see whether I had the intellectual capacity to pass the MRCP examination! He concluded that I did.

So off we went to Edinburgh and Scotland to tackle the MRCP leviathan. I obtained a position as senior resident at Stratheden Hospital in Cupar, Fife. This position had the huge advantage of providing a good-sized, heated apartment for our growing family. I also registered for a three-month, full-time course of preparation offered by the University of Edinburgh, for students aspiring to sit the examination. For the duration of this prep period, I rented a room in a boarding house in Edinburgh, where I lived from Monday to Friday, returning by train to Cupar and the family for the weekends. I completed the course in December 1963, and sat the MRCP examination in January 1964, passing it at my first attempt. Holding this degree now rendered me eligible to practise as an internist, although I never, in fact, did so.

While at Stratheden, I worked mainly in the admissions unit and, in my capacity as a senior resident, believed I had clinical autonomy in the management of my patients. One of the psychiatrists on staff at the hospital thought otherwise, and on several occasions, he prescribed ECT on my patients without discussing it with me, when I did not think ECT was indicated. He reminded me of my first chief at Warley Hospital in Essex, who gave ECT to almost all his patients, without considering the appropriate indications. Then, as a junior, novice psychiatrist, I could do nothing; now with a DPM tucked under my arm, I was in a stronger position. So, I confronted that psychiatrist, and we had a stern argument in which I told him to back off and stop interfering in the management of my patients. He interfered on several more occasions before finally getting the message.

During my senior residency at Stratheden Hospital, together with a colleague, Dr. Archie Morrison, we set up a rehabilitation program designed to activate and socialize patients in the long-term back wards of the hospital, and a number became well enough to be discharged home.

While I was in Edinburgh, the Kennedy assassination occurred, and I shared the shock of the world at this awful tragedy. I recall, with disbelief, the Dallas police chief stating, after Ruby shot Oswald, "The Kennedy case is now closed."

Sarie and I enjoyed our time in Scotland and the Scots, with their lilting accents and lively customs. We even took a liking to haggis—as long as it was accompanied by a good single-malt scotch, to terminate any living creatures remaining therein. We made a glorious circuit of the Highlands in a camping trailer, stopped to search (unsuccessfully) for the Loch Ness Monster, and visited the remarkable gardens at Inverewe, situated in a warm micro-climate area on the west coast of Scotland, full of beautiful rhododendron, fawn lily flowers, and Wallemi pine trees native to New South Wales, amongst many others.

While we loved our Scottish sojourn, it was tempered for Sarie by the responsibilities of motherhood. Sixteen months after Nicolas's birth, Andrew, our third son, was born in St. Andrew's, just fifteen kilometres from Cupar, site of the world-famous golf course. As the home filled with boys, I was studying almost full-time at home, working in the hospital during the day, or away in Edinburgh; hence, I was quite unavailable to help when the children got sick, as of course they did with chickenpox, measles and mumps. Sarie carried the increasing workload that came with a growing family loyally and with equanimity, for which I am eternally grateful.

With the MRCP under my belt, I was ready now for an academic appointment, but where? Neither Sarie nor I wished to remain in the United Kingdom; in any case I still had no contacts in academia. Returning to South Africa was not an option, and I was not keen to enter the United States maelstrom, where I also had no contacts. That left Australia or Canada. I spotted an advertisement for a senior lecturer in psychiatry at the University of Adelaide in South Australia, and I duly travelled down to London to be interviewed by the department head, Professor William Cramond. He offered me a job on the spot. The position had the huge advantage of first-class fares on the mail boat from London to Adelaide for the whole family for ten pounds! We signed on.

Both Sarie and I were attracted to Australia because of its similarities, in many respects, to South Africa—without the racial conflicts. It was far from family and friends, but as this seemed my only entry to an academic position, we took the plunge. By the time of our departure from London in August 1964, Sarie was five months' pregnant with our fourth child.

The mail boat, the *Oronsay,* left London and took three and a half weeks to reach Adelaide, with stops at Gibraltar, Naples, Port Said, Aden, Colombo, and Perth, including a splendid sail through the Suez Canal. At Naples we visited the ruins at Pompeii, and it rekindled my fascination with ancient Roman history, first stimulated by Gussie Ferguson at Grey High School. I subsequently read a number of books about Ancient Rome and collected them in my home library. At Colombo, we visited Buddhist temples and the beaches south of the city. Everywhere we went the locals were engrossed and gathered around this young mother with three boys under four, and visibly pregnant with the fourth!

Our first encounter with Australia at Perth for just one day was memorable. It was springtime; we went for a stroll in a park on the Swan River, and were dazzled by the strikingly original and beautiful red and green kangaroo paw flowers, growing wild. Returning to Oronsay for the final leg of the journey, we found vases on the boat filled with these fine flowers.

Our arrival in Adelaide went smoothly. The university had provided temporary housing, and in January we purchased a bungalow near the seafront at Tennyson's lovely beach. It was made of solid brick with white-washed veneer, and a green corrugated iron roof. The roof caused a cacophonous roar overhead when it rained, totally the opposite of the delicate, drip-drop sounds of Chopin's Raindrop prelude. It was to be our home for the next eight years.

Dear little Paul was born in Adelaide on January 14, 1965. Regretfully, I missed his birth as I had to drive to Melbourne to pick up Sarie's mother, who had come to Australia by boat to help with the birth and aftermath. On my return, I found a lovely, healthy little boy, with fair colouring, like Sarie, and a full head of blonde hair. Another miniature masterpiece.

Tragically, little Paul died, a crib death (Sudden Infant Death Syndrome, or SIDS) on March 13, aged two months, just as he was beginning to smile and engage with his surroundings. Sarie's mother had put him down in his cot at seven, after his evening meal, seemingly healthy. I went to check him two hours later and his little body was already cold. He was lying prone with his face in the pillow. I tried to resuscitate him but it was hopeless. I noticed post-mortem lividity had already set in over his stomach and chest wall, indicating he had been dead for quite a while. I could not help wondering whether he had died by smothering in a pillow while in a deep sleep.

Sarie and I were devastated. To arrive in a new country, have a child, who then died at two months, all within six months of arrival, was not easy to cope with. We were fortunate to have the help of Sarie's mother, and Yvonne and Joe Scanlon (a psychiatrist), who stood in as godparents at Paul's baptism a week before he died, and who became good friends. The priest at our parish wanted to take Paul away, and bury him somewhere anonymously. Fortunately, I was able to dissuade him, and he celebrated a funeral Mass for infants. Paul now has his own little grave in a cemetery near Glenelg, a suburb of Adelaide. We bought a plot for him. Following the Mass, we retired to the cemetery. I recall his small white coffin disappearing into the deep, gaping hole in the ground, and the anguish that followed. Some months later we had a headstone carved out of granite with the following words inscribed:

> In Loving Memory
>
> Of our baby
>
> Paul Bernard Mai
>
> "Nothing is loss compared
> with the privilege of
> knowing Jesus"
>
> Philippians 3,8

I remember Yvonne saying, when consoling us the night of Paul's death, "Just think; Paul is now happy, in heaven, and doesn't have to face all the traumas of life we have here on earth!" I still wonder what sort of a boy and man he would have turned out to be. I know he would have been handsome. It took us many months to get over the shock. It also had an adverse effect on our relationship, as we tended to blame each other for his death.

Some of these tensions may have been caused by differences in attitude; Sarie is outgoing, verbal, easily aroused, and has difficulty coping with stress and changes. I am more passive, inward-looking, and have more difficulty verbalizing my feelings. With provocation, however, I have a nasty temper. Paul's death likely also had a detrimental effect on our surviving children, as we became overly protective of them. We decided the best way to overcome our grief and shock would be to have another child, and just over a year later, in June 1966, to our joy, our fifth and youngest son, Quentin, was born. Sarie had a fast labour, and the obstetrician arrived late at the hospital, so I had to deliver him myself, but all went well. He was a healthy and handsome child.

We were trying to get settled into the South Australian lifestyle, both socially and academically. This was not difficult. Australia is a welcoming place for immigrants and we quickly made friends, and having young children made this easier. Many would ask, "How can you have and raise four children in six years?" We felt blessed with our four living and loving children. Sarie especially was young and energetic and a fine mother to them.

Spiritual Musings

The death of Paul forced me to ponder whether suffering had any meaning. Pain is an experience that is likely universal in humanity. How can God, who is good, allow pain and evil in the world? This question has transfixed philosophers and theologians for centuries but each human being has to answer it in their own personal lives. Many people deal with the problem by ignoring it, but inability to find an answer is purposeless, and can lead to cynicism and/or despair.

Suffering has meaning only if it is placed in a spiritual context. God has allowed suffering because there is evil in the world. He has *allowed* the evil, not created it. Evil and suffering test us, and there can be ultimate benefit or reward through spiritual growth, maturation, or heavenly repose. Christ gave us his example by his awful death on the Cross: "Forgive them, Lord, for they know not what they do." I believe it is not possible to understand pain and evil without giving them a spiritual dimension. As John Bunyan said in *The Pilgrim's Progress*, "In times of affliction we commonly meet with the sweetest experiences of the love of God." These factors, and the promise of meeting Paul again in the afterlife, enabled me to come to terms with the hurt and bereft feeling of his death. It was an acid test of my faith.

In his novel *The Plague* (*La Peste*), the French author Albert Camus gives us vivid insight into the problem of evil in the world. A young boy dies a prolonged and painful death from bubonic plague. A priest-character, Fr. Paneloux, who previously presented as a pompous, arrogant ass, watches the boy die, then undergoes a profound change of heart. In a subsequent sermon, he analyzes the problem of evil on earth, with particular reference to the child's awful death. Paneloux says the existence of such evil demands from Christians a deep-felt, almost irrational Act of Faith in the goodness of God, as symbolized by Christ's death on the cross.

An agnostic humanist himself, Camus displays a deep understanding of the dilemma of the Christian in the context of evil in the world. The personal, social and psychological impact of plague on the people of Oran, as described in the novel, are hauntingly familiar in the context of our recent COVID-19 pandemic.

In 1966, I was elected chairman of the Newman Association, the local Adelaide Catholic university graduates' group. With the help of Peter Davis, an eminent academic biochemist, we set up and published a monthly journal called *Accent* in which articles on controversial social, religious, and political topics were published.

I became friendly also with Chris Hurford, a member of the Newman Association, and through him, became involved in Australian politics. Chris stood for parliament for the Australian Labour Party in the 1969 general election. I worked the streets and telephones on his behalf and was thrilled when he was elected to represent Adelaide Centre, overturning the conservative Liberal incumbent. He later took on various ministerial positions when Labour came into power. In 1988 he became the Australian Consul General in New York, where we met him again, with Lorna, his delightful wife. Lorna had her own career as a social worker, and was very involved in the arts and ballet scene in Adelaide. She died in 2005, and Chris in 2020, at the age of eighty-nine.

Lorna and Chris Hurford, with Sarie and me in 1988 in New York.

The 1960s were the time of the Vietnam war, with Australia taking part on the American side. I took a public stance against Australia's involvement. Although the anti-war movement was initially a minority, it became powerful by the early seventies, and played a part in moving Australia toward a more independent foreign policy.

In 1967 Pope Paul VI brought out his long-awaited encyclical *Humanae Vitae*, in which he called for the church to maintain its ban on all forms of artificial contraception. This was contrary to what many of his experts were advising him, and also contrary to the teaching of leading theologians, who recommended that it was time to update the church's teaching on contraception. The Adelaide Newman Association organized a public meeting to protest the encyclical, and Peter Davis and I visited Archbishop James Gleeson of Adelaide to make sure the hierarchy were aware what married practising Catholic laypeople thought about it. Our journal *Accent* published several articles questioning the theology and legitimacy of Paul VI's ruling.

Several weeks later, Peter flew to Rome to attend an international conference that had been called to present the layperson's point of view to the church authorities. Our lobbying and strong recommendations, of course, had no effect on the church's teaching. It remains in effect to this day, even though studies have shown that a majority of married, practising Catholics ignore the church's teaching, and have decided that use of contraceptives is a matter of individual conscience. Some Catholic hierarchies gently dissented from the pope, including the Canadian bishops, who published the *Winnipeg Statement* two months after *Humanae Vitae* came out, stressing the role of individual conscience for Catholic couples in decision-making.

Personally, Sarie and I struggled with this issue, and eventually, from the early 1970s until the 1990s, I lost my faith, in part because of my conflict about contraception. During this twenty-year period, I had no belief system other than what can loosely be called "secularism." My attitude and behaviour at that time were self-centred and harmful to others. I only returned to the faith when I realized that the church, for all its faults, has admirable teachings on spirituality, holiness, and the relationship between God and human beings, and on human inter-relationships. These guidelines, if followed, give meaning to our lives, and lead to personal fulfillment of our destinies on earth. I regret now those years when I rejected the faith.

Many Catholics, priests, nuns, and laity left the church in the late 1960s and 1970s, only in part because of *Humanae Vitae*. Other factors were also at play, such as the rise of the Women's Liberation Movement, the widespread availability of the birth control pill, and changing social mores, which culminated in the Woodstock counter-culture festival held in 1969.

Sexual Abuse

I am deeply dismayed by the dreadful crisis the church is going through regarding the sexual abuse of young boys and girls by priests, and male seminarians (priests-in-training) by senior clergy, and of the cover-up attempts by the hierarchy. Everything about the crisis is contrary to the teachings of Christ—priests breaking their vows of celibacy, the abuse of their power and authority over young people, the protection and cover-up of abusers by those in authority, all going on for years on end. It is nothing short of a moral catastrophe, a deplorable and heart-breaking situation. It recalls the disasters that affected the Church in the fifteenth and sixteenth centuries, when the appalling behaviour of popes such as Alexander VI and Julius II, notwithstanding their support of the arts, disgraced the church. Both popes had mistresses and children to whom they awarded favours, and these derelictions of duty were amongst the immediate causes of the Reformation and religious wars that followed. The whole episode reminds me of the adage that the miracle of the Catholic Church is not that it has survived 2,000 years of persecution, but that it has survived 2,000 years of Catholics.

Many blame the sex abuse crisis on the requirements of priests to take the vow of celibacy, and the inability of some to keep that vow. This undoubtedly plays a part, but it is not the whole story. The culture of secrecy, in which priests and bishops look after their own, plays a key role. It literally has taken our secular society's strong conviction that sexual abuse of minors is a serious criminal offense to persuade the church to cleanse itself of this internal sickness.

There is a requirement in church Canon Law to avoid scandal. So, priests who get involved in abusing children were moved to other parishes where they abuse children again, whereas they should have been thrown out of the priesthood altogether. The result of this short-sighted policy is that a more massive scandal has occurred.

The tragedy is that it is a small minority of priests—perhaps only 5 percent—who are guilty of abusing minors, but it is the whole church that gets painted with this brush. Church leaders, including several recent popes, have been extraordinarily short-sighted in not anticipating this epidemic.

There are loud demands, from both Catholics and others, for the church to change its policies on both the vow of celibacy and on admitting women to the priesthood. Personally, I would accept both these changes. Pope Francis, despite his mostly progressive views, has come out against these initiatives, and this is understandable, given the church's long tradition on these matters. There is a strong conservative wing in the church, exemplified by the substantial support given by Catholics in the United States to the many immoral and false statements, policies, and behaviours of Donald Trump.

There is no biblical or even traditional justification for clerical celibacy. St. Paul, in his Epistles, says that bishops (whom he calls "presbyters") should have no more than one wife, and married clergy were common in the first thousand years of the church's history. Furthermore, there already are married

Catholic priests, in certain Eastern Rites such as the Ukrainian and Rumanian Eastern Catholic churches. If a married Anglican or Orthodox priest converts to Catholicism, he can remain married. Celibacy is justified as an ideal in which a man or woman (the latter if entering the Sisterhood) vows to live their life as closely to the teachings and example of Jesus Christ as possible. If the church were to change its policy on the celibacy of the priesthood there would be huge economic implications. This, rather than theology, is likely a major factor delaying a change in this doctrine.

In my clinical practice I treated few patients who were victims of clerical abuse. In our department at the Ottawa General Hospital, we had a child and family clinic in which Sarie worked as an art therapist, and many were cared for there. Individual and group therapy, in addition to art therapy, are effective in helping people cope with the horrendous long-term effects of childhood, including clerical sexual abuse.

My hope and expectation are that, in the end, the church will survive this crisis, just as it did the Reformation crisis in the sixteenth century, and that it will purify itself as it should have done right from the beginning, when the disaster first broke. This purification will only happen when the church becomes transparent in its dealing with the issue and ends all attempts at cover-up.

Chapter Ten
A Slippery Slope

I knew that to get on in the world of academia, one had to write papers and publish in peer-reviewed journals. *Publish or perish* is the famous cliché applied to budding academics. Now, in the twilight years of my life, I look back and feel a little guilty about having fallen for this line, when it may have been more productive to focus on teaching or patient care. I find writing very labour-intensive; each of my papers and books has taken months or years to reach publishable quality, although the finished product gives me great satisfaction. I seem to have that human talent, sometimes of doubtful value, of being able to postpone gratification.

My first paper was published in the *Medical Journal of Australia* in 1966, entitled "General Hospital Psychiatry: Data Analysis of a Unit." I tried to show that psychiatry could be practised fully, freely, and successfully in a general hospital setting, and that the presence of an in-patient unit enhanced the quality of all medical care in that institution. Until the 1950s, psychiatry was based in mental hospitals, and treating the mentally ill who required hospitalization in a general hospital rather than a mental hospital was a novel undertaking. The data from my paper also showed that a higher percentage of first-generation immigrants than non-immigrants required psychiatric hospitalization.

Other papers followed in prestigious international journals, including an article on "Personality and Stress in Coronary Heart Disease." Here, I demonstrated that anxiety and personality factors were common antecedents in men who developed **ischemic heart disease**, especially **angina pectoris.**

I had decided to make the interface between psychiatry and medicine—sometimes called "psychosomatic medicine" or "liaison psychiatry"—my sub-specialty area. I considered my expertise in both psychiatry and general medicine to be an asset, given my dual qualification in both areas.

I decided also to write an MD (Doctor of Medicine) thesis. Australia follows the British medical educational system, wherein a physician is awarded an MD on the basis of a major research project, called a thesis, following reception of the basic MB, ChB degree. The MD degree is equivalent, therefore, to a PhD in the North American system. Professor William Cramond, my chief and supervisor, suggested the topic of the psychological aspects of infertility. We had an active and cooperative infertility clinic at the Queen Elizabeth Hospital where I worked, under the leadership of Drs. Lloyd Cox and Robert Munday, so I took it on. Of course, I was teased mercilessly by friends for doing research on infertility when I had fathered five children in six and a half years! "What underlying conflicts are you defending against?" they asked. "I am only trying to help childless couples have children," I replied innocently. The teasing became even more merciless when I began inviting my fertile couple-friends to be part of the control group.

My thesis was finally completed and I was awarded the MD degree by the University of Adelaide in 1970. I was only the third psychiatrist to be awarded this degree by the university. One of the others was Professor Sir Aubrey Lewis, head of psychiatry at the Maudsley Hospital in London, who had been born and graduated in Adelaide. When I wrote to tell him about my degree, he replied in a typically laconic researcher way of thinking, "You have increased the number of psychiatrists from the University of Adelaide with an MD degree by 33 percent." My thesis led to twelve papers published on the topic in various prestigious journals around the globe, the key one being "Psychiatric Interview Comparisons between Infertile and Fertile Couples." This paper has been cited 114 times. The results of my research, not unexpectedly, were that infertile women showed more anxiety and personality trait abnormalities than fertile women, and although most infertile women reacted adversely to their infertility, a substantial minority were ambivalent in their stated wish for a pregnancy.

Graduation, Doctor of Medicine, University of Adelaide, 1970. Sarie smiling serenely; Nicolas and Martin smiling mischievously.

There is a folk tale that infertile women who adopt a child are more likely to conceive following the adoption than those who do not adopt. One paper considered this issue and I concluded, "Although conception following adoption may not be a fact, it has yet to be proven a myth."

I found that a small minority of infertile couples could be diagnosed as having "psychogenic infertility." Despite their wish for a child, at a deeper level, they did not really want one. Two of the fifty infertile couples in my cohort were in this category. These couples showed behavioural techniques for avoiding pregnancy, by avoiding relations at mid-month during the ovulatory period of the wife's menstrual cycle. The power of the unconscious mind.

Another result of interest was that men in the infertile group smoked more cigarettes than men in the fertile group, and the smokers had lower sperm counts.

In October 1971, on the strength of this research, I was invited to attend a week-long workshop on infertility sponsored by the World Health Organization (WHO) in Geneva. In that delightful city, I met twenty infertility experts from around the world—obstetricians, gynecologists, pathophysiologists, psychologists and others—who fertilized my receptive mind. Regretfully, the WHO never published a report on the proceedings.

During the eight years we were in Adelaide, we made three fascinating long-distance trips *en famille*, using a rented camping trailer, called a "caravan" in Australia. The first was to the magnificent mountains in the north part of South Australia called Wilpena Pound. The high elevation and encircling mountains give it a micro-climate that is very different from the surrounding desert that covers much of central Australia. It is now part of the Flinders Range National Park and has breathtaking mountain views, and eucalyptus aromas.

Trip number two was to Sydney to visit our friends George and Dawn Parsons. Like me, George was an alumnus of both Grey High School and the University of Cape Town Medical School, but he was a couple of years ahead of me. After graduating he became a specialist in ophthalmology. For much of the way, we followed the Murrumbidgee River upstream, as it flows west from the Snowy Mountains, and viewed the beautiful countryside along the way, complete with hopping "roos" and galloping emus in the wild.

On the third trip, I went with just Martin and Nicolas. We visited the Eyre Peninsula west of Adelaide, where the wreck of the steamship *Ethel* is located, in a desolate region on the west coast of the peninsula. A three-masted barque travelling from South Africa, the *Ethel,* ran aground in a storm in 1904 with heavy loss of life, and now rests on the beach. The area was wild and deserted and we spent a few hours playing on the beach and the wreck. In retrospect, it was likely reckless to travel along empty, unpaved roads in the height of summer. If we had had an auto breakdown, there was no help, no cell phones, we could have perished from dehydration in no time.

Later, we made a shorter trip, taking a ferry to nearby Kangaroo Island, where we lived in a small cabin close to the beach for a week, and saw kangaroos, emus, koalas, and seals. Martin, aged eight, cut his foot badly on some broken glass hidden in sand under the water. There were no clinics or doctors on the island, and, surprisingly for a doctor, I had no first aid kit. My only recourse was to stitch up the wound, without local anesthetic, using one of Sarie's sewing needles and a short length of nylon fishing tackle, both sterilized by boiling. Even though the wound healed well, for him it was a memorably painful event. Every scar tells a story.

Despite these trips with the family, I know my parenting skills must have left much to be desired. I started married life with an idealistic concept of the sort of father I was going to be. I had resolved to be actively involved in their everyday care, and be the father to my children my father had not been to me. But because of my excessive dedication to my career, I know I failed on this scoresheet. On occasion I would read stories to the boys before bedtime, and loved this quiet time with them. Other times I would help with homework, as long as it was within the realm of my knowledge. Martin learned the clarinet and Nicolas the violin and I loved listening to them practise, or performing on the piano with them. These were exceptions, and I left the bulk of parenting to Sarie. There is remorse about this neglect in me and I know some of my sons have been hurt by my inattention when they were young. Unwittingly, I continued the fatherly neglect to my children I had experienced myself as a child.

The University of Adelaide generously offered its full-time staff sabbatical leave benefits of one year after six years of service. One of the world centres of excellence in psychosomatic medicine at the time was McGill University in Montreal, so in 1969 I duly wrote to Dr. Robert Cleghorn, at that time head of the department of psychiatry, asking him if I could spend my sabbatical leave there. I was shocked by his reply, advising me not to come! Isolated in the wilds of South Australia, we were unaware of the rising political tensions in Quebec, on account of the separatism issue. Canada has ten provinces, not including the three northern territories, and Québec is the only one where French is more widely spoken than English. Just under 25% of Canada's population lives in Québec, and there has been an historic pull on the part of many French-speaking Quebeckers to separate from the rest of Canada. This pull reached its height in the 1970s and 1990s when two separation referenda were held, both of which failed, the second by a whisker-thin majority. Political tensions had a devastating effect on university budgets and research projects in that province. Regretfully, I dropped the idea of going to Montreal.

The other major centre of excellence for psychosomatic medicine in North America was Rochester, New York, where the liaison psychiatry section was headed by Dr. George Engel. Engel subsequently became famous for introducing the concept of **biopsychosocial medicine** into the medical literature. I wrote to Engel and received a positive and enthusiastic reply, offering me a one-year fellowship, with the possibility of a one-year extension. We duly made our sabbatical leave arrangements to be away from Adelaide from April 1970 to April 1971. The plan was to travel to South Africa and spend one month there visiting Sarie's family, then on to London, England, for a month to visit my family, and then to Rochester for the rest of the period. It was exciting for our young boys at last to meet and get to know their extended family across the world.

Our return to South Africa was especially stirring, it being our first visit together since we got married. All my family, excepting Christiane, had left South Africa but Sarie's family welcomed us with open arms and hearts. On arrival in Cape Town, Sarie and I, with our four young sons in tow, immediately went up the 3500-foot Table Mountain by cable-way, and, it being a beautiful day, scrambled down the stony, steep Platteklip Gorge, with me having to carry four-year-old Quentin a good part of the way. Muscles and feet ached, but with pleasure, for days thereafter.

In London we reconnected with Maman and Papa, older and greyer than when we last saw them. This was to be the last time we were to see Papa. I reconnected with William Sargant at St. Thomas's Hospital, and we showed the children some of the sights of London, including Trafalgar Square and Tower Bridge, and the excitement of traveling on the Underground. Our sons attended the local school for the month we were in London, and learned how to speak English English, though their accents did not survive the return to Australia.

In Rochester, George Engel became the second great mentor of my career, the other being William Sargant. One cannot imagine two more different people. Sargant was a big man with a huge physical presence. A man of few words, he possessed features and body language that radiated optimism and positivity. Engel, on the other hand, was a balding, bespectacled man, small in stature and quietly spoken, who chose his words carefully, but everything he said carried gravitas. He undercut that with a charming sense of humour. Sargant was an extrovert and a world authority on physical and pharmacological treatments in psychiatry; Engel was an introvert and a world authority on the psychological and social aspects of general medicine.

François with George Engel, London, Ontario, 1974,
at our home near Dead Horse canyon.

He taught me the subtle and crucial art of clinical interviewing, using tape recordings. Together, we would listen to my tape-recorded clinical interviews, and he would comment on my questions, stressing the need for them to be concise, appropriate, and non-directive. A non-directive question is one that does not suggest an answer; there is no right or wrong answer to such a question. I was extraordinarily fortunate to spend many hours in one-to-one contact with him. My ten-month stint in Rochester transformed my life and my philosophy of medicine. It also transformed Sarie's life. While in Rochester, with the four boys now all at school, Sarie registered for an arts course at the Rochester Institute of Technology, and this became the foundation for her career in painting and art therapy.

In his biopsychosocial view of medicine, Engel argued that the previous concept of "biomedicine" was inadequate to explain causation and progression of diseases. Psychological, social, and personality factors all had to be taken into account when trying to understand the pathophysiology of diseases. Biological, psychological, and social issues interplayed with each other in the causation, course, and prognosis of all diseases. Although Engel's concept has been criticized, it has stood the test of time, and is still the standard by which modern medicine is taught and practiced.

In a letter to my family shortly after starting my fellowship in Rochester, I wrote:

> "I am getting organized on a research project on the psychological aspects of stroke, which has been an interest of Dr. Engel's, but also has a bearing on my own interest, the use of the interview in research, and my previous work on coronary diseases. Dr. Engel has a theory that stroke and coronary disease are part of a similar underlying process, and I shall be testing this theory. He is an excellent man with a very clear and lucid brain and a great empathy for others, qualities rarely combined in the same person, so after a rough start I am expecting the rest of the year to be more rewarding. From next week I shall be heavily involved in the undergraduate teaching program, as the teaching of psychiatry to medical students in Rochester is taken very seriously."

Unfortunately, my stroke project never was published, partly because I did not stay in Rochester long enough, and partly because the preliminary findings were equivocal. I did not assess a sufficient number of patients to conclude with certainty that psychosocial factors played a part in provoking the onset of stroke.

Engel was also famous for his psychological and behavioural observations of a young girl, Monica, born with oesophageal atresia. This is a condition in which there is congenital absence of the oesophagus, the tube that connects the pharynx in the throat with the stomach. Prior to Monica, it was invariably fatal. Pediatric surgeons at the Strong Memorial Hospital devised a three-stage procedure to treat her, the first time these operations had ever been performed. The first stage involved opening a surgical fistula into the stomach, so the infant could be fed directly into that organ. At the same time, an opening was made connecting her pharynx with the skin surface, so when she swallowed, fluid would emerge in her neck at the fistula, and be discarded. The third procedure, carried out in her third year, was to bring a portion of the intestine through the thorax so it became a substitute oesophagus, connecting the pharynx with the stomach.

With his colleagues, Engel studied Monica's feeding behaviour from infancy, using movie projector recordings, and noticed that Monica's mother was forced to feed her while she was lying flat on her back on a table, so she could drop milk and food directly through the fistula into the stomach. During her second and third years of life she was not being adequately nourished, became withdrawn and depressed, and failed to thrive. She recovered with treatment, particularly following the third surgical procedure in her third year. During my time in Rochester, I did not myself meet Monica, but saw the movies made about her.

Monica survived all these procedures and interventions, while Engel continued his discreet observations and recordings. Eventually she graduated from school, got married and had a daughter herself, who turned out to be quite normal, her organs all intact. However, Monica was unable to breastfeed, and she bottle-fed her child by lying her on a table on her back, in the identical posture that she herself had been fed as an infant! She said she felt "uncomfortable" if she cradled her infant in her arms against her torso in the manner that the great majority of mothers hold and feed their babies. No one told her that this was the way she should feed her child. It can only be inferred that long-term muscle memory caused her to repeat this singular feeding pattern.

Engel wanted me to spend another year in his department, but events in Adelaide sabotaged that plan. William Cramond, who had recruited me from Britain to the University of Adelaide in 1964, had been offered an appointment in England and resigned his position as head of department. Although realizing I was relatively young and inexperienced in administrative matters, I decided to apply for the position, so I returned to Adelaide at the scheduled end of my sabbatical leave. I did not get the position, and became quite depressed: I considered giving up on academia and going into private practice in Adelaide, but did not relish this option either. I could not imagine myself being confined to a consulting room, eight hours a day, five days a week, listening to personal stories for the rest of my life. No other suitable academic positions were available in Australia. However, while in Rochester I had visited nearby Toronto and Hamilton, and met with senior psychiatrists in medical schools there. I contacted Dr. Vivian Rakoff in Toronto, whom I had known when we were interns together at Victoria Hospital in Cape Town, and Dr. John (Jock) Cleghorn in Hamilton. They put me in touch with Dr. Gilbert Heseltine, who was setting up a new and expanding department of psychiatry at the University of Western Ontario in London. Heseltine offered me an associate professorship at the newly built University Hospital, so I signed up. I was fascinated by the idea of Canada, with its Anglo-French roots and culture, since I myself was a product of an Anglo-French upbringing in South Africa. It was not until I came to Canada, with its unique Anglo-French character, that I came to terms with my Frenchness.

In Canada, I came to describe myself, when asked, as originally a "French-South African," or a *sud-africain français*, although basically there is no such thing as a French-South African, because South Africans with a French background form such a tiny minority. This designation resonates with Canadians, however, and also explains my peculiar accent. I speak both English and French with a South African cadence.

My time in Rochester had been enormously fruitful. Not only George Engel, but other members of his staff such as Bill Green, Art Schmale, and

Robert Ader had carried out excellent groundbreaking research into the relationship between psyche and **soma**, and they all fertilized my young mind. Ader's animal experimental work was of special interest; he found that stress and other psychological factors could affect the immunological system, either detrimentally or beneficially. This research became crucial in theories concerning the role of psychosocial factors in the pathogenesis of disease.

I continued my relationship with George Engel by correspondence until the end of his life in 1999, when he died of heart failure at the age of eighty-six. We discussed our respective writings and research projects. In particular, he was complimentary of my work on hysteria, and the psychological aspects of heart transplantation. In one of his letters to me, dated April 4, 1984, there is a fascinating paragraph concerning his teaching technique. The letter was written to honour correspondence he received celebrating his seventieth birthday. He wrote,

> "The album of letters is a great treasure for me, not only for the fond memories it brings back, but also for its testimony to the effects of the educational experience we all shared together. Especially in the early years, I've often wondered how many of you realized that I was bluffing, or at least encouraging the illusion that I was qualified to act as an instructor. Actually, the most important thing I have come away with from that experience was the realization that the most effective and stimulating learning experience takes place when it is a shared enterprise and everyone is learning from and with each other. That gets more difficult as the age gap widens, but I am convinced it is an attitude all teachers should cultivate if they hope to continue to be effective in their later years."

His comments in the final two sentences are indicative of his wisdom, but I don't think any of his students would agree with his comments that he was bluffing. He was a good actor, sure, as any good teacher must be, but he knew his stuff, and his students hung on his every word.

His final letters to me recounted the sad events of the illness and death of Evelyn, his dear wife of many years, and his own health issues that led to his admission to a residential care facility. At my last visit to him in 1998, a year or so before he died, he presented me with two wonderful gifts: Four excellent volumes of Denis Diderot's *Encyclopédie*, published in 1751, and a copy of Euclid's *Geometry*, published in the seventeenth century. The *Encyclopédie* I donated, in turn, to my cousin Marie-France Goodliffe, who is a world authority on Diderot, having written her PhD thesis on the philosopher; Euclid's *Geometry*, I still treasure.

My ten months in the United States were highly fulfilling, and set me on a trail that was to reach its culmination after I moved to Canada a year later. Personal opportunities that had been stirred by my experience in Rochester were developed to a higher level by the fairness and transparency I encountered in the Canadian political and academic scene.

Chapter Eleven
Becoming Canadian

In August 1972, we left Adelaide for Vancouver aboard the P & O liner *Arcadia*. We did not know it at the time, but the days of travel by sea as a passenger were numbered, as air travel took off. The *Arcadia* converted to cruising full time the next year. The first half of the voyage, from Adelaide to Honolulu, went well, stopping at Melbourne, Sydney, Auckland, Western Samoa, Fiji, and Honolulu. In Sydney we were treated to a spectacular performance of the musical *Jesus Christ Superstar*, and in Western Samoa (now Samoa), we took a cable-car to the mountain-top from which we had a magnificent view of the surrounding islands and ocean. In Honolulu we cavorted on Waikiki beach for the day.

However, the segment from Honolulu to Vancouver was disastrous. An epidemic of influenza broke out, and both Quentin, aged six, and I became seriously ill. We were in recovery mode by arrival in Vancouver. But another crisis awaited us. We had arranged to travel Vancouver to London, Ontario, by train, and the agent who booked our travel in Adelaide assured us all expenses for the train were included in our fare. Not so; only the sleeping compartments and breakfast were included. Moreover, our cash had run out! The trip across Canada was four days and five nights. We survived by filling our pockets at breakfast with bread rolls, peanut butter and jam, and scrounging what food we could from sympathetic waiters in the train's restaurant. On arrival in London, Dr. Douglas Bocking, dean of the faculty of medicine at the University of Western Ontario, generously gave me an advance on my first month's salary to pay for our family's essential needs. When I last saw him five years ago, aged ninety-four, he still remembered that event with amusement.

Desmond ffolliott, my boyhood friend from Grey High School who had moved to London some years previously, met us at the station. He and his wife, Joan, quickly replenished our empty stomachs. Joan and Desmond were extraordinarily helpful in getting us settled and adjusted to our new surroundings, and for the next few years, we saw each other regularly as personal and family friends. Regretfully, over Christmas and New Year in 1974, we became estranged. Desmond had sent around a Christmas letter in which he had criticized the French in Québec, then led by Premier René Lévesque, who were trying to separate Québec from Canada, a move strongly opposed by the rest of Canada. I thought it inappropriate to mention a contentious political issue in a Christmas brief, but instead of ignoring it, which I should have done, I criticized him when next we met. Desmond never spoke to me again.

Looking back, I admit I was oversensitive on this issue. Later, in 1995, at the time of the second referendum on Québec separatism, we were residents of Québec and voted against separation. Hence, we made a small contribution to the defeat of the separatist proposal, which lost by a paper-thin majority of less than 1 percent. Nevertheless, I was sympathetic to the yearnings of the French in Québec, trying to maintain their language and their cultural identity, surrounded, as they were, by a sea of Englishness in North America. Desmond's critical reference to the Québec French in the letter was really a trivial matter, and it would have been sensible to disregard it, but the damage was done.

In 1994, I wrote to him apologizing for my contribution to the estrangement, suggesting we get together again, but he never replied. Years later, I googled him only to find he had died. I remain heartbroken by the break-up and non-reconciliation of this, one of my oldest friendships.

I've kept one special souvenir from Desmond. Shortly before our estrangement, and to celebrate my fortieth birthday, he gave me a binder-bound copy of poems we studied together when we were in Dudley Clear's English matriculation class at Grey High School in 1950. It was the tenth of ten copies Desmond had published, and the collection includes "The Rime of the Ancient Mariner," which we both loved. The opening page of the book contains a charming personal dedication to me, in which Desmond refers to our time together in Mr. Clear's English class.

We arrived in London in September of 1972, in time for the opening of University Hospital, and this turned out to be a spectacular event. The day was marked by the arrival at the hospital, by helicopter, of Bill Davis, the premier of Ontario, for the opening ceremonies. In addition to Davis, two eminent Canadians, Wilder Penfield and Marshall McLuhan, had been invited to give presentations at the university during the days following. Both were to be awarded honorary doctorate degrees from Western University. I was familiar with the writings of these great Canadians. Penfield was the founder of the Montreal Neurological Institute, and was famous for developing the surgical treatment of certain types of epilepsy, while McLuhan was world-renowned for his writings on the media and its effects on modern society. Penfield also wrote two novels, entitled *No Other Gods* and *The Torch*. Years later, I wrote an essay on Penfield as a writer of fiction. *No Other Gods* is a fictionalized rendering of the life and wanderings of Abraham and Sarah, until they settled in the Promised Land of Israel. *The Torch* describes the imagined life of Hippocrates, also known as The Father of Medicine, in ancient Greece.

Penfield respected the genius and precepts of Hippocrates. The ancient *Hippocratic Oath* still governs the ethics of medicine today, despite the liberties our society is taking regarding some of its basic tenets. "I will benefit my patients according to my greatest ability and judgement, and will do no harm or injustice to them. Neither will I administer a poison to anybody. . .. I will abstain from intentional wrong-doing and harm, especially from abusing the bodies of man or woman."

University Hospital had famous Canadians on staff, notably in the field of neurosciences. Dr. Charles Drake had identified and developed a widely used surgical treatment for cerebral aneurysms, and Dr. "Barney" Barnett was later to head a major international study on the value of aspirin in the prevention of stroke. Both were inspiring clinicians, teachers, and researchers. I was awed by this introduction to Canadian medicine. The hospital itself was ten-storeys high, beautifully constructed, with up-to-date technology, and sited right on the grounds of Western University. It was all very impressive.

After writing my MRCP examination in Edinburgh, I thought I was done with exams. However, following my arrival in Canada, I found I had to undertake two more—the fellowship of the Royal College of Physicians, and the licentiate of the Medical Council of Canada. The fellowship was straightforward, as it was pure psychiatry. The licentiate was much more difficult, as it dealt with general medical and surgical issues I had not studied for years, so required many months of study and preparation. The examination consisted of five three-hour multiple-choice tests on three successive days. It was quite amusing, as I had to write it simultaneously with many senior medical students whom I had been teaching. Having completed the answers, the medical students vacated the examination hall an hour or more before the scheduled end of the three-hour test, whereas I, together with a handful of other older, transplanted physicians, struggled to complete the answer-sheet in the allotted time. To my relief, I managed to pass both these examinations.

Seven months after our arrival in London, Papa died, at the early age of seventy-one. He had been diagnosed with both cardiac and liver problems, and his condition was not helped by his excessive use and enjoyment of scotch whisky. He was admitted to a hospital in London, and died there suddenly within a few days. I flew to England for the funeral and to provide support for Maman. The funeral took place in Westerham in Kent, Denyse's hometown at the time, where Papa is buried. It was a melancholy occasion for the entire family. I remember seeing the hearse containing his remains driving by, my first ever family funeral, and, with shock, thinking to myself: *My father is in there.* His final years were not happy, especially with his anxiety about David's continuing health issues, but Maman provided him with loyal and stoic support.

Over the years I had my difficulties with Papa. He had an outgoing and demanding personality and expected the best of himself and his family, and those who worked for him. As a child I felt intimidated by him, but during my teens he became a hero to me. He had a tender side to his personality, and he, more than any other, guided me in my choice of medicine as a career. I was fortunate to be able to meet his expectations academically and he respected me for this, but we had other areas of conflict, particularly with regard to the French political scene that marked our relationship in his final years. It was heartbreaking to see the change from the strong, independent entrepreneur he had been in his fifties, to the ill and helpless man at seventy. Although I cannot say I ever felt close to him, he was an involved and generous father to his five children.

My job at University Hospital was to head and run the consultation liaison section of the department of psychiatry. Shortly after I took up my position, I decided that one of the first outpatients I saw required admission to the psychiatric ward for treatment of his depression. He was the first admission to the spanking new unit, which could accommodate up to ten patients. Each patient had their own room and toilet facilities, and the bed design and décor were state-of-the-art. I asked him to remain in the waiting room while preliminary arrangements were being made. By a remarkable coincidence, a man with the same name was also in the waiting room. While my patient was temporarily out of the room, the nurse invited the second (and wrong) man to come to the ward to be admitted. At first, he meekly complied, believing no doubt that this was the usual procedure when a person had been referred to a psychiatrist. It was only when he was shown his room and asked to undress to await a physical examination that he protested he had not seen a doctor yet. The nurses checked his name and found he had a different first name from the patient who was to have been admitted. Tragically, this unfortunate man, my patient, later committed suicide. Toward the end of his admission and seemingly on the road to recovery, while home on a weekend pass, he took cyanide he had somehow obtained from a chemical laboratory. Over my lifetime he was one of three patients who have suicided while under my treatment. The first was a young woman who developed a **puerperal** depression following the birth and subsequent adoption of her illegitimate child. I had been seeing her weekly for supportive psychotherapy. One week, after she failed to show up for her appointment, I discovered she had taken a fatal overdose. The third was an older man who had a combination of depression and heart disease. Following an angiogram, in which the cardiologist had inserted the catheter through the femoral artery, he went to the toilet, cut open the angiography wound, and exsanguinated into the toilet bowl.

Canada does not have a good record in suicide statistics. With regard to risk of suicide, Canada is ranked thirty-seventh in the world. More men than women commit suicide. Amongst males, the incidence per 100,000 population is twenty, and it is five amongst females. The incidence is higher in Indigenous people, and in Nunavut the risk is one of the highest in the world. In my practice, though three is three too many, it is likely average for the lifetime of most psychiatrists. One always feels shocked by these events, and guilty as to whether one could, or should, have treated them differently.

In the human race, there are many casualties. One of my patients shot himself in the head with the intention of killing himself. Remarkably, the only structure he damaged, other than his skull, was the optic chiasma, the point at the base of the brain where the two optic nerves from the eyes meet, and cross over on their way to the ophthalmic cortex at the back of the brain. As a result, he was totally blind. He recovered well mentally with anti-depressant therapy, but his blindness was permanent.

Another patient was a middle-aged woman with the referral diagnosis of hysterical paralysis of both arms. Her history revealed she had fallen whilst under the influence of liquor, sustaining head and arm injuries. She had a past psychiatric history and I witnessed her histrionic manner as she recounted her story. I decided to carry out a physical examination, and found she had **crepitus** in both arms, strongly suggesting fractures of both humeri, the long bones in the upper arm. This was confirmed by radiological examination. The referring physician had carried out only a cursory physical examination, and missed the broken bones that had caused the so-called paralysis of her arms. There would have been social and legal pandemonium if she had been discharged home with those undiagnosed broken bones. She was referred to an orthopedic surgeon for proper treatment of the fractures.

I had two patients with hysterical '**conversion**' symptom, one with blindness, the other with torticollis (wry neck). Conversion is the term used to describe the condition in which a physical symptom or impairment results from an underlying psychological conflict. Both responded well to treatment with intravenous sodium amytal, although the woman with torticollis had to be treated several times before recovery.

Liaison psychiatrists are often the end of the road for patients in the referral system, especially for patients with complex psychosomatic problems. They have seen many specialists, and had many tests and special investigations, with no serious physical illness being uncovered, or perhaps but a minor abnormality, insufficient to explain the severity of their symptoms, so the referring physician decides, *Let's try psychiatry.* The patient is often resistant to this, stating, or thinking, *you're telling me it's all in my head;* hence, they decline the referral. For those who agree, however, it is an opportunity to render the patient less sensitive to psychopathology that may be contributing to their apparent physical illness. Using George Engel's biopsychosocial model, I would explain to the patient something along these lines: "The mind and body are one. Emotional and social changes affect the body and the body affects one's emotional health and social adjustment. Sometimes this can work like a vicious circle that revs up as it goes around. Treatment requires breaking, or slowing down that cycle. Psychiatrists can help you do that." When portraying psychiatric therapy in these terms, most patients willingly accept it for their problems. I have summarized these treatment recommendations in more detail in a publication entitled *Somatization Disorder: A Practical Review,* which has received 124 citations in the medical literature.

A cognitive therapy approach is best for treating such patients, and this can be done on an outpatient basis, where they are seen weekly or biweekly initially, and then less frequently as treatment progresses. In these late stages of the illness, the patient is often on a variety of pharmaceuticals, and I have found that the first step in treatment is to reduce or stop these drugs. This in itself may help them feel better because many of their symptoms are caused by the side-effects of the medications. After reducing or stopping the drugs, one is then better able to identify and deal with the underlying issues.

The final crucial step in the management of such patients is to ensure that the smallest number of physicians (preferably one) becomes responsible for their long-term care, be it the psychiatrist, family physician, or a selected specialist. So often, the problems are perpetuated by the involvement of many physicians in their management, or the tendency of doctors to refer them needlessly to colleagues, transmitting to the patient the idea *I don't know what's wrong with you so I'll try specialist Dr. X.* If more than one physician is involved, they need to ensure they are in regular communication with each other about any treatment procedures or changes.

I'll illustrate the principles of cognitive therapy by describing how it might have been applied to the young man called Steven, mentioned in Chapter Eight, a patient of William Sargant at Belmont Hospital, who was preoccupied with his gait. At an early interview one would ask him, "What are your treatment goals?" Steven might reply, "I want to stop worrying about my gait" or, "I want to change my gait." The therapist proceeds by giving him practical, daily techniques for achieving these goals, which are written down and a copy given to the patient. If anxiety is the main problem, he may be taught meditation/mindfulness; if he wishes to modify his gait, he may be given practice sessions to show the specific changes he desires. Steven is required to make a daily written record of his practice sessions to demonstrate and encourage his motivation. The therapy program is always individualized for the needs of each person. Visible progress with relief of symptoms reinforces recovery. Steven will be seen on a regular scheduled appointment basis. In so doing he will learn how to deal with minor issues himself, without calling on the therapist whenever a problem occurs.

Studies, such as those by Demers, Gaulin, and others, have shown that hard-to-treat patients with chronic symptoms often have complex biological, psychological, and social issues. Although small in number, they make a disproportionately heavy demand on health-care services, emergency departments, and family doctors. These studies found the mean cost-per-patient for their ambulatory care was much higher than normal. I believe that managing them in the manner I've described above will help reduce the demands they make on health-care services. Moreover, this approach will help the recovery of the patients themselves. These treatment principles have been expanded in an excellent, recently published manual that I reviewed in a report, *Understanding and Managing Somatoform Disorders: A Guide for Physicians.*

The management of such hard-to-treat patients is amusingly demonstrated in the Netflix movie series *The New Amsterdam Hospital,* set in New York City. Max Goodwin, the character who plays the part of the hospital's medical director, discovers a homeless "patient" who costs the hospital over a million dollars a year for his repeated unnecessary admissions and tests he undergoes. Goodwin arranges for the hospital budget to pay for the man to live in rental accommodation, thus preventing his expensive hospital stays. The "dean," Dr. Peter Fulton, Goodwin's boss, is initially shocked by this deal, calling it "socialism," but finally agrees with Goodwin that this simple arrangement actually did save hundreds of thousands in hospital funds.

Life in London

Sarie and I spent sixteen great years in London. We purchased a lovely home on the banks of Dead Horse Canyon in the city's northwest suburbs, within walking distance of University Hospital. There were a number of other families on the street with young boys, so friendships were easily made. Our sons quickly learned how to skate; play hockey; and throw, hit, and field a baseball; and adapted to the new school system. Fortunately, all four had a natural flair for sports, in particular, hockey. They also did well academically.

Now that Quentin, our youngest son, was attending school, Sarie had to make big decisions about her own life and career. In Rochester, she had attended the Institute of Technology and completed a course in art, and on return to Adelaide, she had trained as an art therapist. Unfortunately, in London, no positions for art therapists were available. One of the rooms in our home had large skylights, so she converted this to a studio, and started painting and teaching adults and children how to paint. She is a verbally expressive person and a natural-born teacher. Her adult teaching group dubbed themselves "The Mai Bees" and they had a number of successful art exhibitions in London. Later, Sarie was able to obtain an art therapist position in the local cancer clinic at the Children's Hospital. There, she did magnificent work supporting children with cancer, which was written up in the *Canadian Medical Association Journal* by journalist B. Trent, and in the *Toronto Star* by Paula Adamick. Trent writes, "To begin with, the children are very silent and withhold a lot of feelings, once they start to paint and draw about it, a whole new area of communications opens up." Adamick states, "Art therapist Sarie Mai helps young cancer patients deal with their fears and feelings about their condition through colours and symbols they choose themselves. Staff get insight into their state of mind from the drawings." Sarie gave inspiring presentations and workshops on these topics, in Canada and other countries, and authored a textbook, *The Mai Colour Glossary,* describing a new technique for assessment in art therapy that has become widely used nationally and internationally. In it, she describes how colour selection by her client can be used to identify areas of psychopathology in feelings and relationships. For example, one person may associate the colour red with danger; another with love or sex. Each person has a different colour code that can be used for therapeutic purposes.

We also did some sailing, although that was less successful. Sarie had no experience of sailing in her life, although I had done some in Australia on friends' sailboats and loved it. I bought a twenty-six-foot Grampian, which had a spacious cabin and cockpit, and we went on a week-long sailing course to learn the ropes. I named her *Winter Dream,* indicative of my thoughts during the long Canadian winter, and she was a safe cruising craft. Sarie tried hard to enjoy it but never adjusted to the boat movements. Realizing this, I eventually sold the boat but it became a family joke that I had to make a choice between my boat and my wife. If so, I made a wise decision.

Then there was the day Quentin, our youngest son, brought home a day-old chick his class had incubated and hatched as an educational exercise. Our whole family became attached to this chicken, whom we dubbed *Chirpy.* During the night, Chirpy slept in the garage, and in daytime would follow anyone of us around in the garden, seeming to have imprinted on the human figure. Our neighbours were highly entertained to see the local psychiatrist walking around the circle, followed closely by a chicken.

We were unsure of Chirpy's sex, but one morning found an egg in the garage, and this was followed by many more. As a child on Papa's farm, I had learnt how to cluck like a hen, and crow like a rooster, so Chirpy and I often chatted in chicken.

The downside was that Chirpy messed up our garage. One morning we got up to find that she had roosted overnight on Sarie's car and fouled (fowled) the whole windscreen. Chirpy was unceremoniously dispatched to friends who had a chicken run on a farm. I missed my fresh morning Chirpy egg.

My academic writing flourished during the years in London. I collaborated with Harold Merskey, who had an international reputation in the field of chronic pain, and who had moved to London from the United Kingdom. We published landmark articles on the contribution the nineteenth century French physician Pierre Briquet made to the diagnosis and treatment of **hysteria**. Its name was changed first to somatization disorder, and it is now called somatoform disorder. For a while in the 1970s, Guze and a group of eminent American psychiatrists based in St. Louis recommended that hysteria be renamed Briquet's syndrome in his honour. Merskey and I read, translated, and published key sections of Briquet's book and even subjected some of his clinical data to statistical analysis. Little was known about statistics in 1859, when Briquet published his book. For example, Briquet's data showed that the children of "hysterical" mothers had a higher death rate than children of non-hysterical mothers. Using his data, we showed that this difference was highly significant statistically. In 1983, as a result of this research, I was promoted to full professor in the University of Western Ontario, and also elected as a Fellow of the Royal College of Physicians of Edinburgh (FRCP)

In 1982, I visited Paris to attend a psychiatric conference, where I was scheduled to give a presentation, in French, on Briquet. In my readings on Briquet I had found that some nineteenth-century documents had given his first name as "Paul" and others said it was "Pierre." On the title page of his monograph only the letter P is written. After much reading and investigation, I decided that Paul was more likely correct, and this was the name I used in my subsequent writings. It was also the name I used in the title of the presentation I was to give.

The day before my presentation, I visited the Père Lachaise cemetery and inquired whether Briquet was buried there. Sure enough, he was. I located his grave, which had a catafalque over a metre high, so I climbed to the top but found the grave untended, and the inscription illegible because of the growth of lichen and moss. I had no tools with me, so I climbed down again, found a solid stick that I could use as a scraper, and climbed back up. All these activities were complicated by the fact that it was a rainy day. Once the vegetation had been scraped away, I discovered that the inscription on the tombstone indicated that his first name was Pierre, not Paul! At my presentation the next day, I had to explain in my opening remarks, that in the light of "very recent research" in the Père Lachaise cemetery, I had ascertained, without shadow of doubt, that Briquet's first name was Pierre and not Paul.

Old habits die hard, however. Although I immediately published my findings about the name correction, many authors who have written since on Briquet, and cited my work, continue, wrongly, to give his first name as Paul.

Working with colleagues in London, we secured a substantial research grant from the Canadian Research Council to study the hormonal changes that occurred in people who had depressive conditions. Our findings showed that changes occurred in the secretion of prolactin in depression, with particular differences evident between pre- and post-menopausal women. These results were consistent with the hypothesis that changes in dopamine levels play a role in the development of depression.

My other major field of research in London was the psychological and social aspects of heart transplantation. From time immemorial the heart has been regarded as the seat of the soul, even though science has now shown that it is merely a remarkably efficient and effective biological pump. I was fortunate to collaborate with Drs. Bill Kostuk (cardiologist) and Neil McKenzie (cardiac surgeon), who carried out the first successful heart transplant operation in Canada, in 1981. The first recipient survived twelve, and the second, thirty-two years. To date, over 450 such procedures have been carried out in London.

McKenzie completed his medical training in Aberdeen, spent two years on a British Heart Foundation scholarship in Upsala, Sweden, and was recruited to London, Ontario, by Dr. Raymond Heimbecker, the well-known Canadian cardiovascular surgeon. Together with the organ transplant team in London, McKenzie carried out many of the early research studies on cyclosporine, a potent and novel immuno-suppressive agent.

Neil McKenzie, the cardio-thoracic surgeon who carried out the first successful heart transplant operation in Canada, in 1981

Our published collaborative work on the psychiatric and psychosocial aspects of heart transplantation was a world first on this topic. I had been fascinated by transplants ever since Chris Barnard, Sarie's cousin, had performed the world's first in 1967. The major finding of our study was that patients who survived surgery did very well from the psychological, physical health, and activities point of view, but not so well from the occupational function perspective, i.e., whether or not they were able to work. We published related papers in the Canadian, and the British *Journals of Psychiatry* and, together, these papers have received 191 citations in the medical literature. I also spoke at meetings in the United States, South

Africa, France, Belgium, and Germany, as well as Canada. The presentation in Cape Town, South Africa, was given as part of our Class of 1956 fortieth reunion in 1996. We'd all aged, some of us had died, but we connected *tout de suite,* as if we were all teenage students again.

I asked myself whether heart transplant recipients were affected by the age, sex, or race of the donor. Often attempts are made to keep the identity of the donor heart anonymous, but this does not always succeed. I investigated these issues and found that the majority of recipients were not interested in the donor or the donated heart; they were just happy to be alive and that the heart worked. I interpreted this as their use of the mechanism of denial. A small proportion showed anxiety about the age and skin colour of the donor, and were curious to know, or even to meet the family of the donor. When they did so, it appeared to be satisfying to all parties. A few patients went further in their thoughts about the donor. One told me, four months after her surgery, "I feel guilty that I am alive and he [the donor] is dead. I'm trying to see his heart as my heart. It took me a long time to adjust to the fact that I'm walking around with somebody else's heart inside me. I couldn't accept that . . . it wasn't me. I was somebody put together." Another, with a glint of humour, twelve months after surgery said, "I think about the operation every day. The new heart is amazing. I dream about being in hospital but not about the new heart. I wouldn't mind doing it for someone else, but it would have to be a second-hand heart." I concluded that these findings showed support for the traditional role of the heart in human feelings and relationships, and that post-transplant adaptation was promoted if the patient is given "a time for silence."

Whilst in London I also published a satirical article entitled "New Diagnostic Instrument Brings Psyche into View." It purported to show that, by attaching a complex lens system to the eyes and ears of an individual, one could actually peek into the head, and view an image of the psyche in the brain, including visualization of the ego, superego, and id. I called the device a "psychoscope." By so "viewing" the brain, the psychiatrist could make a diagnosis such as schizophrenia, or bipolar or personality disorder.

Here are some of the highlights of the article. You may want to place your tongue in your cheek while reading it:

"As the name implies, the psychoscope is a technique for bringing the psyche into view. With this instrument, psychiatrists for the first time will have available a technique that will provide a true physical sign. It will be possible to make diagnostic inferences by visually observing psychic phenomena.

The psychoscope is constructed with a double lens system so as to permit binocular viewing by the observer. Built into the instrument is an intricate prism and mirror system to provide for simultaneous bi-visual and bi-aural examination of the patient. A built-in laser system connects to a standard 120-volt wall outlet and provides deep penetrating power so the psychic core can be visualized in the three spatial dimensions, as well as the temporal dimension.

The examiner can focus on the psyche using both low- and high-power focusing devices as required. The latter enable the ego, the superego, and the id to be differentiated clearly from each other.

Examination of patients with schizophrenia showed that the most striking feature was that the psychoscope enabled the observer to share the hallucinatory experiences of the subject just as they were occurring, so no longer will their presence be based solely on the subjective report of the patient.

The manic-depressive psyche was visualized . . . and here the most prominent feature was a rapidly oscillating body never witnessed before. We have provisionally termed this organelle the "oscilith."

In patients with personality disorder, the most distinctive were the sociopaths, where the psyche could be seen pulsating vigorously at rhythmic intervals, and with high-power magnification large vacuoles were visible in the superego. The id of patients with psychosexual disorder showed polychromasia with scattered cellular structures, some having a rounded concave form, and others an elongated fusiform shape. Further research is required to ascertain the precise diagnostic significance of these curious bodies.

Note that the procedure is non-invasive and will make it an office routine for all practicing psychiatrists. Unfortunately, the complex lens-lased power system will mean that the initial capital outlay will be in the order of $4,500 without options, but this may be reduced if, as expected, the psychoscope becomes widely used and mass-produced.

The fact that the examination involves a <u>procedure</u> with a highly specialized <u>instrument</u>, and not a mere clinical interaction, will place it into a separate category with reference to Medicare benefits. Indeed, use of the psychoscope may render the traditional assessment psychiatric interview obsolete. The degree of complexity and sophistication and the quality of expertise required to interpret the data is considered to be analogous to a colonoscopy, hence application is being made to health insurance organizations for at least equivalent coverage. As with a colonoscopy, Medicare benefits (OHIP) will be based on a sliding scale, which will vary according to the depth of penetration, permitting a maximum benefit of $111.20 [1983 dollars] for the most extensive examination."

There was a serious message behind the satire. Payments to physicians by the Ontario Health Insurance Plan are heavily weighted toward those specialties that have a procedure. Specialists who use a procedure, be it surgeons or gastroenterologists with an endoscopic examination, are rewarded far more generously on an hourly basis by provincial health insurance plans than specialists such as psychiatrists, paediatricians or rheumatologists who do not have available a diagnostic or therapeutic device. The psychoscope, at a cost of $4,500, would change all that because psychiatrists would now have a procedural diagnostic tool that would greatly add to their incomes. Surprisingly, the article had no impact on the way that physicians were remunerated.

There was an amusing sequel. I received numerous hilarious letters from colleagues expanding on the use of the psychoscope in all sorts of bizarre ways. For instance, here is an extract of a letter to the editor that appeared in the *Ontario Medical Review*, where the original article appeared.

"As the article mentioned, the psyche is visualized by the psychoscope as an oscillating body; variations in the characteristics of the oscillation correspond well to various disease states. Modification of a given pattern of oscillation is made possible by adding a waveform generator in a parallel circuit with the laser of the psychoscope. It was determined by the late Dr. I. Dimwiddy that profound alterations in a person's emotional and intellectual functions could be achieved in this way.

Dr. Dimwiddy, in a characteristically selfless gesture of ardent stupidity, elected to be the first subject of the modified psychoscope (now known as "the Dimwiddy device" in his memory). The resultant fragmentation of a previously semi-integrated personality had tragic consequences. One of the newly emerged personalities, a violent paranoid schizophrenic named Chip, strangled Dr. Dimwiddy with a length of Foley catheter and thus committed suicide.

The scientific community, stunned by the loss, bravely carried on as if nothing had happened. But the federal government, horrified at the prospect of such a powerful device being utilized by inexperienced academics, slapped a security cordon around Dr. Dimwiddy's offices. The populace greeted with a sigh of relief the news that the Dimwiddy device had been turned over to the RCMP, who will use it to treat the many psychopaths known to them. . . ." This letter was signed by a medical student using the nom-de-plume "Rufus T. Firefly."

Another colleague wrote, "Dear François, my warmest congratulations on your development of what will, I am sure, prove to be a major development in the armamentarium of psychodiagnostics instrumentation. For far too long psychiatrists have struggled in the wasteland of psychodiagnostic formulation (Freudians and Jungians pitted in the murky molasses of unconscious determination). Please record my tentative order for 400 psychoscopes, to be delivered as soon as the instrument becomes commercially available. For a long time, I have shared the view that psychiatry needs a good $400 procedure. Your outstanding achievement makes that aspiration a clinical reality. My warmest congratulations. If (Pierre) Trudeau fails in his bid for a Peace Prize, I shall see that Council seriously considers the psychoscope as an alternative."

Yet another wrote: "I have been complaining bitterly this week that no one seems to have any sense of humour nowadays.

"Then yesterday the Ontario Medical Review arrived and I read your article, which immediately restored my faith in human nature! Congratulations and many thanks—please have the article circulated as widely as possible."

On the other hand, a number of physicians who wrote me did not grasp the satire, believed the psychoscope was for real! They thought I was on to a whole new chapter in psychiatric diagnosis. They asked that I send them a replica of my psychoscope for their own use in their clinical practices. With a little difficulty, I resisted the temptation to ask them to send me the $4,500 first, and the (non-existing) psychoscope would be sent them by return of mail. In the end, I ignored these pleading letters.

Our recreation activities prospered in London. Sarie and I enjoyed cycling together and on two occasions we joined forces with our friends Marybeth and John Drake and cycled in France, in the Valley of the Loire, and in Holland. Visiting the chateaux of the Loire by bicycle was memorable, though cycling up the hills with heavy panniers was challenging. I would use a bungy cord to hook the back of my bicycle to the front of Sarie's, and give her a lift up the hills.

We played much tennis in London, both recreational and competitive. Sarie especially won several tournaments, both in singles and doubles.

Tennis vacation in Florida. L to R: Paul Pennington, Tom Feasby, François, and Brian Wheeler

Late one afternoon we stopped at a hotel for the night in the ancient cathedral town of Loches. John and I went in to negotiate our rooms, while Sarie and Marybeth waited outside, guarding the bicycles. When we came out, they were seated in the street on the kerbside, looking for all the world like two forlorn waifs, sweaty, dusty, and exhausted from the day's ride. We got to our rooms and, an hour later, lo and behold, both were transformed into beautiful, well-dressed young women, ready to toast the town.

I also carried out a long-distance cycle tour alone, from Windsor, Ontario, to Niagara Falls, following Highway 3 for 400 kilometres along the north shore of Lake Erie. This was a lovely route with little traffic and much historical relevance. I strolled through the quaint, historic village of Sparta, a few kilometres northeast of Port Stanley, in the middle of nowhere. Founded in 1813, Sparta features houses, streets and shops that seem to have changed little in the last 200 years.

For six months in 1985 I took a sabbatical, and remained in London, with the intention of writing a book on psychosomatic medicine. Up till then, the standard texts were those of Flanders Dunbar, Weiss, and English, and, above all, Franz Alexander, who had published *Psychosomatic Medicine: Its Principles and Application,* in 1950. Alexander had been dubbed the "Father of Psychosomatic Medicine" because of his attempts to integrate psychological, physiological, and pathophysiological data into a single coherent framework. He introduced the theory of "specificity" into the jargon of psychosomatic medicine. By "specificity," Alexander meant that a specific conflict, usually based on psychoanalytic theory, was at the basis of the psychological factors that lead to each disease. Mind and matter, in other words, were at each end of a two-way street, with traffic flowing between them in both directions.

The objective of my book was to update and integrate knowledge on the interface between the psyche and soma, in the light of research after 1950, the year of publication of Alexander's book. I was trying to get psychosomatic medicine away from the psychoanalytic structure bequeathed by Alexander. It has always been a challenge to persuade internists and their multiple subspecialties of the reality of psychiatric and psychophysiological aspects of medical diseases. Focussing on psychoanalytic theory, as he did, rendered that task difficult.

By the end of the sabbatical, I had completed drafts of five chapters on disorders of the rheumatic and connective tissues; and the gastrointestinal, central nervous, respiratory, and cardiovascular systems. Each chapter dealt with specific diseases under the headings of psychosocial antecedents; mediating factors; pathophysiology; psychosocial sequalae; personality traits; conditioning and stress; and the psychiatric aspects of management.

The book never reached publication stage, as I ran out of time, perhaps having bitten off more than I could chew. At the end of my sabbatical, I went back to work and never again had the time or incentive to complete it. Though I was not able to, the gap has been filled by books that appeared later, such as *Psychosomatic Medicine: An Introduction to Consultation Liaison Psychiatry,* by Amos and Robinson, and *Handbook of Liaison Psychiatry,* by Lloyd and Guthrie.

I was getting itchy feet in London. Although I had been promoted to a full professorship in 1983, I had failed in my efforts to obtain a senior administrative position such as departmental headship, and began looking around in the rest of Canada to see what was available. At the 1986 annual meeting of the Canadian Psychiatric Association, held in London, at which I chaired the Local Arrangements Committee, I met Dr. Yvon Lapierre, newly appointed head of the department of psychiatry at the University of Ottawa. He invited me to apply for the position as head of the department at the newly built Ottawa General Hospital. I did, and was duly offered the position.

I have to confess that Sarie was very unhappy about my desire to leave London, and I know I treated her poorly over it. She was well-settled, with a job as an art therapist. She also had a coterie of good friends, was an active and successful tennis player, and had her art and painting groups that were doing well. Plus, we had a lovely home. By now, our youngest son, Quentin, was preparing to leave home so we had an empty nest coming up. Sarie, bless her, reluctantly acceded to my request (demand?) to move to Ottawa.

Chapter Twelve
A Capital Adventure

I started my job at the Ottawa General Hospital on leap year's day, 1988, while Sarie stayed behind in London, trying to sell our home, which, in the end, took six months. Even though this was thirty years ago, I still feel bad about how I treated her during those early years in Ottawa, though, fortunately, she has a generous and forgiving nature, so we were able to resolve these issues.

For the first five years in Ottawa, we lived in a bungalow home in Rockcliffe, a village suburb and a Heritage Conservation District, but the space and surroundings felt confined, so we put it on the market in 1993 and bought our *chateau* in Chelsea on the Gatineau River. Thus, we unwisely owned two expensive homes simultaneously. While waiting for the Rockcliffe house to sell, we decided to rent our new Chelsea home for the summer. It so happened this coincided with repairs being carried out at Rideau Hall in Ottawa, the residence of the governor general, Raymond Hnatyshyn, and his wife, Gerda. The Chelsea home was duly rented to the Hnatyshyns, with all the accompanying security paraphernalia. It was a privilege to get to know this delightful couple, albeit briefly. Hnatyshyn was of Ukrainian extraction, though born and raised in Saskatchewan, and is best known for opening up the grounds of Rideau Hall to the public, in sharp contrast to Jeanne Sauvé, his predecessor, who had closed the property to outsiders. The stunning grounds and gardens, in particular the rose garden developed by Gerda Hnatyshyn, and the grandly attired guardsmen, are a star attraction for visitors to Ottawa.

Raymond and Gerda Hnatyshyn at Rideau Hall, 1993.

I managed to arrange for Sarie to work as an art therapist in the Child and Family Unit of the hospital, helping children and adults who had been abused. The job also helped give her financial autonomy. Her work was written up again in the *Canadian Medical Association Journal*. She still encounters former patients in the street who thank her for all she did to help them.

Almuth Lutkenhaus-Lakey was one of these clients. She was a Canadian who emigrated from Germany after going through highly traumatic experiences during World War II. She became a well-known sculptress, her best-known exhibit being the *Crucified Woman,* displayed at Emmanuel College, University of Toronto. In December 1989, hundreds of mourners came to pray, weep, and hold vigil at the sculpture after the shooting death of fourteen young women engineering students at Polytechnique École in Montréal. Another of her masterpieces is *The Sun,* a three-metre-high sculpture exhibited in the gardens of the Museum of History in Ottawa. We have a small-scale replica of this sculpture in our home. In her dreams, recounted to Sarie, Lutkenhaus-Lakey formed pictures of childhood traumatic events. She converted these into paintings, one being of a mother being forced to abandon her daughter because of her abusive husband.

Crucified Woman. Sculpture by Almuth Lutkenhaus-Lackey, located in grounds of Emmanuel College, University of Toronto. Photo by François Mai.

Another notable client was Amy McCaughey, a successful real estate agent who became crippled following a right-sided embolic stroke in her early fifties. The recovery of movement and speech was minimal, yet she lived on for over twenty years. Gradually, Sarie taught Amy to paint using her left-hand and arm, although she had always been right-side dominant. She became a talented artist and, in 2011, her paintings were exhibited at the Canadian Stroke Network meeting in Ottawa. Strikingly, her early paintings were split-screen, with stark differences between the left and right sides of the painting, as if to symbolize the split between the left and right sides of her brain caused by the stroke. Amy's speech had been destroyed; the only words she could utter were "nothing good," and these she repeated endlessly in conversation. Yet amazingly, when prompted, she was able to sing "Happy Birthday to You" completely and faultlessly. The words and tune of this well-known ditty must have been transferred to, and imprinted in, the still-functioning right side of her brain. The power of music.

Amy McCaughey displaying her pictures

I had worn a ring since our wedding in 1959. However, the ring fitted too loosely on my finger, and easily slipped off. One Sunday morning, while walking and waiting in the grounds of St Stephen's Church in Chelsea to attend Mass, I noticed it was missing. I assumed it had dropped off on the driveway and searched the grounds, without success. The next day, a Monday, I rented a metal detector and once again combed the church driveway. I found an immense number of useless and discarded metal objects, including several sets of car keys, but no ring. This was in October, and the next day it snowed, making further search futile. I gave up on the ring and Sarie gave me her father's ring as a substitute, which fitted me more snugly. Seven months of winter rolled by, and I forgot about the original ring.

In May, the following spring, I decided to do some gardening and put on my gloves that had not been used since the previous fall. On completing the gardening, I took off the gloves and, lo and behold! There, back on my finger, was the lost ring! It had lain hidden in the glove for the entire winter and had found its own way back on my ring finger. To me it seemed like one of those seemingly coincidental events that are in fact small miracles that occur periodically in our lives, with a hidden message. Ours was to confirm the recommitment to our marriage Sarie and I had made when we moved to Chelsea.

I now wear two rings, the original and my father-in-law's. Many ask why and I reply, facetiously, but also a little truthfully, that it is because I have been married twice -- but to the same woman.

We lived in Chelsea for twenty years, from 1993 until early 2014, and had endless battles with intrusive local fauna, in particular squirrels, mice, crows, and raccoons. One warm summer night around one a.m., I was awakened by a noise downstairs in the kitchen, Followed by Sarie, I gingerly crept down the staircase, naked other than the upper part of my pyjamas and, on entering the kitchen, found a mother raccoon with her three kits on the countertop, helping themselves to bread, cheese, and fruit we'd left there. On seeing us, the mother grabbed a baguette and headed for the screen door we had mistakenly left slightly ajar. She had to drop it when she found the baguette too long to exit the opening. I chased the three kits around the kitchen with a broom until they too found the exit. We noted the raccoons' discernment in choosing their menu; they'd taken the camembert but left the cheddar, eaten the juicy peaches but not the apples.

Shortly after we moved to Ottawa, I carried out another long-distance cycling tour alone, from Ottawa to London and back, following Highway 2 on the out-trip, and Highway 7 on the return journey, for a total of around 750 kilometres in each direction. I did not carry my own camping gear but slept in hotels, sometimes cockroach-infested, along the way. On this trip, I completed the maximum distance I have ever ridden in one day—200 kilometres, from Peterborough to Perth, helped by a strong wind on my back. Along the way, with no one around, I even had a refreshing skinny-dip in Silver Lake.

Our four sons were all developing their lives and careers. All are tall, have athletic builds, and are university graduates. As young boys they had excellent voices and sang in a quality church choir. Martin also played the clarinet, and Nicolas the violin. All four were cunning hockey players. Martin and Quentin have extravert characters, like Sarie; Nicolas and Andrew are more introspective, like me.

Sarie and François with four sons. Martin and Andrew at rear (latter cradling Kryssi). Quentin and Nicolas at front. London, Ontario, 1987.

During the year Martin spent at Ridley College at St. Catharines, Ontario, he had taken up rowing, and eventually trained to Olympic level. He represented Canada at the Pan-American Games at Caracas in 1983, and won the bronze medal in the heavy fours. He just missed the cut for Canada's team for the Olympic Games at Los Angeles in 1984, where the heavy eight crew won gold. I went to Montréal to watch his crew take on the heavy four team that had been selected to represent Canada at the Games. It was a madly exciting race that Martin's crew lost by less than a boat length.

After Ridley College he returned to London, went to Western and has since had a successful career as a teacher, including terms as Principal at International Schools in Syria, Bangladesh, China and Egypt, and at a private school in Victoria, British Columbia. He is married to Barbara, also a teacher, and has four children from his first wife, Jennifer: Danielle, Paul, Maureen, and Martha.

Nicolas went first to Western University, obtained a degree in geography, then completed post-graduate studies at Simon Fraser University in Vancouver. Subsequently he moved to Victoria, married Amei, had two children, Thea and William, and today teaches mathematics at Camosun College. Amei is a principal in a high school. Nicolas has developed remarkable skills as a creative builder, a talent he must have inherited from his maternal grandfather. He passed a building diploma test, and has constructed a lovely *chalet* on Saltspring Island.

Andrew was accepted in the medical school program in Toronto, and graduated in 1987, after which he completed the family medicine program in London, Ontario. He is an excellent and caring physician, and in this respect did not fall far from the tree. After spending time practising in BC and Nova Scotia, he returned to Ottawa, where he now practises as a palliative care and rehabilitation physician. For a time, he was director of the Maycourt Hospice in Ottawa. He was then married to Carolyn Clark and they have two children, Aaron and Sarah. He has one child, Emily (September), from his first wife. Andrew is now married to Nancy, a yoga instructress from California.

Quentin obtained a renaissance history degree at Western, went to Capilano College in Vancouver, spent time working as an English teacher in Japan and then with a gold-mining company in Indonesia. Quentin has in his possession a stunning and rare copy of a document, written in calligraphy, describing the trial, early in the fourteenth century, of Jacques de Molay, head of the Knights Templars in France, on charges of heresy. King Philip IV of France had become jealous of the power and wealth of the Templars, and despite the intervention of Pope Clement V in their support, de Molay and many of his fellow Templars were found guilty and burned at the stake. The king was able to confiscate their wealth without resistance.

Quentin now lives in Calgary and is a successful manager with Freeman Gold, a mining investment company. He has one child, Isabelle, from a previous relationship, and another, Desmond François, from his marriage with Rainu. He is now a single father. Sarie and I have a total of eleven grandchildren and, so far, no great-grandchildren.

When the boys were young it was our custom to have dinner together every evening. On celebratory occasions, we would have talent shows in which each family member would demonstrate an artistic gift or skill. At our forty-fifth wedding anniversary party, Martin performed on the clarinet, Nicolas and Amei played a violin duet, Andrew performed on his didgeridoo, and Quentin displayed his dancing skills. Sarie and I also danced a waltz, as we had done at our wedding forty-five years earlier. Sarie was a spectacular ballroom dancer when young, and I a good follower. On another family occasion to celebrate our fifty-fifth anniversary, Phil Jenkins, a well-known Canadian singer and song-writer, performed on his guitar for us. One piece he played as a special request was the Beatles' song "Ob-La-Di, Ob-La-Da." It brought back memories of a glorious week-long holiday we spent on Beachcomber Island in Fiji, where the family vacationed on our return to Adelaide from Rochester in 1971.

Sarie has remarkable skills as both a chef and a hostess, and we had lovely and lively parties, in which I was much the add-on in preparing for these dinners. After the boys left home, I developed a few skills in the kitchen, with but a limited repertoire of dishes. One day, when Quentin came home for a visit, I told him proudly, "Quentin, I'm learning how to find my way around the kitchen." He replied, "Dad, you've got to find your way _to_ the kitchen, before you can find your way _around_ the kitchen."

Maman, aged ninety-four, visited us at Chelsea in the summer of 1994. She could not travel alone and flew from London with Martin Dives, my nephew and Christiane's oldest son. It was at that visit I noticed the first signs of dementia. She would wake up every morning and ask, "Where am I?" She would react in disbelief when we oriented her in time and place. Despite the impaired cognitive function, she was still able to play the piano and mix a French mayonnaise.

She returned to England via New York to visit Vincent, and died eighteen months later, at the age of ninety-five, in a nursing facility in Canterbury, Kent, close to Denyse's home. Her death occoured the day after my sixty-first birthday, and eleven years to the day after David's death. She had two falls, and in the second, fractured her pelvis. She'd lived twenty-five years after Papa's death and, with the exception of her sorrow about David's health, I believe these were happy years for her. For most of the year she lived alone in a small apartment in Sevenoaks, Kent, and would travel to spend a few weeks with one or other of her children, doting on them and her grandchildren. For someone who was given up for dead from tuberculosis at age forty, she lived a long and productive life.

Despite her age I was saddened by her death. I was close to her, likely closest of her five children. We had similar somewhat introverted personalities and were both passionate about music, something that did not interest Papa much. Sarie tells me that Maman once told her that I was a "dark horse." I think she was something of a dark horse, as well, good at keeping her feelings to herself. Once she had recovered from her recurring bouts of tuberculosis, she was a loyal and devoted mother to her children, and despite our wide geographic separation, she kept us together and well-informed about one another, like a good shepherdess. Papa, Maman, and David are buried together in the churchyard at Westerham in Kent. The cemetery is behind the church on its north side, and is in a lovely setting, surrounded by trees and bushes. Some of the tombstones date back to the sixteenth century and even earlier.

I became immersed in my new job as head of the department of psychiatry at the Ottawa General Hospital, that I took up in February 1988. Morale had become low, and finances were in a chaotic state. I was able to recruit several excellent new staff members, and let a few others go. With the advice of James Morrisey, an accountant and partner with the firm Ernst and Young, who later became a good friend, I was able to set up a new partnership agreement that distributed income more fairly among the staff psychiatrists, and that also promoted teaching and research, essential functions of a university department.

I divided my time with approximately 50 percent spent in patient care, half that spent in administrative responsibilities, and the remaining time devoted to teaching and research. With the assistance of Dr. Robert Swenson, we were able to set up a medical-psychiatric in-patient unit as part of the department of psychiatry, and with the help of Dr. Vincent Russell, we established an acute care day hospital. Both were novel ideas in Canadian psychiatry. The results of these enterprises were presented at national conferences and published in the *Canadian Journal of Psychiatry*. The day hospital was a particularly novel approach, intended to fill a gap in psychiatric care for patients who had been seen in the emergency department, who were not ill enough for admission, but could not wait several weeks, or even months, for follow-up in the outpatient department. Other psychiatrists who developed fine programs were Drs. Paul Cameron in psychotherapy teaching and supervision, Jean-Yves Gosselin in the francophone teaching program, Lily Varan on the in-patient unit, and Hifziya Bajramovic in managing the outpatient program. For the year 1991-1992, Gosselin was invited to be president of the Canadian Psychiatric Association, an honour not only for him but for the whole department. Through the partnership, we established a sabbatical leave program, and two members took advantage of it; Dr. Luc Bourgon left for six months to learn about modern developments in electric shock treatment, and Dr. Hany Bissada completed a course in the management of an eating disorders program, setting up a unit on his return. Eating disorders such as anorexia nervosa and bulimia are becoming an important part of psychiatric practice, especially in these pandemic times.

The accomplishments of all these department members gave me great satisfaction.

As a psychiatrist, one periodically has to appear in court when a patient gets into trouble. One day I arrived at work in the morning to find I had a court appearance scheduled that afternoon. It being a warm summer day, I had dressed smart-casual, with a tie but no jacket.

What was I to do? It is not acceptable court decorum to appear as an expert witness without wearing a jacket. Going back home, a return drive of ninety minutes, was not an option. I thought of borrowing one from a colleague, but there would be problems about the fit; besides which, I was too embarrassed to admit my stupidity in not bringing a jacket to work when I should have known I had a court appearance that day. I thought of buying a new one, but the needless cost was prohibitive.

I finally decided to go to the Salvation Army store to purchase a discounted jacket. While at the store, I made myself as inconspicuous as possible, to avoid meeting friends or patients of mine (snobbish, I know), and eventually found one, for eight dollars. Within my budget, I decided. The jacket looked new as the pockets were still stitched together. It fitted me well around the shoulders, but the left sleeve was halfway up my forearm. A minor impediment, if I hunched my left shoulder as much as possible. When I got to the check-out, I found on that day, all prices in the store were reduced by 50 percent. Two toonies for the jacket, I decided, was not excessive.

That afternoon, I successfully defended my patient in his court hearing, hunched left shoulder and imitation of Richard the Third notwithstanding. Next day, I surreptitiously returned the jacket to the store.

Opportunities for my personal research were reduced from what they had been in London. I was not successful in obtaining a research grant to study compliance with treatment in complex medical therapies such as renal dialysis, but nevertheless published a paper on this topic that has received twenty-one citations. We were able to demonstrate a new reliable measure of compliance that could also be used in patient education. Many patients with chronic renal disease have difficulty following the complex requirements of treatment. The questionnaire I developed helped both patients and their therapists better manage their disease.

I also published papers on topics related to the history of medicine, and a review of psychiatrist's attitudes to multiple personality disorder, a paper cited thirty-three times in the literature. The article surveyed all psychiatrists living in Ottawa, Kingston, and London. Of those who returned the questionnaire, almost one-third doubted the existence of multiple personality disorder as an entity, confirming a split in the profession on the topic. My own view is that it does exist, but is over-diagnosed. I had one patient who presented with chronic lower abdominal pain, and who had been sexually abused by an uncle when ten years old. Most of the time she appeared a caring and compassionate person. At times, with minor provocation, she'd become like a tigress, irate and belligerent, to the point of physicality, an attitude that could last for days, before the "caring" personality reappeared. Her condition improved with individual cognitive behaviour therapy.

In 1994, at the end of five years, I was appointed for another five-year term. This was not as successful, or as satisfying, as the first term. Major financial problems in hospital funding loomed on the horizon. Mike Harris, with his so-called "Common Sense" revolution, became premier of Ontario, and hospitals had to be "restructured" to function more efficiently. As a resident of Quebec at election time, I played no part in his election. We were fearful that our departments or hospitals were to be closed. Many in fact were. Tensions and conflicts between department heads and individuals grew, each vying to defend their territory. For some years I had wanted to take a sabbatical leave at the University of Cape Town, my alma mater, and planned this for 1998, just as disruptive hospital restructuring was at its height. Thinking, wrongly, that I was needed to help with restructuring, I canceled my sabbatical. In fact, restructuring continued over my head, and I had zero impact on the result. Three hospitals—the Ottawa General, the Ottawa Civic, and the Riverside—were amalgamated into one huge hospital complex, The Ottawa Hospital, on three different campuses. Likewise, the three departments of psychiatry at the General, the Civic, and the Royal Ottawa Hospital were amalgamated. By 1999, I had come to the end of my second term so had to step down as director of psychiatry at the General Hospital.

Now aged sixty-five, and scheduled to retire my university professorship in July of 2000, I spent my final year working as an ordinary physician in the department, without position or role. I had hoped to be offered an emeritus professorship in the University of Ottawa, knowing I had the academic credentials to be thus honoured. If I may blow my own horn for a moment, I had published over 150 articles, of which sixty-five were in leading international peer-reviewed journals, including the *British Medical Journal*, the *American Journal of Psychiatry*, the *Archives of General Psychiatry*, *Psychosomatic Medicine*, the *Journal of Psychosomatic Research*, the *Canadian Medical Association Journal*, the *Canadian Journal of Neurology* and the *Canadian Journal of Psychiatry*. Moreover, I had been a full professor for seventeen years, beginning at the University of Western Ontario. In my role as department head at the Ottawa General Hospital, I had promoted research, and a number of young psychiatrists whom I recruited, including Drs. Paul Cameron, Alison Freeland, Robert Swenson, Amanda Sutherland, Hany Bissada, and Vincent Russell, had taken leadership positions in teaching, research or administration, in Canada and abroad. However, for what I believe are personal and political reasons I was not offered an emeritus professorship. It took me some years to recover from this disappointment.

At the time, I did not know or understand the back-room intrigues that take place when deciding who gets to be promoted or offered an emeritus professorship. I suspected I did not have the support of the department. This likely occurred because during the restructuring battles of the 1990s, I had argued strongly that the general hospitals, rather than the mental hospitals, needed to play a major role in the restructured department of psychiatry.

On two occasions I visited the dean of the Faculty of Medicine. On the second occasion I had in my hand a copy of the letter from McGill/Queens University Press accepting my scholarly book *Diagnosing Genius: The Life and Death of Beethoven,* for publication. Both times he refused the offer of an emeritus, without explanation.

I do not believe personal differences arising from disagreements over policy should override academic merit. I suspect there may have been members of non-psychiatric departments on the committee who could not appraise the leading-edge quality of my writings on infertility, hysteria, Briquet, and the psychiatric aspects of heart transplantation.

"Men are ruled by toys," said Napoleon, when asked why he awarded medals to soldiers who had distinguished themselves in battle. An emeritus professorship may be a "toy," but it is also a recognition of services rendered, an offer to continue academic activities in the university, and perhaps even an invitation to provide future financial support to University Foundation funds. I had every intention of continuing to carry out research, writing and publishing after my retirement, as in fact I did. I would certainly have contributed financially to the univer sity, had I been offered an emeritus professorship.

There is no appeal mechanism for decisions of the promotions committee at the University of Ottawa, so I considered the possibility of contacting a lawyer and contesting the decision through an external civil court process. I knew that a few years earlier, a member of the department of medicine took this route and was ultimately successful in obtaining an emeritus professorship. I chose not to do this on the grounds that obtaining an award through an external court decision disparaged the value of the award.

Fortunately, Dr. Yvon Lapierre, former head of the department of psychiatry in the university, was able to arrange for me to obtain an adjunct professorship in the department of psychiatry at Queen's University in nearby Kingston, under the headship of Dr. Roumen Milev. Like Lapierre, Milev had a national and international reputation in the field of psychopharmacology. Hence, I was able to continue to participate in academic functions at Kingston, and did so through on-line contact particularly with the department's research committee, and presentations and attendance at Grand Rounds.

I have been disappointed by the route psychiatry, indeed medicine as a whole, has been following in recent years. The Diagnostic and Statistical Manual of Mental Disorders, Fifth Edition (DSM-5)[6], published by the American Psychiatric Association in 2013, replaced DSM-IV, but other than changing terminology and the grouping of categories, it is doubtful that it has advanced psychiatry much. Like medicine, psychiatry has lowered the threshold for making a diagnosis.

---

6 For obscure reasons, the American Psychiatric Association decided to use an arabic numeral to designate DSM-5, while using roman numerals for the first four DSMs.

DSM-IV was published in 1994 and DSM-III in 1980. The rising number of psychiatric diagnoses is reflected in the exponential increase in the size, weight, and cost of each newly published DSM manual. This increase benefits the American Psychiatric Association, but few others.

In medicine, Welch, Schwarz, and Woloshin state that many diseases can now be diagnosed with relatively minor criteria, compared to previously. Dubbing this "overdiagnosis," they call this "the biggest problem posed by modern medicine." Doctors are diagnosing diabetes and hypertension, and a number of other conditions such as elevated cholesterol, osteoporosis, and cancer of the prostate, at a stage where patients have no symptoms. They are then given treatment that makes them feel sick, whereas they did not feel sick before. There is no great benefit from the treatment in terms of extended life expectancy, and improved quality of life.

Similarly, in psychiatry, using DSM-5 criteria, conditions such as personality disorder, post-traumatic stress disorder, and attention deficit disorder can be diagnosed with relatively minor symptoms. Once diagnosed, the condition becomes eligible for treatment, which usually means medications. A high percentage, around seventy percent of psychiatrists and others who framed the DSM-5, had connections with the drug industry and, although they claimed transparency, most of the meetings were held in secret. Publicly declaring that they had conflicts of interest did not mean these conflicts did not affect the descriptive and diagnostic decisions that they made. Remarkably, despite this apparent leaning toward the role of biological factors in the causation of mental illness, there is barely a mention of organic factors in the **etiology** of mental illness in the DSM-5 document.

Two eminent American psychiatrists, Robert Spitzer and Allen Frances, amongst others, have heavily critiqued the DSM-5, in particular the secrecy with which the committees met. Spitzer, who headed the DSM-III review system in 1980, apparently went "bonkers" when he heard that the DSM-5 panels were meeting in secret. Frances, head of the DSM-IV panels, has made a more sustained and incisive criticism of the DSM-5. Making a diagnosis renders a patient eligible for health insurance coverage, which, in turn, qualifies them for medication treatment. Two prominent Canadian psychiatrists, Joel Paris and Paul Garfinkel, have taken a similarly critical view of DSM-5, in particular its promotion of overdiagnosis in psychiatric disorders.

With regard to the personality disorders, DSM-5 gives no recognition to the criticism of psychology associations that the symptomatology of these conditions lies on a continuum with normality, rather than a defined categoric system, which forces the psychiatrist to classify the patient as either "ill" or "not ill." In other words, we are saying a patient's diagnosis is either black or white, and there are no shades of grey. Making a psychiatric diagnosis is a form of labelling, and can promote therapeutic nihilism. This attitude is exemplified by those who turn a diagnosis from an adjective into a noun, for example by stating that this person is a "schizophrenic," a "bipolar," or a "borderline," rather than reporting that they have a schizophrenic, bipolar, or a borderline condition or <u>disorder</u>. Employing such terminology to patients with psychiatric illness implies they are without hope, and will be that way for life, whatever treatment they are given and however they respond to therapy.

Edward Shorter, the well-known Canadian medical historian, similarly has strongly criticized the psychiatric diagnostic system, Big Pharma and, by implication, psychiatrists. He states there is little empirical evidence that the selective serotonin reuptake inhibitor drugs (SSRIs) are more effective in the treatment of depression than were the tricyclic antidepressants (TCAs) and mono-amine-oxidase inhibitors (MAOIs) that preceded them. Many double-blind trials on the efficacy of SSRIs compared them to a placebo, not to a previously available effective medication. Yet the SSRIs are far more expensive, and heavily marketed by the pharmaceutical companies: psychiatrists fell into the trap of prescribing them in huge quantities. I admit that I, too, fell into this trap. At its height in the 1980s and 1990s, when almost every psychiatrist was prescribing an SSRI to their depressed patients, I would have felt quite out-of-sync with my colleagues if they heard I was prescribing a TCA or MAOI as a first-line treatment of depression.

There is dissension amongst psychiatrists about the place of psychotherapy in treatment. Those with a psychoanalytic orientation continue to treat a handful of patients with daily therapy, sometimes for years on end, even though it has been shown by Lam and others that cognitive behavioural therapy (CBT) is equally effective, where the patient is seen but once a week for a much shorter period. Cognitive behavioural therapy is a form of structured psychotherapy, in which the patient is taught certain skills and problem-solving techniques on a time-limited basis. If CBT were more widely used, more patients could be treated, and some of the backlog in those requiring therapy could be reduced.

On the same theme, Gardner and Kleinman, in an excellent paper in the *New England Journal of Medicine,* argue that, "something has gone wrong in contemporary psychiatry. Checklist amalgamations of symptoms have taken the place of thoughtful diagnosis, and trial-and-error 'medication management' has taken over practice to an alarming degree." The authors go on to say, "psychiatry needs to be rebuilt. Biologic and dynamic psychological considerations can complement one another. Psychiatric training programs can promote epidemiology, social science, cultural expertise, community studies prevention and consultation-liaison work—and, most important, psychotherapy."

"Let's try XXX [insert name of latest expensive pharmaceutical]" is a common refrain psychiatrists use when changing or adding medications. Use of the word "try" is not likely to instil a patient with confidence in their physician.

It has been found that older psychiatric patients and those with a chronic condition are often on a multitude of medications (a situation derisively called "polypharmacy") with no indication or understanding how they interact with each other, or whether they are benefitting the patient. As a clinician, I used to joke, only half facetiously, that I got most of my therapeutic successes by stopping, not starting, medications. The side-effects of the medications were causing these patients more harm than good.

Mine and others I've mentioned are still voices crying in the wilderness, and have yet to make an impact on orthodox psychiatric thinking, teaching, and practice. Psychiatry needs a strong world leader, as Kraepelin was in the nineteenth century, who can reconcile its biological and psychosocial bases into a single theoretical and practical framework. Kraepelin was a German psychiatrist who wrote a famous textbook in which he clearly defined and categorized psychiatric conditions. His influence is still felt now.

It is likely fortunate I am no longer an active clinical psychiatrist. I would have difficulty in toeing the party line in teaching the subject to students and residents.

What was I to do in my retirement from the hospital and the university? It is in my nature to need a continuous project on the go: I do not enjoy milling about, or even participating in recreational activities such as tennis or golf to occupy my time. I need to feel that what I am doing has a useful purpose and an end result that will benefit me—and, hopefully, others.

During the 1990s I had taken up piano playing quite seriously. I found a wonderful teacher, Anne Weiser, made good progress, and was able to perform in public at a recital given at the Unitarian Church in Nepean, where an excellent grand piano is located. I used both narrative and slides to enliven the concert. For example, I played pieces by Eric Satie, famous for performing at night clubs in Paris in the early 1920s, so showed slides of the décor at *Le Moulin Rouge* while I was playing.

On two occasions I produced a compact disc, in which I performed on my baby-grand Knabe piano, and the concert was professionally engineered by Michael Weiser, Anne's son. I donated the CDs to the Ontario Schizophrenia Society for fundraising purposes. The recordings included Beethoven's *Sonata No. 17, Opus 31, No. 2 (the Tempest)* and pieces by Debussy and Chopin, and the jazz music of William Bolcom, Scott Joplin, and others. I also played in small ensembles, and particularly enjoyed performing with cellist Stans van Wijk, and my friend and colleague Paul Grof. In addition to being a renowned world authority on bipolar disorder and the use of lithium salts in therapy, Grof is an accomplished clarinettist.

I thought of returning to school, becoming a music student, and getting a degree in music in order to perform professionally. Sadly, events in my health made this impossible. Some years previously I had developed Dupuytren's Disease, a condition in which fibrous tissue collects in the hands, causing the fingers to curl over and become immobilized. In addition, I badly injured the fifth finger of my left hand, while lowering myself to sit in a lounge chair. My finger was caught in the hinge, and it was cut right off, halfway along its length. Although a plastic surgeon stitched the separated piece back on, it was never the same. The finger proved sensitive to trauma and cold, and eventually the surgeon suggested it be amputated at the proximal inter-phalangeal joint (the first knuckle). With this handicap, I decided it did not make sense to make music performance the focus of my post-retirement years.

Dupuytren's Disease also turned out to be familial. My father had a bad case of it, requiring amputation of a finger. My sister Denyse and brother Vincent also have the disease. In the next generation it has affected our sons Nicolas and Andrew. Nicolas has had a number of surgeries and still has a badly clawed left hand. The genetic transmission apparently has been tracked back to the Viking invasions of Northwest Europe during the ninth and tenth centuries, and this Viking influence may explain some of the Mai family's character, such as its determination, and perhaps also its stubbornness!

Having made my peace with my musical aspirations and let go of them, I applied for and obtained a federal government position as medical adviser in the medical expertise division of the human resources department, which reviews Canadians who apply for a federally granted disability pension. If a Canadian before the age of sixty-five develops a "serious and prolonged disorder" (terms that are legally defined), they can apply for a disability pension. If the pension is denied, it goes through four levels, the final two of which involve legal procedures. I enjoyed this job. It was not too onerous, yet kept me on my toes with general medical and psychiatric knowledge. It also involved travel to various parts of the country for legal hearings closer to where the applicant lived, and this gave me the opportunity to get to know Canada better. I visited every province bar Saskatchewan, and in Ontario worked in such out-of-the-way towns as Thunder Bay, Timmins, and Windsor.

The department's mandate did not include northern Canada, but I visited Nunavut in 2017, when Vincent, my brother, and I went on a cruise of the Northwest passage, ending up at Ilulissat, in Greenland. The cruise boat stopped over the wreck of the *Erebus*, one of the recently re-discovered ships lost in the famous, disastrous Franklin expedition of 1845. It also called at Gjoa Haven and Pond Inlet, and sites in Nunavut such as Beechey Island, where lie the graves of three members of the expedition who died there. It was an awesome voyage of discovery, and brought home the vastness of Canada.

I was also able to carry out research while working in the department. In discussion with my colleagues, I noted there was a perception amongst psychiatrists that, if their patient had a psychiatric diagnosis, they were less likely to be awarded a disability pension than if they had a medical (physical) diagnosis. In fact, the research, carried out jointly with my colleagues Andrew Ember and Catherine McCourt, showed the reverse: a large minority of those receiving a pension did so because of a psychiatric condition—in particular, depression. Hence, those with a psychiatric diagnosis were not, as was thought, at a disadvantage. The data showed that the percentage with depression increased from almost 12 percent in 1990 to close to 30 percent in 2008. By the latter date, of all recipients on CPPD benefits, those with a psychiatric condition represented a majority.

I presented these findings at a psychiatric conference, and it was our intention to publish them in a journal. However, permission for publication was denied by my superiors in the government bureaucracy. No reason was given, but I suspect it was because they were afraid it might reflect poorly on government policies. I thought we might get a different decision following the change of governing party from Conservative to Liberal in 2015, because the latter had promised more openness and transparency in the lead-up to the election. But the request for permission to publish was again denied. Our completed paper never saw the light of day. So much for government promises and government transparency.

When my Dupuytren's Disease made it impossible for me to continue playing the piano, I decided instead to take up my pen and write about music. The two or three hours each day that I had previously spent practising the piano now became time spent in research and writing. From the age of eight, I had been enthralled by the music of Ludwig van Beethoven, and puzzled as to how he could compose such awe-inspiring music while being unable to hear. Reading about his life, I discovered he suffered not only from deafness, but had a multitude of other medical—including respiratory, musculo-skeletal, and psychiatric—problems. Few physicians had authored articles or books about these issues, so I decided to write a monograph, which eventually became my book, entitled, *Diagnosing Genius: The Life and Death of Beethoven*. In it, I argue that his health problems, including his deafness, paradoxically enhanced his creativity. The book was favourably reviewed in such prestigious journals as the *New England Journal of Medicine*, the *Journal of the American Medical Association,* and the *Literary Review of Canada*, among many others.

How did Beethoven compose beautiful music while being deaf? Surely a composer needs auditory feedback to be sure that the nuances of sound and expression he is writing down, are exactly what he wants his audience to hear. In my book I concluded that, because of his intensive musical education while young, Beethoven was able to internalize musical notation and that enabled him to "hear" music on the written page. Even then, I considered this an inadequate explanation for his remarkable talent.

I now consider Beethoven to have been a synesthete. Synesthesia is the condition in which a sensory stimulus of one organ is perceived in another sense organ. For example, an auditory stimulus, such as a musical note, is perceived as a colour, such as red. There are multiple types of synesthesia, as any pair of the five sense organs may be involved.

The following are two examples, written by Beethoven's contemporaries, of him being able to hear music he saw written on a page before his eyes, qualifying him as a synesthete:

From Anton Schindler, *Beethoven As I Knew Him*.

> "His deafness (to which practically everyone attributes the alleged flaws in Beethoven's notation of pitch) has nothing to do with these reasons, for *the master had no more needed to hear with his ears what he had written down than another person needs to read aloud a letter he has just written.*" [my emphasis].

From Gerhard von Breuning, *Memories of Beethoven*.

> "See, I received these as a gift. . .. they have given me great joy. . .. Handel is the greatest, the ablest composer; I can still learn from him." Breuning adds that Beethoven kept on saying these and similar things in "happy excitement."

> Beethoven asked Breuning to bring the books, one after another, to him to his bed. Breuning states, "He leafed through one volume after another as I gave them to him, sometimes stopping at particular passages. . ... [He] then put one volume after another to his right on his bed up against the wall, finally making a heap that remained there for hours, because I found them still piled up when I returned in the afternoon. And again, he started to sing the praises of the great Handel and to call him the most classic and most accomplished of all composers."

This facility, together with his likely capacity for perfect pitch, enabled him to compose the miraculous music of the final ten years of his life, when he was quite deaf.

One of the outcomes of my book was to perform in public a talk entitled "Emotional Expression in the Music of Beethoven." Using selected recordings of Beethoven's music, and, on occasion, a professional pianist or string quartet, I would recount an anecdote about an event in Beethoven's life, or read an appropriate section out of my book, and then play a recording, or the pianist or quartet would perform a selection of his music that expressed, in music, the emotional content of the event I had recounted, such as depression, anger, or love. I delivered invited performances in Edmonton in 2007 with a string quartet, at the Ottawa Chamber Music Festival in 2010 with pianist Justin Kolb, and an invited performance as a warm-up recital for the Winnipeg Opera's performance of Beethoven's opera *Fidelio* in 2014, with pianist Richard Konrad. *Fidelio* was produced to coincide with the opening of the magnificent Museum of Human Rights in Winnipeg, because the theme of *Fidelio* is the battle over human rights between the people and an autocratic regime. On many other occasions, I gave the talk using recorded music only.

One of the sad anecdotes I recounted during these presentations was the time, in 1826, when Beethoven went for a walk on a country road one evening, while visiting his brother Nikolaus's estate outside Vienna. Dressed in bedraggled clothes, he began singing loudly and gesticulating, as if conducting an orchestra. A passing policeman thought this behaviour very odd, arrested him, and locked him up for the night. The authorities refused to believe his claim he was Beethoven, the great, widely known composer. They thought he was just a local, deluded, psychotic hobo. They only released him when his identity was verified by a neighbour.

One day, in the early 2000s, when I started writing about Beethoven, my granddaughter Emily, then aged seven, came into my study and asked, "What are you doing, Papa?"

"I'm writing a book about Beethoven," I replied.

"That's cool," she replied. "I know all about Beethoven."

My heart swelled with pride that she would know all about the great composer at such a tender age.

"Where did you learn about Beethoven?" I asked.

"Oh, I saw the movies about Beethoven, the dog," she replied, with a broad smile.

I then had to learn about the canine rendition of the unfortunate composer.

In 1953, as a third-year medical student, I had gone to France and seen my Grandpère for what was to be the last time. He gave me a family tree of the Mai family, written in his own hand, going back just four generations to his great-grandfather, Martin Mai. Every name on the tree had a birth-date and a death-date (where appropriate) with the exception of this ancestral Martin Mai. I became intrigued by this man, the family progenitor, about whom nothing was known other than his name, and the fact that the family had come from a small village at the foot of Vimy Ridge called Givenchy-en-Gohelle. It is within walking distance, little more than one kilometre, from the famous World War I Canadian War Memorial on Vimy Ridge, surrounded by cemeteries, trenches, tunnels, and other relics of that awful conflict. Grandpère had told me that all family records and archives had been destroyed in the war.

My brother Vincent and I speculated where the name might originate; the surname "Mai" is rare in France but common in Germany. Vincent's opinion was that it derived from a German-Jewish family called Mai who had moved to France. I thought the original Martin Mai was likely a German soldier who had joined Napoleon's army, then settled in Givenchy at the end of the Napoleonic wars. It turned out we were both wrong.

In the course of a visit to Givenchy in 2003, I went to the *Mairie*, (the Village Hall) and asked the clerk if she had information about the birth of Jules Mai, Grandpère's father. She turned around, took a tome off the shelf, opened it on the appropriate date, and there was Jules's birth information, including the names and ages of his parents. She said if I wanted any further information, I should go to the genealogical archival records maintained by the Mormon Church in Salt Lake City! While in Givenchy I also found the Mai burial plot, which held about ten members of the family. The inscriptions on the headstone were unkempt and so faint as to be barely legible. I could read them only in bright sunshine, so in the morning I read and wrote down the names of those inscribed on the east side of the monument, and returned to the gravesite in the afternoon to read those inscribed on the west side. I then arranged for a local stonemason to make a new inscription of all the names, and re-inscribe them on the tombstone.

On my return to Ottawa, I went to the local Mormon church, and they sent my request for archival information from Givenchy to Salt Lake City. The microfiche documents duly arrived a month later.

I spent days poring through these files, squinting through the lens at a projector, as the whole family history appeared on the screen! It turned out the original Martin Mai, the family progenitor on Grandpère's family tree, was born illegitimately in May 1776. He was christened Martin pierre (the family name lower case presumably because he was illegitimate), and he changed his name to Mai in the early 1800s; his death record in 1837 stated, *"Père, Inconnu"*—Father, Unknown. In other words, the family members who reported his death to the authorities regarded this information as important enough to record on his death certificate.

In the Mormon Church microfiche documents, I discovered that Martin pierre married Clementine Cavigneau and the couple had five children. The first two, Martin-Louis and Jean -Baptiste, were born in 1799 and 1801, respectively, and were surnamed "pierre," while the younger three, Bonne-Augustine, François Joseph, and Amecie, born in 1805, 1809, and 1814, respectively, were surnamed "Mai." Hence, he changed his family name from "pierre" to "Mai" between 1801 and 1805, between the births of his second and third children.

From 1793, for thirteen years, France abolished the Gregorian calendar that we all use, and the country followed the Revolutionary calendar, in which each of the twelve months had different names based on the four seasons. Examples are the months of Brumaire, Nivose, Floreal, and Thermidor, each representing an autumn, winter, spring, or summer month respectively. A week was divided into ten, not seven days. For example, the first day was primidi and the tenth day was decadi, a day of rest depicting Sunday. Napoleon's coup d'état occurred on *18 Brumaire An VIII* (September 9, 1799). The calendar has even entered folklore. The Lobster Thermidor—lobster meat served in a rich wine-based sauce, with cognac added to provide heat—was prepared in Paris in 1891.

Introduced in September 1793, the calendar caused such chaos that it was finally scrapped by Napoleon, in 1806. The Catholic Church was one of the groups that strongly opposed the new calendar, and Martin pierre and his family, judging from the birth, marriage, and death records I unearthed from the Mormon archives, were devout Catholics.

Martin pierre was born May 3, 1776, and it is my contention that he changed his surname as a political act to express opposition to the new calendar. The family name he chose, "Mai," was the month of his own birth in the old Gregorian calendar. It was also his way of rejecting his lost paternity symbolized by his given surname of 'pierre, with its lower case 'p'.

I was fascinated by these few scraps of information about his life, and believed it had the makings of a book. My historical novel *Father, Unknown* is the result. It is a fictionalized rendering of the life of this original Martin Mai, his name changed in the book to Marcel Juin for the purposes of (admittedly thinly disguised) anonymity. In the novel I speculate as to why Martin pierre changed his family name to Martin Mai.

I also suspect strongly that Grandpère was aware of this skeleton in the family closet (so to speak), but did not wish this information to be transmitted to future generations. One of his uncles, Victor Mai, died and was buried in Givenchy-en-Gohelle in 1919, i.e., after WWI. At that time, Grandpère was in his late forties, and living in Boulogne, just an hour's drive away. Even if he did not attend the funeral, he must have known about the death of his uncle, and the fact that many of his family ancestors were buried in that cemetery, including his great-grandfather, Martin pierre, later Mai. Martin-Louis Juin is the character in my novel who does not wish to know or transmit to future generations the fact that his father was illegitimate.

Many families in our contemporary society have skeletons in their family closets, such as illegitimacy (as in mine), criminality, psychiatric illness, suicide, or adoption. There are some in every family who wish to deny or suppress knowledge about these secrets. Families have divergent ways of dealing with secrets, and there is nothing egregious or blameworthy about such skeletons. I believe that all people have a right to know the names and identities of their parents. This is so relevant nowadays where infertility clinics are using sperm from anonymous donors to fertilize women's ova. Increasingly, we are seeing the adult product of these test-tube babies searching fruitlessly for their fathers. Ensuring that anonymous sperm is not used to fertilize ova may reduce the availability of sperm donors, but it will also ensure that a child's right to knowledge about its parental background is respected.

Another ancestor, revealed in the research, caught my attention, a Catholic priest named Abbé François Mai (1809-1857), third son of the original Martin Mai. My interest was partly because he is my namesake, although I am not named after him. By contacting the Catholic seminary in Amiens, I discovered that he died in a village called Martinpuich, south of Arras, in northern France. In October 2018, Vincent and I, accompanied by his son Timothy, travelled to Martinpuich to see if we could find any evidence of his existence, such as a plaque in the church or a headstone in the cemetery. Two weeks earlier I had written to the *prétre-en-charge* of the church, alerting him to our visit, and to ensure that the church would not be locked up, it being a weekday. I received a response, not from the priest-in-charge, but from the mayor of Martinpuich, M. Jean-François Dercourt, stating that he would be at the church to meet and greet us at the appointed date and time.

On arrival at the church, we were greeted not only by the mayor, but also by his wife and several of his assistants, who gave us red-carpet treatment, including a bottle of genuine champagne! Dercourt was a small, lean, and affable man, likely in his mid-fifties. To our astonishment, the mayor's wife, using a different database from my own, had created a genealogical table of the Abbé François Mai that was nearly identical to mine, and in some respects even more informative. She told us that, after his death, Abbé François' remains were transported back to Givenchy, his birthplace, for burial.

The original church in Martinpuich was totally destroyed in World War I, and there was no memorial plaque to the Abbé in the new church. We decided therefore to invite the church in Martinpuich to erect a plaque to commemorate him, and also commemorate our visit to the village. It was our way of thanking the mayor, his wife, and his retinue for their effusive welcome. The church steeple had been badly damaged in a storm, and Vincent made a substantial donation for the repair, with part of the donation being used for installing the commemorative plaque as follows,

CETTE PLAQUE EST ÉRIGÉ À LA MÉMOIRE DE

L`ABBÉ FRANÇOIS MAI

CURÉ DE CETTE PAROISSE DE 1854 JUSQU'A SON DÉCÉS EN 1857

IL EST ENTERRÉ AU CIMITIÉRE DE GIVENCHY-EN-GOHELLE,

PAS-DE-CALAIS

ÉRIGER POUR COMMÉMORER LA VISITE A MARTINPUICHE

EN OCTOBRE 2018 DE CES DESCENDANTS FAMILLIALES

LE DOCTEUR FRANÇOIS MAI DU CANADA

ET

M. VINCENT MAI ET SON FILS TIMOTHY, TOUT DEUX DES ÉTATS-UNIS

(This plaque was built to the memory of Father François Mai, parish priest from 1854 until his death in 1857. He is buried in the cemetery at Givenchy-en-Gohelle, Pas-de-Calais. Erected to commemorate the visit to Martinpuich of his family descendants, Dr. François Mai from Canada, and Vincent Mai and his son Timothy, both from the United States)

I remain in regular correspondence with Mayor Dercourt, and he sends me a copy of the annual *Bulletin Municipal,* complete with colourful photos. Reparations to the church are proceeding apace, and the plaque commemorating our visit will be erected shortly.

Chapter Thirteen
Physician, Heal Thyself

My wife and I loved our waterfront property on the Gatineau River in Québec, twenty kilometres north of Ottawa. The house had a modern design and was large enough to accommodate our extended family, and the plot was well-treed, with spectacular views of the river. The home had a modern style, with beam-and-post interior design. Beautiful, solid pine beams lined the ceiling on the lower-level dining and sitting room areas, giving the space a lovely, light-yellow hue. Floor-to-ceiling windows fronting the river gave the feeling of being part of the surrounding woods.

The time had come, we decided, to gear down to a smaller home, and February 28, 2014, was the closing date for the sale. Two and half months before closing, on December 16, 2013, we held a final celebratory party. On a memorable moonlit evening, in front of about thirty good friends and musicophiles, the eminent German pianist Hinrich Alpers, gave us a spectacular rendering of Beethoven's *Moonlight Sonata* to celebrate both Beethoven's 243rd birthday on December 16, and my seventy-ninth birthday on the seventeenth. Alpers is a great admirer of Beethoven's music and has performed all thirty-two of Beethoven's sonatas at the Ottawa Chamber Music Festival, and recorded all the piano music of Robert

Schumann and Maurice Ravel. That night he also performed music by Schumann and Ravel.

Hinrich Alpers, winner of the Telekom Beethoven competition in Bonn, Germany, and Laureate of the Honens competition in Calgary, Canada.

Packing boxes to vacate the property started next day. Sarie and I were distressed about having to sell the property to which we had become much attached during the twenty years we'd lived there, but it was something that had to be done. Because of advancing age, we were having increasing difficulty managing the property.

Six weeks later, early in February 2014, I had my annual medical examination, which included a prostate specific antigen (PSA) blood test. A few days later my family doctor phoned to say that my PSA report had come back at the very high level of forty-three. A normal PSA is four or less.

"Did you have sex before the test?" he asked, then added, "Intercourse can elevate PSA levels."

"No, I did not," I replied truthfully. Unfortunately.

"Well, in that case I'd better send you off for a pelvic scan." And he made the arrangements.

For a few days, and because I had been feeling so well, I thought little further about this conversation—an attitude psychiatrists call denial. I did not wish to know the truth. Then suddenly, while walking to work on the Alexandra bridge across the Ottawa River, on a cold, dull, overcast day, it hit me like a blow to the head: "I'VE GOT PROSTATE CANCER." Even though my doctor had not mentioned these words. I leaned on the parapet and wept, then phoned Andrew, my physician-son who lives in Ottawa. He confirmed my suspicions.

I phoned my doctor and asked him to refer me to a urologist as soon as possible. He told me my pelvic scan was booked for late March. Like many before me, I was sure I had prostate cancer, yet I would have to wait over six weeks for a scan, let alone a biopsy or any form of treatment. Everything then happened in the final week of February, my *septem horribilis,* horrible week; the examination by the urologist, the biopsy, the report of the biopsy, and all the legal machinations regarding the sale of the house. I have an agenda filled with all the bunched-up medical, legal, and bank appointments I had to meet during those awful five days.

The digital rectal examination carried out by the urologist Dr. James Watterson confirmed that the prostate was hard and roughened, typical of that found in cancer. The biopsy was particularly unpleasant—a pain in the ass, in fact. The anesthesiologist, working through the anus, used a needle to pierce the wall of the rectum into the prostate, and took about ten tiny specimens of tissue for later microscopic analysis. Although I had been given a local anaesthetic, it was nevertheless extremely uncomfortable. At the end of the procedure, he asked me, *"Did I do OK?"* Seething inside, I mumbled a non-committal answer.

At home, subsequently, I was unable to pee, and felt progressively more uncomfortable as my bladder filled up during the rest of the day. I had visions of returning to the hospital to have a catheter inserted, and did not relish that plan, because the urethra was already damaged by the biopsy. It could be further damaged by the catheter. So, once again I phoned Andrew, who suggested I soak myself in a warm bath. While on my elbows and knees in the bath, a large blood clot that had been blocking the urethra suddenly popped out, and my bladder quickly emptied, followed by a huge sigh of relief.

Next day I returned to the hospital to get the results of the biopsy. It showed a score of nine on the Gleason grade of malignancy, where two is low grade and ten the most severe level of malignancy. The Gleason score depends on the microscopic appearance and character of the cancer cells. A patient with a Gleason score of five or less can often be treated with watchful waiting, especially in older men. Those with a score of six or more require treatment. My Gleason score was nine, almost as malignant as can be. Men with a high Gleason score and a high PSA level have a high expectation of death within five years. It was the one time in my life I would have preferred a lower grade.

I was shocked, almost speechless by the news. This reaction of course, was quite irrational. I was seventy-nine years of age, had already outlived the biblical three-score and ten life-span, and was at an age when cancer and many other conditions can occur with increased frequency.

Yet, for some reason I never imagined myself getting cancer. Again, denial. For one who took pride in knowing and being honest with myself about my real and potential failings, it was a serious reality check.

I had already decided to retire from my position as a physician with the medical expertise division of the human resources department of the federal government. I was in the process of writing a novel, and had other books and essays I planned to write in the future. I still had much to do in my life and was not ready for a fatal illness. I had imagined myself rolling along until my nineties, like my mother.

Over the next few weeks, I had further tests, including a pelvic scan and a bone scan, to identify whether the cancer had spread to other organs. Yes, it had spread to the pelvic lymph nodes and, no, it had not spread to the vertebrae or any other bones or organs in the body. Because the cancer was now outside the prostate, it was classified as Stage 4 manifestation of the disease. As such, it was not suitable for surgery or radiotherapy, and Dr. Watterson recommended I start on anti-androgen hormone therapy. The drug chosen was Firmagon, given by subcutaneous injection into the abdominal wall. It is slowly released into the system, and has to be repeated every three months. The injection by a medical resident was unpleasant, to say the least. I had an allergic reaction, and over the next week my abdomen became red, inflamed, and painful, leading to sleepless nights and the need for analgesics, distressing me even more about my situation. Eventually the inflammation subsided. Dr. Watterson told me that despite the therapy, the cancer would likely recur in a year and a half, and kill me in four.

I knew the implications of starting anti-androgen therapy: feminization of my body, weight gain, shrinkage of the genitalia (rarely mentioned in the lists of the side-effects of these hormones), hot flashes, loss of libido, and a rapid decline in the quality of my tennis. Sure enough, these effects began quickly and have been continuous since. For the next injection the drug was changed to Zoladex, and this did not cause the allergic reaction I had had with Firmagon.

My state of shock lasted for the next six months, during which time I was emotional and inconsolable. I could not control my feelings, and would tell anyone and everyone about my condition, then throw myself tearfully into their arms for consolation. On one occasion I even clearly visualized myself lying in my coffin in the aisle at the Notre Dame Basilica in Ottawa.

I was also angry. I had recently changed physicians, and it was my new doctor who carried out the PSA test and found it to be high. Investigating the records of my previous physician, I found that although he had been carrying out blood tests, he had not been doing the PSA. He belonged to the group of physicians who believe that carrying out PSA tests does more harm than good. I don't object to his beliefs about the PSA test, but I do object to his lack of candour in denying me the option of having the test done regularly. My disease might have been discovered earlier if a PSA test had been carried out at previous annual medical examinations. To my mind, to stop using the PSA as a screening test is throwing out the baby with the bathwater. A better approach is to "watch and wait" if the PSA is slightly elevated, and only treat when the diagnosis and tumour character is clearly established.

Some medical authorities have criticized the use of the PSA test as a screening tool, on the basis that it leads to unnecessary biopsies and treatments. Other screening tests, such as the Stockholm3 and the mpMRI are coming down the pipeline, but until they are validated and widely available, the PSA, properly used, is the best available. For me, the PSA may not have saved my life, but it would have enabled the cancer to be diagnosed at a relatively early stage. I was not able to accept having an aggressive form of cancer of the prostate that would recur in eighteen months' time, and kill me within four years.

The prostate gland is a golf ball-sized structure situated below the bladder and directly in front of the rectum. It completely envelops the urethra as the latter emerges from the bladder, and then flows through the penis to the exterior. As a gland, its function is to secrete a fluid that mingles with the ejaculate, aiding the motility of sperm, and it also produces prostate specific antigen that, in turn, helps sperm survive in the uterus and vagina. The prostate also produces hormones and enzymes involved in secondary sex characteristics. Diseases of the prostate are common in men, and become increasingly so with age, the commonest being benign prostatic hypertrophy.

Cancer of the prostate has been found at autopsy in over fifty percent of men over eighty who die of other causes, indicating that cancer is not only common but usually symptomless, and not necessarily lethal. Prostate cancer is the most common form of cancer in men in Canada. An estimated 21,300 men were diagnosed with the condition in 2017 and 4,100 died from the disease. The good news is that death rate has been slowly falling over the last twenty years.

What are the risk factors for developing prostate cancer, if any? Family history is the strongest one. If a man has a close blood relative who has had the disease, the likelihood of him also getting it increases at least twofold. My paternal grandfather died from cancer of the prostate. There was no PSA test in the early 1950s when he developed his disease. By the time of diagnosis, I suspect it had spread far and wide. Prostate cancer is also more common in Black men and in the presence of obesity. What about the effect of diagnostic X-rays? It is said they have no effect but, in my thirties and forties, I had two episodes of renal colic caused by kidney stones. On both occasions I had numerous examinations by intravenous pyelogram (IVP), a test frequently used at that time but rarely now, in which substantial doses of X-rays are used to track the stones through the genitourinary tract, and ensure they were properly excreted, like a bouncer showing unwanted guests to the door. I have asked my physicians about this and all have assured me that a connection between a large X-ray dosage and the later development of cancer of the prostate is unlikely. I question the accuracy of this opinion.

Hormone therapy works because the growth and spread of many prostate cancers is powered by testosterone secreted by the body. By suppressing testosterone secretion, one is controlling the spread of the disease. Unfortunately, the cancer cells commonly become resistant to hormone suppression, allowing the cancer to spread.

The long-forgotten scientist who first found that suppression of testosterone was effective in the treatment of prostate cancer is a Canadian, Charles Huggins. Born in Halifax, Nova Scotia, Huggins completed an arts degree at Acadia University in 1920, went to medical school at Harvard, moved to Michigan, then on to Chicago where he carried out his scientific studies. His work was published in 1941, and it took twenty-five years before he was finally honoured with the Nobel Prize for Medicine and Physiology in 1966 for this groundbreaking work. In his paper, Huggins described the beneficial effects of castration and the administration of estrogens in advanced prostate cancer, and the value of serum enzymes in monitoring its progress. I am glad to say that castration is now rarely performed as a treatment for prostate cancer, nor are estrogens used. Modern hormone therapy depends on a shelf-full of synthetic drugs such as Firmagon and Zoladex, which act on the pituitary gland and interfere with the production of Luteinizing hormone, a chemical that stimulates testosterone production in the testis. There also are drugs such as enzalutamide, that act on the androgen receptors in the body, interfering with the action of testosterone. I have been on all these medications, Zoladex since shortly after my cancer was diagnosed and enzalutamide more recently, when I had a recurrence. My serum testosterone levels have consistently been very low or undetectable. With all these physical and chemical changes in my body, I would not get far in mixed martial arts at present.

Charles Huggins with some of his awards.
Portrait owned by David Teplica and used with permission.

Huggins was a truly remarkable man. Dr David Teplica, a reconstructive plastic surgeon in Chicago, knew him well and admired him as a mentor. Teplica himself has become widely-known for his research in genetic studies, and describes Huggins as witty and gregarious. He was proud of his Canadian origins and between 1971 and 1979 Huggins was Chancellor of his alma mater, Acadia University in Wolfville, Nova Scotia. Teplica reports one of Huggins' aphorisms, "If you can measure it, measure it. If you can't measure it, find a way to measure it." This epigram is highly relevant to research in psychiatry, where many of our phenomena are intangible and hard to quantify.

After his discovery of the effects of testosterone ablation in prostate cancer, Huggins wrote, "I was excited, nervous and happy. That night I walked home, about a mile, and had to sit down several times, my heart was pounding so. I thought, this will benefit man forever … a thousand years from now people will be taking this treatment of mine." This was, indeed a major discovery, the first time it had been shown that cancer growth can be curtailed by changing its biochemical milieu.

My sister Denyse and her family owned a beautiful old home near the small village of Saillans, situated on the Durance River of the La Drome region, in the foothills of the Alps, not far from Valance in the south of France. In order to get away from Ottawa and give me a break from the miseries of my cancer, Sarie and I decided to rent their home for two weeks in September 2014. Saillans has the beauty and charm of a medieval village, with ancient cobblestones, narrow streets, and old stone buildings leaning toward the street with age. Both Denyse and Vincent came to spend a few days with us while we were there. We had what came to be called our first annual sibling "rave" to celebrate our family togetherness, and were joined by our cousin Marie-France and her husband Henry, who lived nearby, and our friends from Quebec, Madeleine Blière and Gaëtan Belec, both now deceased, who accompanied us on our driving tour through France. All our raves have been sedate affairs, but have given Denyse, Vincent, and me, and Christiane when she was alive and well enough, a chance to share old memories, and repair old hurts, related mainly to childhood sibling rivalry.

On our way home to Canada, we decided to make a detour through the pilgrimage town of Lourdes, in southwest France. Lourdes is the small village where, in 1858, the Blessed Virgin Mary appeared to a fourteen-year-old girl, Bernadette Soubirous. A spring appeared at the site, and shortly after, it was discovered that many people with serious illnesses were cured when bathing in its waters. Bernadette had endless difficulties with church authorities, persuading them of the reality of her visions, but they finally came to believe her and she was canonized a saint of the Catholic Church in 1933. Her story has been beautifully portrayed in the 1943 movie *Song of Bernadette*, where the title role is played by Jennifer

Jones. She is remembered also in the "Song of Bernadette" by Leonard Cohen. The village has now grown to a sizable town, and is the venue for many thousands of pilgrims, not only Catholics, who go there for prayer and healing.

I was raised a Catholic, as I have said, and lost my faith for twenty years between the ages of forty and sixty. I believe in the possibility of cure by divine intervention, but my intention in going to Lourdes was not to obtain a cure for my disease. It was more the desire to get help in coping with it. A more modest intervention, but still worth trying for.

Despite the large crowds, it was a strangely silent and spiritual experience. There were separate entrances to the spring and grotto area for men and women, and each pilgrim lined up on long rows of benches. One slowly shuffled forward along the seat until one's turn came. Groups of six men at a time were ushered into a changing area, and were asked to strip to their underpants. Following this, one man at a time was taken into an enclosed area in which there was a large bath of slowly flowing water, perhaps three metres in length, and a metre a half wide in width and depth. Steps led down from the side into the bath. An attendant then wrapped a cold, wet towel around your body and asked you to remove your underpants under the towel. He then led you to the top of the steps, and asked you to make your petition, and say the Lord's Prayer. My petition was the request for help in coping with my disease. I did not petition for a cure because I thought this presumptuous, especially given my age. I then walked down the steps of the bath into cold water, which came up to my neck, and then slowly walked to the far end, where we were given a choice between submerging or having a wet towel wrapped around our head, to symbolize immersion. I chose the latter. Then I turned around, walked back up the steps, replaced my underpants while wrapped in the wet towel, and returned to the changing room to get dressed. No dry towels were provided so one dressed over the wet body. Surprisingly, this did not seem to matter; the body and clothes dried quickly. No payment was involved.

The remarkable thing is that, from that moment on, I was able to cope in a much better manner with my disease. My crying spells ceased, I became less angry, felt and slept better, and returned to Canada in a much more hopeful frame of mind. A petition come true.

We also visited the "medical centre," at Lourdes, where the medical histories and photographs of the sixty-nine individuals whose cures have been publicly accepted by the church, are kept. These include people with cancer, tuberculosis, osteomyelitis, and fistulae, amongst other diseases. The church has strict criteria that must be met before formally acknowledging a person as "cured." The cure must be instantaneous, and it must not be explicable on medical grounds. Even if they don't fit the church's tough definition of a cure, many thousands of pilgrims have been helped by bathing in the springs at Lourdes.

I had also been pondering other techniques for coping with the cancer. For many years I had been practising prayerful meditation. I am an admirer of the writings of Thomas Merton, and attempt to follow his techniques, as described in his book, *New Seeds of Contemplation*. They were helpful not only with prayer, but enabling me to relax and sleep at night. Could meditation-relaxation-mindfulness be useful in a more direct manner with the cancer? I wondered. Merton himself sharply distinguished spiritual meditation from relaxation-mindfulness, but I suspect there is an overlap between these processes.

Mindfulness is the process in which one becomes increasingly conscious of their body, surroundings, and state of tension, by starting with the toes and working slowly upward, thereby inducing a profound state of peace and relaxation. It is based on Buddhist principles of meditation, widely used by both psychiatrists and psychologists in therapy, and is akin to self-hypnosis, although its proponents do not give it that characterization. Merton himself became very interested in Eastern mysticism toward the end of his life. Although he was a monk in an enclosed and silent order, he managed to arrange a visit to Asia, where he met the Dalai Lama and other Buddhist dignitaries. A few weeks later, in Bangkok, following a presentation, he died, allegedly from accidental electrocution. A recent book, *The Martyrdom of Thomas Merton,* by Hugh Turley and David Ernest Martin, suggests he may have been assassinated by a CIA hit man, posing as a priest, for his strong and articulate opposition to the Vietnam war. He died in 1968, aged fifty-three, the same year that Robert Kennedy and Martin Luther King were assassinated.

Merton had a premonition that he would die young. In 1962 he wrote, "I think sometimes that I may die soon, though I am not yet old (forty-seven). I don't know what kind of conviction this thought carries with it, or what I mean by it. Death is always a possibility for everyone. . .. So, I have a habitual awareness that I may die, and that, if this is God's will, then I am glad."

In practising techniques of mindfulness, psychiatrists and psychologists teach that one must be attentive to one's body: "Listen to what your body is telling you," as a means of dealing with stress. If you can listen to your body, I wondered, can you not also talk to your body? Give yourself a benign talking-to, as it were?

It is well known that some bodily organs, particularly skin sensation and muscle activity, have representation in the cerebral cortex in the left (dominant) hemisphere. This representation brings skin sensation and muscle movement under conscious control and experience. However, other organs such as the heart, liver, pancreas, spleen, and prostate do not have cerebral representation, and hence are not subject to conscious control or reaction. Psychophysiological techniques such as biofeedback have shown that physiological functions such as heart rate and blood pressure can be controlled, to a certain limited extent, by focused concentration. Through an analogous process, I decided I was going to "speak" to my prostate cancer cells.

Every day or two, I would induce a state of meditation-mindfulness, and visualize my prostate gland and nearby lymph nodes, thereby drawing them into consciousness. I would then "speak" or "negotiate" with the cancer cells, telling them that if they remained in the prostate and nodes, and not spread to other parts of the body, they could then remain in my body, and I would not try to eject them. I first described this technique in detail in an essay published in the *Globe and Mail* newspaper in November 2015.

I am well aware that speaking to cancer cells would not pass muster to a hard-nosed scientist, which I myself have been at certain periods of my life. I am aware also that it would be difficult, if not impossible, to subject it to a double-blind controlled trial, the acid test in evaluating the value of a new treatment technique. However, this approach made sense to me in a rational and empirical manner. Moreover, it was simple and inexpensive. So, I carried out these meditative exercises, and still do so, though with diminished frequency.

I also decided not to battle my cancer. One often sees obituaries in which the deceased died after a "courageous battle" with cancer. I have no doubt about the courage required by the deceased, but do question the need for a battle. I have seen too many people with cancer go to extraordinary lengths to prolong their lives, spending tens, if not hundreds, of thousands of dollars travelling to various countries seeking the magic potion, either a new highly expensive, experimental drug, or an equally expensive naturopathic substance, to little or no avail.

Perhaps some might regard my visit to Lourdes or speaking to my cancer cells as a form of me battling my cancer. As explained above, in going to Lourdes I was not seeking a cure, but help in coping with the disease. In speaking to my cancer cells, I was not seeking to exterminate or excise them from my body, but more negotiating with them.

Every person with cancer deals with the disease in a different manner. Many are anxious and/or depressed, and remain so until the end. Others are angry; they are the ones who fight the disease, sometimes with a degree of bitterness. Others, surprisingly, remain cheerful and accepting. Andrea, a friend of Sarie's and mine, developed cancer of the lung in her early seventies. It was Stage 4 and untreatable. She had been a lifelong smoker so knew the risks. Two months before her death, she came to a meeting of a committee of which we were both members, carrying her oxygen tank, and cheerfully announced to all present, "I'll be leaving you in two months' time." She maintained her cheery attitude until the end. I must admit to being full of admiration for people like Andrea who are able to adopt this positive demeanour. John Kleinschmidt, my brother-in-law, exhibited gallows humour when he was dying from complications of diabetes. When I met him in South Africa three months before he died, I asked him how he was doing and he replied, "Oh, I'm just fine, thanks, François; I've got one foot in the grave and the other foot on a banana peel!"

Although I am certainly better now than when first diagnosed, I still would not classify my attitude toward my cancer and limited life-expectancy as cheerful.

People with cancer experience five phases in adapting to their condition: denial, anger, depression, bargaining, and acceptance. These are analogous to the five phases of grief. I am sure any reader of my story will see that I've been through each of these phases, which have sometimes overlapped one other.

Bill Cameron was a well-known Canadian journalist and television personality, executive producer for the program, *The Journal*. In the summer of 2004, he was diagnosed as having stage 4 cancer of the oesophagus. In a poignant article published posthumously two months after his death, in March 2005, he gave a moving account of the immense difficulties he had in coping with his cancer. He describes his journey into "Cancerland" thus:

> "the world of faith and hope, an enormous Kasbah with huge rooms at the front devoted to conventional treatment, radiation and chemotherapy, and smaller and smaller rooms behind them, some well-lit, some murky: experimental drug therapy, massive infusion of vitamins, new vaccines, the application of powerful light, the insertion of tiny radio-active spheres in the area next to the tumour, distant healing. And then, at the end of the bazaar, the little chambers of the long-shot: goji juice from Asia, blood cleansing, distillation from apricot pits, amino acids, green tea."

Cameron describes his anger about the delay in diagnosis, and the suspicions of his own body that this engendered. He became "stunned and discouraged" when the treatments failed and decided to "throw everything at it." Vitamins, magnesium, acidophils, beta-carotene, biotin, whey protein shakes, milk thistle, fish oil, German enzymes, and sickly-sweet multivitamins. His doctors reacted with "indifference or rage" to these efforts to try everything. "The Cancerland 'war' is prosecuted on the internet, through law enforcement agencies, the police, and the courts," he stated. "If you search for alternative therapies on the internet, there is an instant cacophony, a buzzing, whining, and banging as the traditionalists trade artillery shots with the New Age therapists." He was "uplifted" by the prayers of many, from the Dalai Lama to various churches and "dozens" of freelance worshippers. Cameron concluded his essay on a sardonic note by stating, "Cancer is not the best thing that ever happened to me. Even if, against all the odds, I emerge five years from now, able to walk and talk, cancer will still have been a colossally enervating and humiliating drag, a sudden shunt into old age and infirmity." What powerful words, "a sudden shunt into old age and infirmity"! Yet it also helped him to make friends, and nurtured his role as a father and husband.

Cameron's evident rage over his battle with cancer is very understandable. He was a relatively young man, in the prime of a successful career, with a young family, and a serious type of cancer that gave him little time to adapt to the condition.

Another well-known journalist who lucidly described his reactions to having cancer of the prostate is the Briton, *Guardian* columnist and environmental activist, George Monbiot. His cancer was diagnosed at a relatively early stage, when it was still confined to the prostate; he had many family and friends who were supportive, and he had the National Health Service. In an essay published in 2018, he stated there were three reasons why he was happy with his diagnosis. Firstly, he imagined how much worse it could be, and to do this he developed the "Shitstorm Scale," which he defined as, "How does my situation compare to others with medical problems and family tragedies?" He gave himself a Shitstorm score of two out of ten. Secondly, "Change what you can change; accept what you can't." Thirdly, "Overcoming fear: name it, normalize it, socialize it." Monbiot added, "I will ride this out. I will own this disease, but won't be defined with it: I will not be prostrated by my prostate. I will be gone for a few weeks (having surgery) but when I return, I do solemnly swear I will still be the same old git with whom you are familiar."

In a follow-up article two months later, after surgery, Monbiot described the complications he had—infection, muscle spasms, bowel paralysis from narcotics that required manual evacuation and urinary catheterization. But he also learned the power of human kindness and the value of family hugs in relieving pain. "With the help of the blue pill," he said, even his sexual functions were restored. He has been given a 90 percent chance of surviving five years and is still working. Well done, George.

Stephen Fry, the well-known actor, writer, and television presenter, has publicized his prostate cancer. Like mine, Fry's diagnosis followed the discovery of a high PSA level and, again like mine, his biopsy showed a Gleason Score of nine. In an interview he stated that, "Cancer is a word that grills into your head; it's an awful taboo word. I kept saying to myself; you're not supposed to get cancer. I know it's a cliché but you don't think it's going to happen to you, only to other people. [This is] an aggressive little bugger, all pretty undignified and unfortunate." He ended his interview by recommending that all men have their PSAs done regularly.

A well-known surgeon, Atul Gawande, an author and staff writer for the *New Yorker*, has written a fascinating book, *Being Mortal*, about how society deals with old age, dying, and death. Gawande stresses the need the old and sick have for autonomy, and how health and care services fail them dismally in this regard (he is writing as a US citizen). He gives the example of his own father, also a surgeon, who developed a rare malignant tumour of his cervical cord, and of the long and complicated course he had before dying of the condition. The book is packed with pearls of wisdom in dealing with people in this situation. One quote, in particular appeals to me: "We've been wrong about what our job is in medicine. We think our job is to ensure health and survival. But really our job is larger than that. It is to enable well-being."

Henry Marsh, a British neurosurgeon, describes the shock of getting prostate cancer. "I had symptoms of prostatism for years, steadily getting worse, but it took me a long time ask for help. I thought I was being stoical when in reality I was being a coward. I simply couldn't believe the diagnosis at first, so deeply engrained was my denial …... looking back, I am amazed how willfully blind I was." Every time he has a PSA taken, Marsh waits anxiously for the result to find out whether the cancer has returned. His and my psyches are like two peas in a pod.

Having cancer exposed me to another curious situation. I was often required to undergo various tests such as X-rays and scans, and these involved spending much time in waiting rooms, alongside other patients awaiting the test. This gave me time to talk with them and discover their problems and situation. I was able to look at their issues from a physician's point of view without their knowing I was a physician.

For example, a woman in her fifties, Joanne, was with me in the bone-scan waiting room, and we got talking. She had breast cancer with widespread metastases and was very depressed, crying when recounting her story. She had few social supports, only a son who lived in another town. I reassured her as best I could, and suggested she contact a social worker through her physician to provide sustained support. She appeared relieved at this suggestion and at the opportunity to talk with me.

Dave, a man in his late forties, had chronic back pain. He told me he had had "every treatment under the sun," but was still heavily disabled and distraught by his symptoms, and taking big doses of analgesics. He showed me his X-rays, the report of which indicated he had "mild osteoarthritis disease of the spinal vertebrae." This strongly implied he had a condition called "chronic, non-malignant pain" and that he did not have a serious or a terminal condition. I explained to him that sometimes doctors could not cure diseases, and that a more reasonable approach than trying everything under the sun was to accept the condition, stick with one physician and one treatment, adopt a wait-and-see attitude, and remain as active as possible, within his limitations. He too was heartened with this advice.

Another man, Don, in his early sixties, I met when both of us were awaiting a bone-scan. I asked him if he had prostate cancer and he replied in the affirmative. He had been diagnosed two years previously, had a Gleason score of nine (like me), and had bony metastases that were being treated by radiotherapy. He was very distressed by his situation, as he lived alone, though he had some support from a lady friend. I told him about my illness—a mistake perhaps, because mine was less advanced. We exchanged telephone numbers and emails, and continued communicating for a few weeks subsequently, but eventually he stopped responding to my messages. I suspect that he had discovered that I was a physician and, because of this, had decided that a friendly relationship was not appropriate. I feel I did not help Don much. A year later I read Don's obituary in the *Ottawa Citizen*.

The two remaining pillars of my technique in coping with cancer were physical and spiritual exercises. In May of 2013, nine months before my cancer was diagnosed, I had had a myocardial infarction—a heart attack—for which I was hospitalized for one week. Investigations, including a coronary angiogram, revealed that it was only a branch of the circumflex artery that had been affected. The infarction was deemed minor and thus inserting a stent, or having surgery, was not required.

Following hospitalization, I was referred to the cardiac rehabilitation program at the Heart Institute in Ottawa. There, for eight weeks, together with about thirty other people with heart problems, I went through a rigorous program of supervised exercise therapy. I had always been a physically active person. When young I was a competitive swimmer, and in my forties, fifties, and sixties, a moderately successful tennis player. During those years, friends who were active golfers would ask me when I was going to take up golf. "When I get really old," I replied, to their disgust. In my early seventies I decided I was getting really old so I took up golf, thinking my skills as a good tennis player would transfer quickly to golf. However, it was too late. I am a dreadful golfer, so my friends got the last laugh.

The cardiac rehabilitation program was extremely useful. It taught me the need for regular, focused, structured aerobic exercises and also the importance of carrying out muscle-strengthening exercises, for thirty or more minutes each day. There is nothing new about the importance of this approach, not only in cardiac, but in general health, as well. Carrying them out in a class format on a regular weekly basis led by a health professional, helps to underline their crucial value. Almost every day since, I have ridden my bicycle or exercised indoors on a stationary bicycle in inclement weather, and carried out muscle-strengthening exercises for at least thirty minutes each day. I firmly believe the theory that physical exercise bolsters the immune system of the body.

More recently I have developed a heartbeat irregularity that caused blackouts—brief losses of consciousness when I would fall to the ground. The blackouts have been completely corrected by the insertion of a cardiac pacemaker. Yet, I feel now there is a race between my prostate and my heart to see which one gets to the finishing line first.

Chapter Fourteen
A Rocky Road

My life resumed its character after our return to Ottawa from France and from Lourdes. I had fully retired from clinical medicine, and was in the midst of writing my novel, *Father, Unknown,* and this became my occupation. Sarie and I had to learn how to live with each other on a full-time basis in a relatively small apartment, compared with our château on the Gatineau River. A good friend of mine, also a psychiatrist, told me that, after he retired, his wife one day told him, angrily, "I married you for better or for worse; I didn't marry you for lunch!" Sarie and I had to adjust to having lunch together every day, which we managed, reasonably amicably.

Sarie also has health issues. In 2006, she had back surgery for collapsed vertebrae, followed by a deep vein thrombosis. The surgery helped for a while, but by 2014 she had chronic back pain and had to use a walker to get around. She also had endless problems caused by bleeding, a side-effect of the Warfarin, a blood thinner she was taking. Nevertheless, she continues her extracurricular activities, in particular playing bridge, and I join her from time to time. She also loves swimming, and as often as possible, carries out aqua-fitness exercises. Despite some tensions, I believe we passed the Lunch Test. We came to realize that we complement each other very well. I am the thinker, writer, and ponderer; she is the outgoing, practical speaker and go-getter.

Every three months I was required to have an injection into my abdomen of Zoladex, the anti-androgen drug for my prostate cancer. The side-effects were immediate, unpleasant, and powerful. The injection itself is painful because a wide-gauge needle has to be employed to inject the solid pellet containing the hormone. Hot flashes have been the most persistent side-effect. I have up to seven or eight a day, and have to remove clothing, or go out on our balcony to cool off. Curiously, they occur commonly just as I am dropping off to sleep, thus waking me up. Dr. Watterson offered me an injection of Depo Provera, and I have had this on several occasions with benefit. However, I am reluctant to add yet another hormone to the large doses of those already circulating in my body; hence, I try to put up with hot flashes as best I can.

The holy grail test for prostate cancer that scientists are seeking is a "liquid biopsy"—a minimally invasive test that can be performed on blood or urine and is capable of detecting "the prostate cancer that kills, versus those that don't kill," here quoting Dr. Otis Brawly, chief medical officer for the American Cancer Society. Two tests—the Select Mdx, which measures messenger RNA levels, and the STHLM3, developed in Sweden, which analyzes 200 genetic markers—show great promise.

A week or so prior to each injection of Zoladex, I have blood taken for the PSA test to see whether the level is rising, which could mean a recurrence of the cancer. At my three-monthly visits for the injection, I would wait anxiously to hear the result, as if the Sword of Damocles was about to fall, and heave a sigh of relief on hearing it was still low.

Reading, writing, living an active social life, and physical and spiritual exercises have rounded out my life nicely since the cancer was first diagnosed. In 2016 we purchased a small condo in Victoria, British Columbia, where, at the time, three of our four sons lived. Quentin later moved to Calgary, while Martin and Barbara have returned to Ottawa. Our condo is close to the downtown area, and borders the spectacular Beacon Hill Park.

To escape the Ottawa winter and keep in touch with the family, Sarie and I now spend at least four winter months in Victoria and the rest of the year in Ottawa. Walking or cycling on the trail of Dallas Road, with the snow-clad Olympic Mountains of Washington State visible across the strait in the distance, is an exhilarating experience.

We love Ottawa with its vibrant cultural life, amenities, and natural beauties. From our apartment we have great views of the river, Parliament buildings, the Museum of History, and the Gatineau hills in the distance. Ottawa has been given the Bicycle Trail Community Award by the Share the Road Cycling Coalition of Ontario, and I make full use of the nearly 1,000 kilometres of cycling trails in and around the city. Both Martin and Andrew and their families are our support in the city. Age has made it more difficult to endure the long winters.

Things changed in the spring and summer of 2017. In spring, my PSA went up to 0.9 and, three months later, to 2.14. Dr. Watterson promptly referred me to an oncologist, Dr. Christine Canil, who, after carrying out a pelvic scan showing enlarged lymph nodes, confirmed that the cancer had recurred and spread. She placed me on a new synthetic hormone called Enzalutamide. This comes in the form of large capsules, and one has to swallow four daily, while continuing three monthly injections of Zoladex. I really felt overloaded with testosterone-suppressing chemicals! Meanwhile, I continued my daily physical and spiritual exercise program. At this stage I asked Dr. Canil about my life expectancy and she replied, briefly and factually, "two to three years."

The Enzalutamide quickly brought the PSA down to low levels again, and I have continued this treatment combination since then. My most recent PSA level has remained low, although, as of January 2022, it appears to be slowly rising again. However, bone and pelvic scans in November 2021, and again in May 2022, showed no recurrence of the cancer. So far, the anti-androgen drugs appear to have been a life-saving.

I have been hoping (hope springs eternal, or at least until you pass on) that new research would be the answer to my cancer. What seems to give most promise is immuno-therapy. This depends on isolating the cancer cells in biopsy specimens, culturing them, and creating a genetically engineered receptor cell that is specific for neutralizing or killing the original cancer cell.

The most promising form of immune-therapy depends on the use of the Sipuleucel-T ("Provenge"). This is produced by separating a sample of the patient's white blood corpuscles from the blood by a process known as leukapheresis. They are then processed by growing them with a fusion protein in a special medium, following which the product is reinfused in the patient on three separate occasions, separated by a two-week period. Studies, such as "New Therapies for Castration-Resistant Prostate Cancer," by Dan Longo, have shown that this personalized treatment of hormone-resistant metastatic prostate cancer prolongs life to a significant degree. These products and procedures remain experimental and expensive approaches to the treatment of prostate cancer. However, I am hoping they become more widely available before I expire.

I believe in the power of prayer, and prayers have been offered on my behalf. Jeanne Charron, a good friend who lives in our apartment building, is a practising Catholic, and is friendly with the Sisters of Charity at the Elisabeth Bruyère Convent in Ottawa, whose foundress was Elisabeth Bruyère. She was a holy woman who not only established the first hospital in Bytown (as Ottawa was then called), in 1845, but also set up schools and orphanages and was a great help to the poor and the homeless. She founded a hospital that still bears her name, and treated the sick of all religious denominations during the typhus epidemic of 1847. The process for her canonization has begun, and she was recently declared "venerable," the first step to canonization. One miracle is required for her to be declared "blessed" and another for her to be declared a saint. Other complex church requirements have to be met. Her remains are held in a beautiful stone sarcophagus in a chapel at the mother house of Élisabeth Bruyère Convent in Ottawa. On my own behalf, I pray for her intercession to help me cope with the disease.

The Sisters of Charity, especially Sister Yvette Lalonde, are praying that my recovery (I dare not use the word cure) may become one of the miracles required to promote her canonization. I want to emphasize that I had nothing to do with promoting this petition, but am thankful to Jeanne and the Sisters of Charity for thinking of me and organizing this prayer cycle.

I let the cancer interfere with my activities as little as possible. With age and infirmity, I found my cycling speed spiralling downward, with all riders swiftly passing me by, on the great cycling trails of Ottawa. So, in the spring of 2018, I purchased an electric bicycle, and rode over 2,000 kilometres that summer. In the fall, I made a costly mistake. On a lovely, though cold, day in mid-November, following a snowfall, I went out on my e-bike, rode over a small sheet of black ice on the road, and went for a nasty fall, injuring my left arm and right eye. X-rays showed I had fractured a small bone in my wrist, the head of the radius in my elbow, and, most seriously, the floor of the orbit in my right eye, and had also been concussed. I have recovered well from that stupid sprawl, and the only permanent effect is double vision when I look upward; I shall no longer cycle after snowfalls!

Despite my failure in my second- and third-year medical examinations because of playing too much bridge, I have had a life-long passion for the game. We play bridge regularly with three couple friends, Evelyn and Peter Hustwit, Leona and Ned Kiez, and Madeleine Blière and Gaëtan Belec. Both Gaëtan and Madeleine passed away recently. Gaëtan and Evelyn had experience playing duplicate bridge and acted as our teachers. There is a saying that "bridge means silence." Sarie broke this rule repeatedly[7] by asking for advice, unwittingly revealing the strength or weakness of her hand. This led Gaëtan, teasingly, to call the director (himself) to penalize her. Bridge evenings were always combined with excellent dinners and wines, so as the evening wore on, errors would multiply. Peter would make zany bids, based on the 1950s rules he, alone, followed. This confused not only his opponents, but his partner. The evenings always ended jovially, with the winner and the loser both getting whimsical prizes such as a miniature bottle of scotch or a small writing pad to aid failing memories.

Other than the early days following diagnosis, when I was anxious, depressed, or angry, I have slept well. Most nights I take a mild over-the-counter hypnotic such as Melatonin or an antihistamine, or just Tylenol ES. Recently I have started using a prescribed hypnotic, Zopiclone. I have gained about fifteen pounds since my cancer was diagnosed and, despite

---

7 Evelyn Hustwit also passed away on August 13th 2022, sudden and unexpectedly.

serious efforts, have not been able lose it. This has given me a new-found empathy for obese people who cannot lose weight.

The diet I follow can loosely be described as "Mediterranean." Fruit and vegetables at every meal. Fish three or four times a week and a small amount of meat five or six times a week. Mug of black coffee once a day for breakfast, one or two glasses of white or red wine per day, and a small dessert once or twice each day.

Like many older people, I spend an increasing amount of time pondering my youth and my past. There are many things I would do differently but I have no wish to relive my life, even if I could. I keep in touch with psychiatry by reading journals, and am disappointed in the psychiatric profession for its full-scale use of DSM-5. All of medicine appears to be headed down the road of multiplying diagnoses. Whatever the cause of this change, I do not believe it is an expedient development.

Chapter Fifteen
The Perils of Prophecy

Physicians make medical prognoses based on statistical probabilities; they know that most individuals with a particular condition will survive for a certain length of time, and in most instances, they will prove correct. However, there are always the outliers, in either direction—those who survive either much longer or much shorter than average. One hears of cancer patients (or, for that matter, those with serious heart or liver or other diseases) being given a poor prognosis, and then going on to live for many years. One also periodically hears the reverse: individuals being given a clean bill of health, then becoming seriously ill or dropping dead shortly thereafter. Of the two, the former is preferable, as in my case.

Doctors are not as good as actuaries in forecasting future health and life expectancies. Actuaries base their predictions of life expectancy using complex statistical methods as to what has happened in the past to men and women of a certain age and lifestyle, and include estimates of probability in their calculations. Insurance companies, banks, and government departments depend heavily on actuaries in formulating their policies, and financial and pension planning.

Economists are notoriously poor at predicting what will happen to the economy. Few foresaw the recession in 2007. In his book the *Black*

Swan, Nassim Nicholas Taleb wrote about the perils of predicting financial futures, which are so dependant on human behaviour, which is itself so unpredictable. Taleb suggests the way to protect against the black swan effect is to focus on generalities and expect the unexpected.

I have not been given a good prognosis—neither when I was first diagnosed in February 2014, nor when my cancer recurred in the summer of 2017. Many people, especially medical colleagues, tell me I will likely die of another unrelated condition, as is commonly the case when older men develop prostate cancer. Despite this poor prognosis, I have a number of points in my favour, in addition to my age. As I've said, I follow my recommended medical treatment scrupulously, and am active in the physical, social, and spiritual spheres, all said to be good prognostic indicators. If I live five years or more, it will be a small, perhaps even a big, miracle.

Despite my age and my Catholic faith, I had difficulty dealing with issues of dying and death. As Woody Allen says, reflecting the ambivalence of many toward death, "I'm not afraid of death, I just don't want to be there when it happens." I know and accept that death is a fact of life. Most of my classmates from Grey High School in Port Elizabeth, and from the medical class of 1956 in Cape Town, have died. I spend much time reading the obituaries of friends, colleagues, and other contemporaries who have died, or going to their funerals. In a sense, this book is my auto-obituary. My faith teaches me that there is life after death and I do believe that. Christ, hanging on the cross, told the "good" robber, crucified and dying alongside him, "I promise you, today you will be with me in Paradise." He said this in reply to something the robber had asked him, "Jesus, remember me when you come into your kingdom." These are poignant words uttered between two men dying dreadful deaths on neighbouring crosses.

Yet there is an intangibleness in the world of the spirit that makes it difficult for many to comprehend. Belief at a factual and emotional level does not always follow smoothly from belief at an intellectual level. Many in our secular society have difficulty in believing in God and the world of the spirit, and believers don't make it any easier for them when, for example, they get involved in religious wars such as the Crusades, the wars in Europe of the sixteenth century, or Ireland in the twentieth century, and in the present-day Middle East. Religion is not the only factor at the source of these conflicts. Language and ethnic and cultural differences are also involved.

Another issue that makes it difficult for me to deal with death is that I still feel I have much to do. Completing this book, writing an article on Beethoven's deafness, another on cycling, and an essay on Lord Tweedsmuir, governor general of Canada. I love my grandchildren and would love to see them grow and mature. In addition, there are many family documents and photographs to be sorted out and classified. I also have travel plans—places in Britain, France, and South Africa that I have never seen, such as the Hebrides, the Lake District, Normandy, Brittany, the Kruger National Park, and The Blue Train that runs between Cape Town and Pretoria. All this will take the next twenty years—if I live that long. When I have completed these tasks on my bucket list, I shall be ready to die!

What about my legacy? By far the most important are my children, grandchildren, and future descendants. In my clinical practice, my teaching and in my writings, I have hopefully helped and touched some with temporary or lasting benefit.

In 1959, shortly after starting my career in psychiatry, I watched a BBC *Face-to-Face* television interview with Carl Jung, the famous Swiss psychiatrist and psychoanalyst, carried out two years before his death. John Freeman, the interviewer, asked Jung if he believed in God and he replied, "I know. I don't need to believe. I know." Jung betrayed no doubt about the existence of the world of spirit, and I am strongly encouraged by his <u>certainty</u> of God's existence. The interview is a fascinating account of Jung's childhood, relationships with his parents and with Sigmund Freud, and the development of his theories of personality and of archetypes. It can be seen on YouTube and is worth a viewing.

At present these reflections are a little academic, since I feel well and my death is (hopefully) not imminent. But once the cancer starts spreading to the bones and other organs, these issues will become much more pressing. I have been told that when the cancer returns its growth and spread may be slowed by radiotherapy and/or chemotherapy. I will then have to make the decision whether I want either of these traumatic treatments. When that time comes, I do believe I will have the strength and capabilities to cope with these decisions, and that my faith and hope will help me see this through. Sarie and I have purchased our plots in the cemetery at St. Stephen's Church in Chelsea, near its northeast corner. From 1995 until 2006, I was pianist and organist at the church, and it is there that we will lie, side by side, for eternity. On our tombstone we would like the same epitaph that is on our baby Paul's tombstone in Adelaide.

I know well enough that one has little choice in the timing of death. Every living being has to go through this, other than those who die suddenly, such as from accidents, heart attacks, or strokes, or as a result of violence. John F. Kennedy had no time to accomplish all he had set out to do, or to prepare for death when he was assassinated. The millions of young men—English, French, American, Canadian, German, Russian and others—who killed each other in World War I had no chance to live out their lives. All knew they had a high probability of death, yet hoped it would not happen to them. War carries off the young before they have had occasion to realize their dreams. This was strikingly described by Erich Maria Remarque in his novel *All Quiet on the Western Front*. First published in German in 1929, the book was a huge success and was translated into many languages. It was also banned and burnt in Nazi Germany. In the book, the protagonist, who is Remarque himself (he fought in the German trenches in World War I) speculates on the irony of killing the enemy English and French soldiers, when he knows that in any other context he would enjoy going out to a pub and having a drink with them. Compared to these millions of young men who died in war, it embarrasses me to grumble about death when I've had a full, long, and productive life.

Some go the route of medical assistance in dying (MAiD). I have no desire to do this, and I am disappointed in the medical profession for accepting a role in carrying out this function. I did not become a doctor to kill people. When the time comes, I know I shall deal with death, giving it the dignity it deserves, with the help, if needed, of palliative care specialists. Denial or submerging one's anxieties in drugs or alcohol are useful techniques for many people, and I have no difficulty with these approaches for those who need and benefit from them during their last days on earth, though hope I will not have to take this route. Our generation is fortunate to have the advantages of modern medicine in this regard. Our ancestors often died painful deaths, at an early age, because of the absence of palliative care. Unfortunately, this is still the case in many developing countries. With good quality palliative care, it is now rarely necessary for anyone to die in pain.

It has been a long journey since my isolated beginnings at the bottom end of Africa. A move to England in my twenties, then Scotland, Australia, the United States, back to Australia, then ending up in Canada, first in London, and finally Ottawa. Each move was determined by my wish to climb the slippery academic ladder and, as I gaze back on my life in the proverbial "retro-spectroscope," I do have a sense of accomplishment, mixed with a heavy dose of guilt at what I put my family through, because of my spirited ambition. I now realize how much my ambition was determined by fear of failure. Despite my determination and stubbornness, I am a sentimental old soul and weep when I hear beautiful music, see a stunning painting, or walk past an aromatic flowerbed.

None of the moves has been easy, especially for Sarie, who had to find accommodation, new friends and activities for herself, and new schools and activities for the children at each location. Since our wedding we have lived in five different locations in England, one in Scotland, three in Adelaide, one in Rochester, NY, two in London, Ontario, and four in Ottawa—a total of sixteen moves! Sarie and our four sons have stood by me loyally through all these moves and for this I am eternally grateful. Like Pilgrim in John Bunyan's allegory, *The Pilgrim's Progress,* I and my family have travelled far. As Bunyan wrote, "Music in the house, music in the heart, and music also in heaven, for joy that we are here."

There have been many setbacks on the journey, both academic and personal, an inevitable side-effect of ambition and career-climbing, but eternal hope has carried me through.

Since that *septem horribilis* in February 2014, when I was diagnosed with prostate cancer, when I retired and when we had to say goodbye to our home in Chelsea, I've had time to ponder my situation. I believe I've come to terms with the reality of dying and death and, when my time comes, I know I shall be ready.

"The Soul . . . Rests and expatiates in a life to come." (Alexander Pope)

Chapter Sixteen
Afterthoughts

Why does anyone write their life story? In some respects, it is an ego-trip, all about "I" and "me". Every person's life is unique and we all have gone through unusual experiences, so, anyone is entitled to write a memoir, and many do. A memoir is, of necessity, a selected slice of one's life. Much is left out, some intentionally, some not, some because it is just plain boring.

A life story is also revealing of oneself, far more than an author realizes. I have endeavoured not to paint myself with a halo, because no such halo exists. Perhaps there is a brief glow, balanced by shadows.

With age, I have come to an increasing feeling of wonder and awe at the marvels of creation, from the structure and function of the sub-microscopic RNA and DNA molecules, to the vastness and depth of space at the macroscopic level. Every summer I watch in wonder as a spider spins its web outside my study window. How can an insect, with a brain smaller than a pinhead, have developed the capacity to create an edifice that is so complex, so purposeful and so beautiful? Such phenomena leave me with a profound sense of the divine.

Thomas Merton has expressed these sentiments far more eloquently than me, in his portrayal of pre-dawn and dawn at his monastery near Louisville in Kentucky:

> "How the valley awakens. At two fifteen in the morning there is no sound except in the monastery; the bells ring, the office begins. Outside nothing, except perhaps a bullfrog saying "Om" in the creek. . ... The mysterious and uninterrupted whooping of the whippoorwill begins about three, these mornings . . . sometimes there are two whooping together perhaps a mile away.
>
> The first chirps of the working day birds mark the "point vierge" of the dawn under a sky as yet without light, a moment of awe and inexpressible innocence, when the Father opens their eyes. . ... Their condition asks if it is their time to "be." He answers "yes." Then one by one, they wake up, and become birds. They manifest themselves as birds, beginning to sing . . . and will even fly.
>
> Meanwhile, the most wonderful moment of the day is that when creation in its innocence asks permission to 'be' once again, as it did on the first morning that ever was."

My story has intentionally used the theme of hope as a guideline. There are so many reasons to lose hope in today's world. The advent of right-wing nationalist leaders in many countries echoes the events of the 1900s and the 1930s, both of which led to catastrophic wars in which millions of innocents were killed, maimed, or displaced. Now we have proxy wars in parts of the Middle East, east Europe and Africa, being fought by the big powers who believe they have nothing to lose, but which nevertheless cause untold suffering to the locals. A proxy war can easily lead to a generalized war when feelings, fears, and misunderstandings run high. And now a needless war in Ukraine. A future war could lead to nuclear weapons being deployed with devastating consequences to life on Earth. The so-called balance-of-terror during the forty-two years of the Cold War prevented either the US or the USSR from using its nuclear arsenal against the other, but there is no assurance that this balance would be maintained as smaller countries continue to develop these lethal weapons. The new threats come from the east: North Korea and China.

And then, early in 2020, the COVID-19 pandemic struck. By January 2022, over two hundred million had been afflicted and over five million had died. Perhaps, I hope, it will not prove as disastrous as the Black Death in the fourteenth century, in which one-third of Europe's population died, or the Spanish Flu of 1918-1919, which killed fifty million people worldwide. Nevertheless, it has become highly disruptive of social and economic life around the globe. Our more advanced scientific, political, and social structures should help humanity adjust better to this disease than we did to earlier pandemics. However, no one can tell when, whether, or how it will end. Despite the human talent for knowledge, inventiveness, and control, we seem to be at sea on this one, unprepared on a disastrous scale. There have been many pandemics in the history of humankind, yet there appears to have been a mysterious belief that it could not happen again. Meanwhile, Canada is handling the pandemic relatively effectively, and, hopefully, if the curve of increase is flattened and the pandemic controlled, restrictions may soon be eased. The virus knows no boundaries and affects friend and foe alike, which helps mark our common humanity. Once the pandemic is controlled, some good may yet emerge from its horrors, including the lesson that our greatest enemy is ourselves.

Hope seems to be letting us down with the accelerating pace of climate change, and our failing efforts, so far, to control the destruction and despoliation of our earthly environment. This has been described eloquently but pessimistically in a recently published book, *Civilization Critical: Energy, Food Nature and the Future*. The author, Darrin Qualman, depicts overpopulation, food wastage, production inefficiencies, and environmental pollution as having a catastrophic effect on Earth's natural recycling mechanisms. Like COVID-19, climate change recognizes no political or state boundaries. This is a universal Earth and human life issue, not a country-specific one, yet politicians spend more time fighting one another than developing a unified, coherent, and effective policy to deal with this worldwide problem. Controlling the growth of human population is a key to resolving these issues, and although this is now happening, we are still a long way from coming to grips with it.

The second of the three great theological virtues is hope, the others being faith and charity, yet hope seems to get the brush-off when compared to the other two. If hope goes, cynicism or despair result, often with fatal consequences. Hope has been my life philosophy both in my clinical practice and in my expectation concerning the capacity of human nature to find a solution to the plague of war, and the accelerating pace of climate change. Even though it is late in the day, I have hope in my heart that humanity will control these twin potential catastrophes, if only there is the political will.

Where will humanity go if we destroy life and civilization on earth? Some talk about colonizing the moon or Mars. Neither of these options appears very practical at this stage of our scientific development. There is no planet B. In the event of a nuclear or a climate-change holocaust, a few humans may survive in isolated, self-contained communities, but our culture and our civilizations would be destroyed.

Where is my hope in this alarmist scenario? Most people, and probably even most world leaders, if pushed in all honesty, would admit that a nuclear war, or accelerating climate change, would be disastrous for life on earth. Yet neither leaders, nor the majority of the mass of humanity seem to have grasped the awful reality of these possible developments. We may not grasp them until the so-called tipping point is reached, beyond which time it will be too late to reverse the headlong rush. I do have hope and expectation that the inherent wisdom of our species will see the writing on the wall, and make the required changes of behaviour, before developments become irreversible.

I have been fascinated, as are most people, as to whether there is life Out There, in the Great Astronomical Beyond. For fifty years at least, huge radio telescopes have been trained on the skies, hoping to pick up messages that might have been transmitted by intelligent beings on other planets, so far with zero results. More recently, astronomers have identified thousands of earth-like planets, called exo-planets, which are the appropriate distance from their star, and that could, theoretically, support life. The latest gizmo is the James Webb Space Telescope.

My supposition is, even if there is life on some idyllic exo-planet out there, it is unlikely to be at exactly the same developmental level as we are here on Earth. It has taken hundreds of millions of years for our biosphere to evolve on Earth, and only in the last few decades has it developed to the point where we have the potential to communicate with intelligent life elsewhere. What is the probability of life out there being at the same key stage of intellectual development as is ours? I believe it is close to zero. Alpha Centauri is the star in the sky closest to our solar system, and the third brightest after Sirius and Canopus. Light and radio-waves take over four years to travel between Alpha Centauri and Earth; therefore, it takes eight years for a return message. Eight years, and it's the closest! Astronomical distances are so huge as to make efforts at electronic communication puny in comparison. It could take decades, if not centuries, for a message to be sent, and a reply received from another planetary civilization, if one exists. I am not against efforts to communicate with intelligent beings out there, but my prediction is they will not be successful. Time will tell. The Bard may be right when he got Hamlet to tell Horatio, "There are more things in Heaven and Earth, than are dreamed of in your philosophy."

Alexander Pope was an early eighteenth-century poet who wrote timeless, hope-filled verse. Yet he had a painfully difficult and abrasive personality, alienating family and friends alike. During his childhood he developed tuberculosis of the spine. As an adult, therefore, he was only four feet six inches (1.3 metres) tall. Despite the severe handicaps of a difficult personality and small stature, he was able to write inspiring, optimistic poetry that captured the imagination of his peers in England, France, and beyond. His verse epitomizes the profound wisdom of the poet. Our twenty-first century has much to learn from this almost forgotten English writer.

> Vital spark of heav'nly flame!
>
> Quit, oh quit this mortal frame:
>
> Trembling, hoping, ling'ring, flying,

Oh the pain, the bliss of dying.

I mount! I fly! Oh grave! Where is thy victory?

O death! Where is thy sting?

Alexander Pope

From *The Dying Christian to his Soul.*

THE END

Suggested Reading

(Page number indicates page of the reference in text)

Adami, John George and McCrae, John. *A Text-Book of Pathology for Students of Medicine.* Lea and Febiger, Philadelphia, 1914. (Page 56)

Adamick, Paula. *Art Therapy Can Help Kids with Cancer.* The Toronto Star, February 19, 1987. (Page 126)

Alexander, Franz. *Psychosomatic Medicine: Its Principles and Applications.* W.W. Norton and Co. NY 1950. (134)

Amos, James and Robinson, Robert G. *Psychosomatic Medicine: An Introduction to Consultation Liaison Psychiatry.* Leiden, Cambridge University Press, 2010. (Page 136-7)

Barnard, Christiaan and Pepper, Bill Curtis. *One Life.* George Harrap and Co. London, 1970. (Page 66)

Berton, Pierre. *The Dionne Years: A Thirties Melodrama.* W.W. Norton, Toronto 1978. (Page 10-11)

Biko, Steve, *I Write What I Like.* The Bowerdean Press, London, 1978. (Page 63)

Boileau, John. *Canada's Soldiers in South Africa: Tales from the Boer War, 1899-1902.* James Lorimer & Co. Ltd., Toronto, 2011. (Page 55)

Boraine, Alex. *A Country Unmasked: Inside South Africa's Truth and Reconciliation Commission.* Oxford University Press, Cape Town, 2000. (Page 24)

Boraine, Alex. *What's Gone Wrong: On the Brink of a Failed State.* Jonathan Ball, Cape Town. (Page 98)

Botha, Colin Graham. *The French Refugees at the Cape.* Cape Times Limited, Cape Town, 1919. (Page 52-53)

Briquet, Pierre. *Traité Clinique et Thérapeutique de l'Hysterie.* J.B. Baillière et fils. Paris, 1859. (Pages 127)

Burns, Noel. *Erie: The Lake That Survived.* Rowman and Littlefield, Lanham, Maryland, 1986. (Page 47)

Cameron, Bill. *Chasing the Crab. The Walrus* Magazine, Toronto, May, 2005. (Pages 170-171)

Camus, Albert. *The Plague.* Trans. Stuart Gilbert, New York; Vintage International, 1991. (Page 104)

Carey, Benedict. *Psychiatrists Revise the Book of Troubles, New York Times,* December 17, 2008. (Page 147)

Cheung, Douglas and Finelli, Antonio. *Magnetic Resonance Imaging Diagnosis of Prostate Cancer: Promise and Caution.* Canad. Med. Assoc. J. 191: 18-20, 2019. (Page 163)

Courtney, Bryce. *The Power of One.* Ballantine Books, New York, 1989. (Page 96)

Demers, M. *Frequent Users of Ambulatory Health Care in Quebec: The Case of Doctor Shoppers.* Canad. Med. Assoc. J. 153, 37-42. 1995. (Page 125)

Deruyk, Renéé. *Louise de Bettignies.* La Voix du Nord, Lille, France, 1998. (Page 14)

Diagnostic and Statistical Manual of Mental Disorders. Fifth Edition *(DSM5).* American Psychiatric Association, 2013. (Page 146)

Diar, Prakash. *The Sharpeville Six.* McClelland and Stewart, Toronto, 1990. (Page 63)

Dunbar, Flanders. *Psychosomatic Diagnosis.* Paul Hoeber, New York. 1943. (Page 134)

Dutfield, Michael. *A Marriage of Inconvenience.* Movie, TV Documentary, 1990. (IN) (Page 192)

Dyke, Doris Jean. *Crucified Woman.* The United Church Publishing House, Toronto, 1991. (Page 136-7)

Engel, George. *The Need for a New Medical Model: A Challenge for Biomedicine.* Science, 196, 129-136,1977. (Page 112)

Engel, George. *Psychological Development in Health and Disease.* Saunders and Co. Philadelphia, 1968. (Page 112)

Frances, Allen. *Saving Normal: An Insiders Revolt Against Out-of-Control Psychiatric Diagnosis. DSM-5, Big Pharma and the Medicalization of Normal Life,* William Morrow, New York, 2013. (Page 147)

Freeman, H. *In Conversation with William Sargant.* Bulletin of the Royal College of Psychiatrists, 11, 290-294, 1987. (Page 94)

Friedman, Bernard. *Smuts: A Reappraisal.* George Allen & Unwin, London, 1975. (Page 8)

Gardner, Caleb and Kleinman, Arthur. *Medicine and the Mind—The Consequences of Psychiatry's Identity Crisis.* N. Engl. J. Med, 381, 1697-1699, 2019. (Page 148-49)

Garfinkel, Paul. *A Life in Psychiatry: Looking out, Looking in.* Barlow Books, Toronto, 2014. (Page 147)

Gaulin M, Simard M, Candas B, et al. *Combined Impacts of Multimorbidity and Mental Disorders on Frequent Emergency Department Visits: A Retrospective Cohort Study in Quebec, Canada.* Canad. Med. Assoc. J., 191: 724-32, 2019. (Page 127)

Gawande, Atul. *Being Mortal: Medicine and What Matters in the End.* Doubleday, Canada, 2014. (Page 172)

Guze S, Woodruff R, Clayton P. *Sex, Age and the Diagnosis of Hysteria (Briquet's Syndrome).* American Journal of Psychiatry, 129, 745-748, 1972. (Page 127)

Henderson, D. and Gillespie, R. A. *Textbook of Psychiatry.* Oxford University Press, London, 1927. (Page 46)

Huggins, C. Hodges, C. *Studies on Prostate Cancer: The Effect of Castration of estrogen and of androgen injection on serum phosphatase in metastatic carcinoma of the prostate.* J. of Urology, 167 (2) 948-951, 1941. (Pages 44 and 165)

Hutcheon, Michael. *Book Review: Diagnosing Genius: The Life and Death of Beethoven."* Literary Review of Canada, 15, 27, 2007. (Page 152)

Kedward, Rod. *La Vie en Bleu: France and the French since 1900.* Allen Lane, (Page 18)

Keppel-Jones, Arthur. *When Smuts Goes: A History of South Africa from 1952-2010.* Victor Gollanz Ltd., 1947. (Page 95)

Khomani, Nadia, *Stephen Fry has Prostate Cancer. The Guardian,* February 23, 2018. (Page 172)

Lam, D. Watkins, E. Hayward, P. et alii. *A Randomized Controlled Study of Cognitive Therapy for Relapse Prevention for Bipolar Disorder: Outcome of the First Year.* Arch of Gen Psychiat, 60, 145-152, 2003. (Page 148)

Lehmann, HW, Hanrahan, GE, *Chlorpromazine: a new inhibiting agent for psychomotor excitement and manic states.* Arch. Neurol. and Psychiat. 71, 227-231, 1953. (Page 89)

Lloyd, Geoffrey and Guthrie, Elspeth. *Handbook of Liaison Psychiatry.* Leiden Cambridge University Press, 2007. (Page 135)

Longo, DL. *New Therapies for Castration-Resistant Prostate Cancer.* New England J. of Med, 363, 479-481, 2010. (Page 177)

Luke. 23, 42-43. The Jerusalem Bible. (Page 181)

MacMillan, Margaret. *Paris 1919.* Random House, NY, 2003. (Page 7)

Mai, Martin. *Life Was Not All Wool.* The Toucan Press, Guernsey, 1972. (Page 12)

Mai, Sarie. *The Mai Color Glossary: Instructional Manual for An Art Therapy Assessment Technique*, Second Edition. University of Western Ontario, London, ON, 1987. (Page 126)

Mandela, Nelson. *Long Walk to Freedom.* Abacus Books, NY 1995 (Page 63)

Marsh, Henry. *And Finally: Matters of Life and Death.* Vintage Publishing, London 2022.

McCrae, John. *Letters home*. I have transcribed all the letters that John McCrae wrote home during his sojourn in South Africa in 1900. The originals are kept in the Library and Archives, Ottawa, Canada. (Pages 55-58)

Merton, Thomas. *Conjectures of a Guilty Bystander*. Image Books, 1968. (Pages 167-168)

Merton, Thomas. *New Seeds of Contemplation*. New Directions Publishing, New York, 2007. (Page 174)

Milsanek, Tony. Book Review, *Diagnosing Genius: The Life and Death of Beethoven,* J. Am. Med. Assoc. 297: 2643-2644, 2007. (Page 152)

Monbiot, George. *I Have Prostate Cancer. But I am Happy*. The Guardian, March 13, 2018. (Page 171)

Morrison, E.W.B. *With the Guns in South Africa*. Forgotten Books, London, 2015. (Page 55)

Mullins, Edwin. *The Popes of Avignon: A Century in Exile*. Bluebridge, New York, 2008. (Page 14)

Mutch, Barbara. *The Housemaid's Daughter: A Novel*. St. Martin's Press, London, 2013. (Page 24)

Nutting, Anthony. *Scramble for Africa: The Great Trek to the Boer War*. Constable, London, 1970. (Pages 53-55)

Pakenham, Thomas. *The Boer War*. Weidenfeld and Nicolson, London, 1979. (Pages 52-60)

Paris, Joel. *Overdiagnosis in Psychiatry*, Oxford University Press, NY, 2015. (Page 147)

Paton, Alan. *Cry, The Beloved Country*. Penguin Books, 1958. (Page 95)

Penfield, Wilder. *No Man Alone: A Neurosurgeon's Life*. Little, Brown and Co., 1977. (Page 119-20)

Plosker, GL. *Sipoluecel-T in Metastatic Castration-Resistant Prostate Cancer*. Drugs, 71, 101-108, 2011. (Page 177)

Qualman, Darrin. *Civilization Critical: Energy, Food Nature and the Future.* Fernwood Publishing, Winnipeg, 2019. (Page 188)

Quinn, Kate. *The Alice Network.* Harper Collins, New York, 2017. (Page 14)

Rabin, RC. *New York Times,* Tuesday, December 22, 2015. (Page 147)

Remarque, EM. *All Quiet on the Western Front.* Putnam & Co., London, 1970. (Page 184)

Rosenthal, Eric. *General de Wet.* Simondium Publishers, Cape Town, 1968. (Page 12-13)

Ross, Sue Imrie. *This is My World; The Life of Helen Martins, Creator of The Owl House.* Oxford University Press, 1997. (Page 27)

Sachs, Albie. *The Jail Diary of Albie Sachs.* Harvill Press, London. 1966. (Page 62)

Sandys, Celia. *Churchill: Wanted Dead or Alive.* Castle Books, New York, 2000. (Page 59)

Sargant, W and Slater, E. *An Introduction to Physical Methods of Treatment in Psychiatry,* Third Edition, E & S Livingstone, Edinburgh and London, 1956. (Pages 91-93)

Scamvougeras, Anton and Howard, Andrew. *Understanding and Managing Somatoform Disorders: A Guide for Clinicians.* AJKS Medical Publishing, Vancouver, 2018. (Page 125)

Schindler, Anton. *Beethoven As I Knew Him.* Ed. Donald MacArdle, trans. Constance Jolly, New York, Dover, 1996. (Page 153)

Schoenbrun, David. *The Three Lives of Charles de Gaulle.* Hamish Hamilton, London, 1966. (Page 17-18)

Schreiner, Olive. *The Story of an African Farm.* Collins, London, 1953. (Page 23-4)

Scrivener, Leslie. *Terry Fox: His Story.* McClelland and Stewart, Toronto, 2000. (Page 21)

Shorter, Edward. *Before Prozac.* Oxford University Press, New York, 2009. (Page 148)

Sparks, Allister. *The Mind of South Africa: The Story of the Rise and Fall of Apartheid.* Heinemann, London, 1990. (Pages 52-55)

Taleb, NN. *The Black Swan: The Impact of the Highly Improbable.* Random House, New York, 2007. (Page 181)

Trent, B. *Art in the hospital: treating the mind as well as the body.* Canad. Med. Assoc. J. 135, 1198-1199, 1986. (Page 126)

Trent, B. *Art Therapy Can Shine a Light into the Dark History of a Child's Sex Abuse.* Canad. Med. Assoc. J. 146, 1412-1422, 1992. (Page 126)

Turley, H. Martin, D. *The Martyrdom of Thomas Merton: An Investigation.* Independent Publishing Platform, Amazon, 2018. (Page 168)

Ustinov, Peter. *Dear Me.* Little Brown and Co. Boston, 1977. (Page16)

Vanier, Jean. *Tears of Silence.* Griffin House, Toronto, 1970. (Page 88)

Vanier, Jean. *Becoming Human.* Based on Canadian Broadcasting Corporation Massey lecture series, Anasi, Toronto., 2008. (Page 88)

Versfeld, Martin. *Food for Thought: A Philosopher's Cookbook.* The Carrefour Press, Cape Town, 1991. (Page 61)

von Breuning, Gerhard. *Memories of Beethoven.* Cambridge University Press, 1992. (Page 153)

Weiss, Edward, Spurgeon-English, Oliver. *Psychosomatic Medicine.* W.B. Saunders Co. Philadelphia, 1943. (Page 134)

Welch, HG, Schwarz, Lisa M, Woloshin, S. *Overdiagnosed: Making People Sick in the Pursuit of Health*, Beacon Press, Boston, 2011. (Page 146-7)

Wolf, Paul. "*Book Review: Diagnosing Genius: The Life and Death of Beethoven.*" New England J. Med. 357: 518-518, 2007. (Page 152)

Woods, Donald. *Biko.* Paddington Press, NY and London, 1978. (Page 63)

Personal Bibliography

Mai, Francois. *Psychiatric Aspects of Heart Transplantation*. Brit. J. of Psychiat. 163, 185-192, 1993. (Page 128-29)

Mai F, McKenzie FN, Kostuk W. *Psychosocial Adjustment and Quality of Life Following Heart Transplantation*. Canad. J. of Psychiat. 35, 223-227, 1990. (Page 129)

Mai F, McKenzie NF, Kostuk W. *Psychiatric Aspects of Heart Transplantation: Preoperative Evaluation and Postoperative Sequelae*. Brit. Med. J. 292, 311-313, 1986. (Pages 128-129)

Mai F, Shaw B, Jenner M, Wielgosz G, Giles D. *Nocturnal Prolactin Secretion in Depression*. Brit. J. of Psychiat. 147: 314-317, 1985. (Page 128)

Mai François. Book review of *Understanding and Managing Somatoform Disorders*. Canad. J. of Psychiat. 64, 218-219, 2019. (Page 125)

Mai Francois. *Conception following Adoption: An Open Question*. Psychosomatic Medicine. 33, 509-514, 1971. (Page 109)

Mai Francois. *Somatization Disorder: A Practical Review*. Canad. J. of Psychiat. 49, 652-662, 2004. (Page 124)

Mai Francois. *Wilder Penfield, Man of Letters*. Canad. J. of Neurol. Sci. 39, 845-846, 2012. (Page 120)

Mai, F.M. Busby, K. and Bell, R. *Clinical Rating of Compliance in Chronic Hemodialysis Patients*. Canad. J. of Psychiat. 44, 478-482, 1999. (Page 143)

Mai, F.M. *Personality and Stress in Heart Disease*. J. of Psychosom. Res. 12, 275-287, 1968. (Page 108)

Mai, F.M., *General Hospital Psychiatry: Data analysis of a Unit*. Med. J. of Australia, 2: 986-991, 1966. (Page 108)

Mai, F.M. *Beaumont's Contribution to Gastric Psychophysiology: A Reappraisal.* Canad. J. of Psychiat. 33. 650-653, 1988. (Page 144)

Mai, F.M. *Psychiatrist's Attitudes to Multiple Personality Disorder: A Questionnaire Study.* Canad. J. of Psychiat, 40, 154-157, 1995. (Page 144)

Mai, François and Merskey, Harold. *Briquet's Treatise on Hysteria: A Synopsis and Commentary.* Arch. of Gen. Psychiat, 37, 1401-1405, 1980. (Page 127-8)

Mai, François Martin. *Diagnosing Genius: The Life and Death of Beethoven.* McGill-Queens University Press, Montréal, 2007. (Pages 152)

Mai, François, Ember, Andrew and McCourt, Catherine. *The Increasing Prevalence of Psychiatric Illness among Canada Pension Plan Disability Plan Recipients (CPPD).* Unpublished paper. (Pages 151-152)

Mai, Francois, Munday, Robert, and Rump, Eric. *Psychiatric Interview Comparisons between Infertile and Fertile Couples.* Psychosomatic Medicine, 34, 431-440, 1972. (Page 109)

Mai, François. *A Psychological and Psychosomatic Study of Infertile Marriages.* Doctor of Medicine Thesis accepted by the University of Adelaide, 1970. (Pages 108-109)

Mai, François. *Father, Unknown.* Austin Macauley, London, 2017. (Pages 155-157)

Mai, Francois. *Graft and Donor Denial in Heart Transplantation.* Am. J. of Psychiat. 143, 143-149, 1986. (Page 129)

Mai, François. Letter to the Editor of The Scotsman newspaper, April 15, 1963. (Pages 97-98)

Mai, Francois. *New Diagnostic Instrument Brings the Psyche into View.* Ontario Medical Review. 515-517, 1983. (Pages 130-133)

Mai, François. *Pierre Briquet: 19th Century Savant with 20th Century Ideas.* Canad. J. Psychiat. 28, 418-421, 1983. (Page 127-128)

Russell, V. Mai, F. Busby, K. Attwood, D. Davis, M. and Brown, M. *Acute Day Hospitalization as an Alternative to Inpatient Treatment.* Canad. J. of Psychiat. 41, 629-637, 1996. (Page 142)

Swenson, Robert, and Mai, Francois. *A Canadian Medical-Psychiatric In-Patient Service.* Canad. J. of Psych, 37, 326-332, 1992. (Page 142)

Website Links

www.thecradockfour.co.za/Home.html

www.en.wikipedia.org/wiki/Jonathan_(tortoise)

www.theguardian.com/world/2019/nov/01/south-africans-pin-hopes-on-rugby-win-to-lift-gloom-of-troubled-country

en.wikipedia.org/wiki/Humanae_Vitae

en.wikipedia.org/wiki/Winnipeg Statement

www.theglobeandmail.com/life/facts-and-arguments/abstaining-from-battle-i-decided-to-talk-to-my-cancer-cells-instead/article27282286/

www.youtube.com/watch?v=2AMu-G51yTY Carl Jung Face to Face with John Freeman on BBC.

www.mentalhealthcommission.ca/English/resources/mhcc-reports/mental-health-strategy-canada

Glossary

Anastomosis: Surgical repair or connection of two hollow organs in the body, such as arteries, veins, or intestines.

Angina pectoris: A condition of the heart in which the blood vessels are partly blocked, resulting in chest pain on exertion.

Anhedonia: The negative symptom of schizophrenia in which the person is unable to obtain pleasure or satisfaction in their activities.

Antidepressant drugs: Drugs used in the treatment of depression. There are four main groups of these drugs: tricyclics, mono-amine-oxidase inhibitors, and serotonin and norepinephrine reuptake inhibitors. Each of these groups contains a number of specific drugs.

Biopsychosocial Medicine: The term introduced by George Engel in 1977 to describe the need for medicine to have psychological and social dimensions, in addition to its biological dimension, in its concept of disease.

Bipolar Disorder: A psychiatric condition in which there are swings of mood between elation and depression at different times, in the same person.

Catatonia: Involuntary movements, posturing of body, or jerking of limbs. It occurs in certain forms of schizophrenia and is also a side-effect of phenothiazine therapy.

Cognitive dysfunction: Loss of the ability to carry out intellectual functions such as memorizing or calculating. It occurs in diseases of the brain such as dementia, and is a common negative symptom of schizophrenia.

Conversion: A psychiatric condition in which an emotional conflict is experienced as a physical symptom.

Crepitus: The crackling or grinding sensation that occurs when moving a joint or bone that is broken or diseased.

Electro-convulsive therapy (ECT): A form of treatment that involves producing an epileptic convulsion using an electric stimulus. It is used in severe depression and sometimes in schizophrenia.

Etiology: The cause(s) of any illness.

Flattening of Affect: The negative symptom of schizophrenia if the person shows loss of the ability to react appropriately to emotional expression.

Grand Rounds: A learning and teaching experience in which medical personnel get together to discuss a selected clinical topic.

Herniorrhaphy: Surgical repair of a hernia, which is a protrusion of a portion of bowel through the membranes lining the intestinal wall.

Hysteria: An ancient psychiatric condition in which a patient demonstrates physical symptoms or behaviours that are caused by underlying psychological conflict. Because of dissatisfaction with the term, hysteria was first changed to somatization disorder and it is now called somatoform disorder.

Ischemic Heart Disease: A condition of the heart in which an artery is blocked resulting in impaired oxygen supply to the heart muscle supplied by that artery. Chest pain is a common symptom.

Metastases: Cells and islands of cancer that spread from the primary cancer organ, and settle in other tissues.

Modecate: Another phenothiazine medication. It has the advantage of being given by injection every two weeks.

Narcotic Analgesics: Powerful drugs, mainly related to opium and its derivatives, that are effective in relieving pain, but are also strongly addictive.

Perseveration: A common negative symptom of schizophrenia in which the person repeats certain activities seemingly without the memory that they have just performed that activity.

Poverty of ideation: A negative symptom of schizophrenia in which the person has difficulty in initiating and formulating their thoughts.

Prefrontal leucotomy: Sometimes called a lobotomy, in which surgery was used in some psychiatric patients to cut white matter fibres that connect the frontal lobes to the rest of the brain. It is no longer a recommended treatment, but was commonly carried out from the 1930s to the 1950s.

Psychoanalysis: A concept of human experience and behaviour based on unconscious thoughts, feelings, and emotions, usually of a sexual nature.

Puerperal Depression: A type of depression that occurs following childbirth.

Schizophrenia: A psychiatric condition characterized by loss of contact with reality. There may be positive symptoms, such as delusions and hallucinations, or negative symptoms, such as poverty of ideation, anhedonia, and cognitive deficits.

Sequelae: The consequences or after-effects of certain diseases.

Soma: The body of a person, as distinct from the mind and the germ cells.

Stelazine: An antipsychotic medication belonging to the phenothiazine group of drugs.

Torticollis: A condition in which the head is involuntarily rotated to the right or the left. It is sometimes called wryneck.

Acknowledgements

The idea for writing this personal narrative came from Ken McGoogan when we met on a memorable cruise of the Northwest Passage in September 2017 He also read and reviewed an early draft. *Merci, Ken!*

Many friends and colleagues read innumerable drafts of this book during its five-year gestation period. I value the advice and help of Alex Anstey, Beverley Barron, Phyllis Bohanis, Noel Burns, Tom Feasby, Paul Grof, Jocelyn Kane-Berman, Leila Kulpas, Yvon Lapierre, Vincent Mai, Myron Sandwick, and Carl Stovel. Aaron Mai and Andrew du Toit helped with the complex task (for me) of scanning and uploading the images. Thanks also to Gerda Hnatyshyn, Neil McKenzie and Claire McCaughey for allowing me to use their images. A special thank you to Dr David Teplica for filling me in on the remarkable character and discoveries of Charles Huggins, and permission to use the image of Huggins.

My brother Vincent, sister Denyse, nephew Christopher, and nieces Charlotte and Arabella were especially helpful in filling the gaps in the sad story of my brother David.

I particularly value the perceptive and sagacious support of Phil Jenkins, who kept my feet firmly on the ground, when my mind and pen went wandering amongst the stars.

Finally, I am filled with gratitude to my wife, Sarie, and my sons, Martin, Nicolas, Andrew and Quentin, for loyally standing by me for the major part of my journey through life.

INDEX

Abbé François Mai. 180, 181
Adelaide. 114-116, 118, 119, 124-128, 132, 145, 162, 210, 211, 227
Ader, Robert. 133
Aix-en-Provence. 5, 9, 16, 37, 38
Alexander, Franz. 153, 219
Allen, Francis. 169, 221
Allen, Woody. 208
Alpers, Hinrich. 183, 184
Anglo-Boer War. 4, 12, 19, 27, 63, 65, 69
Anstey, Alexander. 93, 233,
Anstey, Arabella. 93, 104, 233
Anstey, Charlotte. 84, 93, 233
Anstey, Christopher. 84, 93, 94, 96, 233
Anstey (née Mai), Denyse. 9, 17, 20, 37, 51, 52, 80, 81, 84, 92, 93, 104, 138, 163, 173, 191, 233
Anstey, Richard. 52
Anti-androgen therapy. 186, 187, 202, 203
Anti-depressant drugs. 105, 170, 230, 237
Anti-psychotic drugs. 91-94, 105
Apartheid. xiv, 6, 27, 40, 73, 74, 109, 111, 112
Arcadia, 135
Australia. 33, 35, 64, 68, 87, 108, 114-119, 123, 124, 126, 128, 129, 132, 144, 211
Avignon. 15
Backstroke. 45
Bajramovic, Hifziya 164
Bardot, Brigitte. 7
Barnard, Chris. 77, 78, 147, 219
Barnett, Barney. 137
Beethoven, Ludwig van. 31, 50, 51, 199, 167, 172, 174-177, 183, 184, 209, 222-227
Belmont Hospital, Sutton, Surrey. 85, 103-108, 112, 113, 142

Biko, Steve. 73, 109, 219
Biopsychosocial. 128, 130, 141, 230
Bipolar disorder. 148, 170, 172, 222, 230
Bissada, Hany. 164, 167
Bloemfontein. 64, 68, 70, 78, 84
Boberg, Inger. 13
Boetie (Roelofse), 79
Bomb. 44, 45
Boraine, Alex. 27, 112
Botha, Louis. 4, 64, 70
Bourgon, Luc 164
Boxing. 34, 35
Briquet, Pierre.145, 146, 167, 220, 221, 227
Brock, John. 65
Broederbond. 19
Bullying. 34
Bunyan, John. 118, 211
Burns, Noel. 57, 220, 233
Cameron, Bill. 196
Cameron, Bill. 196, 197, 220
Cameron, Paul. 164, 167
Canada. 7, 23, 53, 64-68, 73, 79, 87, 97, 103, 108, 114, 128,132, 134-136, 138, 140, 144, 146,
148, 154, 161, 167, 173-175, 181, 184, 188, 191, 192, 209, 211, 215,
Cape Colony. 35, 36, 63, 64, 70
Cape Town. 13, 14, 22, 23, 44-53, 58, 62, 66-81, 90, 91, 109, 126-128, 132, 148, 166, 208, 209
Catacomb. 84, 85
Cazelet, Peter. 35
Chaplin, Charlie. 7
Charron, Jeanne. 204
Chelsea, Québec. 155, 159, 163, 210, 211
Chemistry. 39, 43, 44, 49
Chevalier, Maurice. 7, 14
Chopin, Frederic. 115, 172
Church, Roman Catholic. xiv, 50, 71, 82, 84, 119-122, 179, 180-182, 191, 193
Churchill, Sir Winston. 18, 69, 80, 81, 224
Clear, Dudley. 42, 43, 137
Cleghorn, Jock. 132
Cleghorn, Robert. 127
Clement VI, Pope. 15, 162

Climate change. 2, 215, 216
Cognitive therapy. 93, 106, 141, 142, 163, 166, 170, 171, 222
Cohen, Leonard. 7, 192
Coleridge, Samuel Taylor. 42, 43
Commission, Mental Health, Canada. 97, 229
Commission, Truth and Reconciliation, South Africa. 27, 112, 219
Communism. 72, 111
Congress, African National. 6, 40, 73, 74, 109, 111, 112
Contraception. xiv, 119, 120
Coronary Heart Disease. 124, 130
Corsica. 16, 17
Courtney, Bryce. 96, 220
Covid. 118, 215
Cradock. 21, 23, 25-32, 41, 88
Cramond, William. 114, 124, 132
Cricket. 37, 47, 89, 90, 93
Crucified Woman. 157
Cupar, Fife. 92, 113, 114
Cycling. 152, 160, 203, 205, 209
Da Gama, Vasco. 61
Dafoe, Allan. 8
Dalai Lama. 193, 196
Davis, Bill. 137
Davis, Peter. 118, 119
De Bettignies, Louise. 15
De Gaulle, General Charles. 18-20, 38, 224
De Klerk, Frederick. 111
de Prat, Eugéne. 98
de Prat, Jean Eric. 82
De Villiers, Dr. 20, 29
De Wet, General Christian. 12, 64, 78
Delattre, Guillaume. 16
Delattre, Joseph. 16
Delpierre, Guy. 52
Delpierre, Stephan. 52
Dercourt, Jean-François. 180, 182
Deruyk, Renée. 15, 220
Diar, Prakash. 73, 74, 220
Dionne, Quintuplets. 7, 8
Disability Pension. 173, 174
Dives, Keith. 98

Dives, Martin. 163
Drake, John and Marybeth. 152
DSM-5. 168-170, 206, 221
DSM-IV. 168, 169
Dunbar, Flanders. 153, 220
Duncan, Patrick. 60
Dupuytren's Disease. 172-174
Durban. 44, 57, 64, 69
Edinburgh. 92, 112-114, 138, 145
Electroplexy (ECT). 54, 100, 164
Elias (née Mai), Christiane. 9, 17, 37, 45, 71, 92, 98, 128, 163, 191
Elizabeth, Queen. 4, 5
Ember, Andrew.174, 227
Engel, George. 2, 128-133, 231
Etzebeth, Eben. 47
Ewen Cameron, Donald. 105
Father, Unknown. 15, 178, 179, 201,227
Feasby, Tom. 152, 233
Feeney, Fr. Peter Paul. 70, 71
Ferguson, "Gussie". 43, 44, 53, 115
ffolliott, Desmond. 43, 136
Fitzgerald, Fr. Joseph. 84
Forman, Frank. 54
Fox, Terry. 23, 224
Francis, Pope. 121
Franklin Expedition. 173
Franschhoek. 62
Freeland, Allison. 167
Freud, Sigmund. 85, 86, 102, 151, 209
Fry, Stephen. 198, 222
Garfinkel, Paul. 169, 221
Gawande, Atul. 198, 222
General Hospital Psychiatry. 123, 167, 226
Genocide. 62
George (city) 78, 79, 89
George, King. 4, 7, 77
Givenchy-en-Gohelle. 15, 37, 52, 65, 66, 82, 179
Gleeson, Archbishop James. 119
Goodliffe, Marie France. 134, 191
Gordon, "Flash". 44
Gosselin, Jean-Yves. 164

Gouws, Gerhardus. 41
Graaff Reinet. 30, 31
Grandchildren. xv, 38, 162, 163, 209
Green, Bill. 132
Gregory XI, Pope. 15
Grey High School. 35-37, 42-46, 90, 115, 126, 136, 137, 208
Grey, Sir George. 35, 36
Groot Trek. 62, 223
Groote Schuur Hospital. 53, 58, 59, 77, 91
Halesowen. 21, 25, 28, 29
Hancock, Marie-Louise. 71
Harris, Mike. 166
Heart transplant. 77, 123, 146, 148, 167, 226, 227
Heart transplantation. 133, 146, 167, 226, 227
Heseltine, Gilbert. 132
History of Medicine. 165
Hitler, Adolf. 7, 81
Hnatyshyn, Ray and Gerda. 155, 156, 233
Hobhouse, Emily. 27, 68
Hope. xiv, xv, 1, 2, 18, 23, 30, 39, 32, 34, 61, 70, 74, 81, 95, 104, 122, 170, 192, 196, 203, 210,
211, 214-217
Hospital Restructuring. 166, 167
Howard, Gat. 68
Huggins, Charles. 51, 189, 190, 221
Humanae Vitae. 119, 120, 229
Hurford, Chris. 118, 119
Hysteria. 133, 145, 167, 221, 227, 231
Infertility. 124, 126, 167, 180
Insulin Shock Therapy. 54, 102, 103
Interviewing. 2, 54, 72, 85, 106, 107
Jameson Raid. 63
Joao, King of Portugal. 61
Johannesburg. 32, 33, 35, 39, 53, 74, 88
John XXIII, Pope. 84.
Jonathan (tortoise). 23
Jung, Carl. 85, 86, 151, 209, 229
Kane-Berman, Jocelyn. 55, 233
Kangaroo Island. 127
Kennedy, John Fitzgerald. 113, 114,
Keppel-Jones, Arthur. 109, 222

Khama, Seretse. 57, 58
Kimberley, 8, 42
Kleinschmidt, John. 195
Kolbe Society. 56, 70
Kolisi, Siya. 47
Kraepelin, Emil. 171
Kruger, Paul. 63, 64, 209
Kwashiorkor. 58
Lalonde, Sr Yvette. 204
Lam, Raymond. 170, 222
Lamb, Mabel. 13
Lapierre, Yvon.154, 168, 233
Laurier, Sir Wilfred. 65
Ledoux, Abbé 10
Legion d'Honeur. 15, 16, 38
Lesotho. 57
Lewis, Professor Sir Aubrey. 124
Lille. 15, 38
Lobotomy. 107, 232
London, Ontario. 50, 129, 132, 135-138, 143, 145-148, 152-163, 166, 211, 219, 225
London, UK. 2, 17, 22, 30, 36, 45, 50, 57, 69, 80, 81, 84, 92, 93, 99, 104-108, 112, 115, 124,
128, 129
Loren, Sophia. 7
Louis XIV, King. 62
Lourdes. 191-193, 195, 201
Louw, James.
Louw, Jan
Luthuli, Albert. 111
Lutkenhaus-Lackey, Almuth. 157
MacMillan, Margaret. 4
Mai, Andrew David. 114, 160-162, 173, 185, 203, 233
Mai, David Bruno. 9, 17-21, 36, 47, 48, 52, 53, 87-98, 138, 163, 233
Mai, Martin (Papa). 5, 8, 9-12, 14-18, 20, 21, 24, 25, 29, 32, 35, 37, 41, 48, 49, 52, 56, 81, 84,
Mai, Martin Francois. 84, 103, 104, 125-127, 160, 162, 202, 203, 233
Mai, Nicolas Fernand. 95, 103, 104, 125-127, 160-162, 173, 233
Mai, Paul Bernard. 115-119, 121, 210
Mai, Quentin Gregory. 117, 128, 135, 143, 144, 154, 160-162, 202, 233
Mai, René (Grandpère) 15, 16, 38, 51, 177-179

Mai, Sarie (née Roelofse). xiv, 75-84, 92, 103, 104, 108, 114-120, 122, 125, 127, 128, 130, 143-145, 152, 154-160, 162-164, 191, 195, 201, 202, 205, 210-211, 222, 233

Mai, Thérèse (Grandmère) 16

Mai, Vincent. 17, 18, 22, 30, 36, 40, 47, 48, 52, 89-93, 163, 173, 177, 180, 181, 191, 233

Mai, Yvonne (Maman), 13-18, 20-24, 31-37, 45, 48, 50-52, 81, 93-95, 99, 128, 138, 163

Medical Assistannce in Dying (MAiD). 87, 210

Malan, Daniel. 3, 5, 40

Marist Brothers. 32-35, 88

Marsh, Henry. 198, 222

Martin (Roelofse). 79, 80

Martin, David. 193

Martinpuich, Pas de Calais. 180, 181

Martins, Helen. 30, 31, 224

Mbeki, Thomas. 112

McCaughey, Amy. 158

McCourt, Catherine. 174, 227

McCrae, John. 68, 219, 223

McKenzie, Neil. 146, 147, 226, 233

McLuhan, Marshall. 137

Merskey, Harold. 145, 227

Merton, Thomas. 193, 194 214, 223, 223, 225

Milev, Rumen. 168

Mindfulness. 142, 193, 194

Miracle. 204, 208

Monica. 131

Moniz, Egaz. 106, 107

Morant, Breaker. 68

Morrison, Dr Archie. 113

Mutch, Barbara. 28

Nadaud, Jacques. 14, 18, 20

Napoleon. 23, 62, 167, 177, 179

Narcosis therapy. 105

Natal. 36, 40, 63, 64, 69

National Catholic Federation of Students (NCFS). 56, 57, 84

Nazi. 13, 18, 19, 38, 39, 210

New Zealand. 33, 35, 36, 57, 64, 108

Newman Association. 118

North West Passage. 173, 233

Nuclear War. 214, 216
Orange Free State. 19, 36, 40, 69, 70, 78
Oronsay. 115
Ottawa (General) Hospital, The. 122, 154, 155, 163, 166, 167
Owl House, The. 30, 31, 224
Paris, Joel. 169, 223
Parsons, George. 72, 126.
Party, National. 5
Paton, Alan. 109, 112, 223
Paul VI, Pope. 119
Penfield, Wilder. 137, 223, 226
Penis, Fractured. 59
Pennington, Paul. 152
Petain, Marshal Philippe. 18
Phimosis. 58
Piano. 31 ,50, 51, 76, 127, 163, 177, 174, 183
Pickford, Mary. 7
pierre, Martin. 178-180
Plains of Camdeboo. 30
Pompeii. 115
Ponsonby, Peter. 46
Pope, Alexander. 212, 217
Port Elizabeth (Gqeberha) 3, 4, 7, 10, 17-22, 27, 29, 30, 332, 35, 37, 39-50, 76, 80, 89-91, 208
Potez. 10, 11, 12
Pretoria. 64, 69, 209
Prostate cancer. 1, 51, 169, 185, 188-191, 194-199, 202, 204, 208, 211, 220-223
Prostate gland. 185-189, 194, 197,
PSA test. 174, 186-190, 202, 203
Psychoscope. 148, 149-152
Psychosomatic Medicine. 2, 124, 127, 128, 153, 154, 167
Psychotherapy. 85, 86, 106, 107, 139, 164, 170, 171
Post traumatic stress disorder (PTSD). 103, 105
Pudifin, Denis. 44
Québec. 64, 65, 80, 128, 136, 166, 183, 191, 230, 231
Quinn, Kate. 15, 224
Racoon. 159
Rakoff, Vivian. 132
Ramaphosa, Cyril. 112
Remarque, Erich. 210, 224
Rhodes, Cecil. 27, 63, 64, 75

Ritchie, Bill. 46
Riverview. 25, 26, 29, 35
Rochester, NY. 2, 128, 129-132, 134, 143, 162, 211
Roosevelt, Franklin. 7
Roubaix. 5, 10
Russell, Vincent. xv, 164, 167, 228
Sachs, Albie. 73, 74, 109, 224
Sakel, Manfred. 102
San People. 62
Sandwick, Myron. 39, 44, 233
Sargant, William. 2, 85, 104-107, 129 142
Schindler, Anton. 175, 224
Schizophrenia. 1, 91-93, 96-98, 101-103, 148, 149, 172, 230-232
Schmale, Art. 132
Schoenbrun, David. 224
Schreiner, Olive. 25, 68
Selzer, Golda.
Shakespeare, William. 42, 56
Shaw, David. 107
Shorter, Edward. 170, 225
Smulian, Ben. 19
Smuts, Jan. 3-5, 40
Somatoform disorder. 142, 145, 224, 226, 231
Soubirous, St. Bernadette. 191, 192,
Spitzer, Robert. 169
St Helena (island). 23
St, Michael's Church. 50, 71
Stigma.
Stratheden Hospital, Cupar, Fife. 92, 113
Stroke. 79, 94, 130, 131, 138, 158, 210
Suicide. 2, 81, 139, 140, 151, 180
Sutherland, Amanda. 167
Swenson, Robert. 164, 167, 228
Table Mountain. 50, 58, 128
Taleb, Nassim. 208, 225
Talent shows. 162
Teplica, David. 190. 233
Toronto. 66, 132, 144, 157, 161, 219, 225
Totteridge Park. 41, 91
Transvaal. 36, 40, 69, 70, 109
Trudeau, Pierre. 52, 151

Tuberculosis. 14, 18, 20-23, 107, 163, 193, 217
Turley, Hugh. 193
Tutu, Desmond. 1, 27
Ukraine. xv, 214
University Hospital, London, ON. 132, 137, 139, 143, 230, 232
Ustinov, Peter. 18, 225
Valkenburg Hospital, Cape Town. 54
Vancouver. 135, 161
Varan, Lily. 164
Vaughan-Williams, Ralph. 13
Versfeld, Martin. 70, 71
Victoria. 95, 161, 202
Vietnam. 119, 193
Violin. 13, 50, 51, 127, 160, 162
Von Breuning, Gerhard. 175, 225
Vorster, Johan. 19
Wagner-Juaregg, Walter. 103
Waring, "Cocky". 43
Washkansky, Louis. 77, 78
Watson, Mrs. 32
Watson-Smith, Harold. 13
Watson-Smith, Hélène. 13
Watson-Smith, John. 13, 38
Weiser, Anne. 172
Westerham, Kent. 80, 81, 93, 94, 138, 163
Wheeler, Brian. 152
Williams, Ruth. 57
Wilpena Pound. 126
Wimereux. 37, 65
Woods, Donald. 73, 225
World Health Organization. 126
World War I. 9, 10, 13, 15, 16, 18, 38, 65, 69, 172, 181, 210
World War II. 4, 18, 19, 33, 52, 69, 78, 81, 103, 106, 157
Zuma, Jacob. 112

CPSIA information can be obtained
at www.ICGtesting.com
Printed in the USA
BVHW011001031222
652250BV00007B/9/J

9 781039 149281